Bakers and Basques

A Social History of Bread in Mexico

ROBERT WEIS

University of New Mexico Press ❖ Albuquerque

© 2012 by the University of New Mexico Press
All rights reserved. Published 2012
Printed in the United States of America
17 16 15 14 13 12   1 2 3 4 5 6

A version of chapter 7 appeared as "Immigrant Entrepreneurs, Bread, and Class Negotiation in Postrevolutionary Mexico City," *Mexican Studies/Estudios Mexicanos* 25, no. 1 (Winter 2009): 71–100.

LIBRARY OF CONGRESS CATALOGING-IN-PUBLICATION DATA

Weis, Robert, 1971–
Bakers and Basques : a social history of bread in Mexico / Robert Weis.
p. cm.
Includes bibliographical references and index.
ISBN 978-0-8263-5146-3 (pbk. : alk. paper) — ISBN 978-0-8263-5147-0 (electronic)
1. Bread industry—Mexico—History. 2. Bread—Economic aspects—Mexico—History. 3. Bread—Political aspects—Mexico—History. 4. Bakeries—Mexico—History. 5. Bakers—Political activity—Mexico—History. 6. Mexico—Economic conditions. 7. Mexico—Social conditions. I. Title.
HD9058.B743M694 2012
338.4'766475230972—dc23
2012012520

BOOK DESIGN
Composed in 10.25/13.5 Minion Pro Regular
Display type is Minion Pro

Para Myrna, que nació con un pan bajo el brazo.

Para Araceli, hija de panadera.

Contents

Illustrations
ix

Acknowledgments
xi

Introduction
1

CHAPTER ONE

"*Zelo y desvelo*"

THE BREAD MONOPOLY AND LATE COLONIAL MARKET REFORMS

11

CHAPTER TWO

"A system that offends the hands of brothers"

SMALL BAKERS AND THE FREE MARKET IN INDEPENDENT MEXICO

24

CHAPTER THREE

"An uncle in America"

CHAIN MIGRATION AND THE SPANISH MONOPOLY

44

CHAPTER FOUR

"Dough Kneaded with Blood"

62

CHAPTER FIVE

"We have no bread"

HUNGER, OPPORTUNITY, AND WAR

83

CHAPTER SIX

The Bakers' Revolution

100

CHAPTER SEVEN

Unionists, *Tlalchicholes*, and *Canasteros*

124

CONCLUSION

147

Notes

153

Bibliography

185

Index

211

Illustrations

FIGURES

Figure 1.	Panadería, Mexico City, ca. 1930	2
Figure 2.	"El Vizcaíno," Mexico City, ca. 1920	57
Figure 3.	Bakers kneading, Mexico City, ca. 1935	67
Figure 4.	Women gathered in front of La Parisina, Mexico City, 1915	91
Figure 5.	"Canastero," Mexico City, ca. 1930	143

TABLES

Table 1.	Mexico City panadería owners, 1867	35
Table 2.	Ounces of bread per real, 1869	37–38
Table 3.	Workers and wages, 1875	64
Table 4.	Budgets from Los Gallos and La Unión, 1915	97
Table 5.	Union affiliation among bakery workers, 1921	115
Table 6.	Investments and capital of Spanish- and Mexican-owned bakeries, 1935	126

Acknowledgments

⚜ FINANCIAL SUPPORT FOR THE RESEARCH AND WRITING OF THIS book came from the University of California Institute for Mexico and the United States (UC MEXUS), the Reed Smith Fellowship, the UC Davis History Department, the Jarena D. Wright Scholarship, the UC Davis Hemispheric Institute on the Americas, the UC Davis Institute of Governmental Affairs, and summer research funding from the University of Northern Colorado. I am grateful for the material and moral support that these institutions have granted me.

Two previously published articles both included aspects of chapters 3 and 4: "Inmigrantes vascos y movimiento obrero en el México porfiriano," *Revista de Estudios Sociales* (April 2008): 65–85; and "El horno no está para bollos: Inmigración, clases sociales y pan en la ciudad de México," *Espacio Regional, Revista de Estudios Sociales* 2, no. 3 (2006): 70–85.

This book reflects the encouragement of UC Davis History Department professors Andrés Reséndez, Chuck Walker, Tom Holloway, and Alan Taylor. Friends and colleagues Pablo Whipple, Kim Davis, Claudia Darrigandri, Lia Schraeder, Claudio Robles, Fernando Purcell, Mathew Osborn, Stevan Ward, Hernán Correa, Ingrid Bleynart, Catherine Komisaruk, Marie Francois, Jeffrey Pilcher, Carolyn de la Peña, Sandra Aguilar, Ignacio Sosa, Eugenia Meyer, Bob Schmidt, Sandra Mendiola, Jeremy Trabue, T. J. Tomlin, Joan Clinefelter, Nick Syrett, and many others offered helpful criticism and support. My colleagues at the University of Northern Colorado have encouraged me with their examples of dedication, rigor, and camaraderie. The historians José Roberto Gallegos and Mónica Lara have shared with me their knowledge, ideas, affection, and inflatable mattress for several years in Mexico City. All have shown me the value of friendship and intellectual community.

Archivists and staff at several institutions aided this research. I am particularly grateful to the superb archivists at the Archivo Histórico de la Ciudad de México, the friendly and expeditious support of Abertano Guerrero Godoy and Raymundo F. Alvarez García at the Archivo General de la Nación, the librarians at the Biblioteca Miguel Lerdo de Tejada, and the Hemeroteca Nacional de México. Clark Whitehorn, editor in chief of the University of New Mexico Press, was very supportive of this book's gradual development. Sarah Soliz and the anonymous reviewers made suggestions and criticisms that vastly improved the prose and the exposition.

I had the privilege of discussing bread and bakeries with the *maestros panaderos* Alfonso Ortega Ríos, Pascual Cortés, Mario Anguiano Trejo, Agustín Moreno, and Carlos Ramírez. The following bakery and flour mill owners also graciously shared their personal and professional histories with me: Julián Castañón, Adolfo Fernández, Darío Ordóñez, Benito Luque, José Sierra, Enrique Segura, and José Luis Fuente.

In Mexico, a newborn who brings fortune to a family is said to carry a piece of bread under her arm. Myrna was born as this research began and has brought endless fortune to our lives ever since. This book is dedicated to her and to my wife, Araceli Calderón, who has contributed to this book more than she could know. Finally, my deepest gratitude goes to our families in Santa Rosa and Tingambato.

Introduction

✢ A YOUNG BAKERY WORKER, MAYBE TEN YEARS OLD, APPEARS IN A photograph from 1930. He stands in the passage that divides the retail section of the *panadería* (bakery) from the workroom in back. Thin and dark, he is dressed in an apron and cloth hairnet and looks at the camera somewhat timidly out of the corner of his eye, one hand reaching across his back to grasp the other arm. Behind a long wooden counter stand three Spanish immigrants—probably the owner, his assistant, and a clerk—one of whom wears the wool beret typical of northern Spain. Another Mexican worker, behind them, has just set down a basket of *bolillos*, Mexico's French rolls, to be added to the piles of bread. Two well-dressed customers, a woman and a man, will take the rolls home so their families can dip them into chocolate or coffee for breakfast and dinner. All the people in the photo together helped make bakeries vital neighborhood institutions and the bread trade Mexico City's second largest industry.

The workers, the immigrants, and the customers all occupy distinct spaces of the panadería. The counter, of course, separates the workers from consumers who went once, often twice, a day for bread. The doorway where the boy stands separates Mexican workers and Spanish employers; it was a passage that divided not only the productional and commercial halves of the shop, but also marked the distinctions of race and class that coincided with the bakery's two sections. The conflicts and negotiations that sprang from these distinctions within panaderías are the focus of this book. From the late nineteenth century until well into the twentieth, Spanish, mostly Basque, immigrants owned most of Mexico City's panaderías. From around 1870 up to the Great Depression in 1929, owners continually brought over relatives

Figure 1. Panadería, Mexico City, ca. 1930. Fondo Casasola, Inventory No. 233. Courtesy of the Fototeca Nacional of the Instituto Nacional de Antropología e Historia.

and countrymen to work the front of the shop until the newcomers opened their own. Meanwhile, Mexican laborers kneaded and baked in the back or often below, in the basement. Occasionally, they managed to set up their own bakeries. But they operated on the fringes of what contemporaries called the "Spanish monopoly."[1]

All of the collective actors represented in the photograph employed varying strategies to pursue their interests. Amid shifting antagonisms and alliances, the rituals of baking, selling, and eating bound together the immigrants, native workers, consumers, as well as government officials. In a broader sense, bread also linked them to the upheavals that characterized the history of Mexico City and contributed to the structuring and restructuring of the state and the market from independence through the decades that followed the Mexican Revolution.

This book takes a long view of panaderías in order to explore how ownership patterns, state intervention, and labor strife contributed to the formation of markets. My original intention was to limit the study to the years when struggles between bakers and Basques were most intense: 1895–1940, a period that is, arguably, long already and unconventional given the established chronologies in Mexican historiography. However, during my research I formed a series of recurrent questions that refer back to at least the late colonial period: Why were some groups, such as the Basque immigrants, able to establish monopolies or a monopoly-like control over the market, while others were forced to operate at the margins or not at all? Why did government authorities almost invariably support these monopolies? And, finally, what role did the conflictive relationships between workers and employers play in the forging of these market configurations between dominant and marginal groups?

I address these questions by tracing the particular interests that linked owners, workers, agents of the state, and consumers. This book is not, therefore, about bread per se but rather about how politics and class struggle contributed to the formation of a market for a particular good.[2] By examining relationships between capital, labor, and politics through a specific trade and exploring the social functions and cultural meanings of bread, I study the intersection of labor history, material culture, and politics.[3] In this sense, the book anchors the processes of state formation and labor in everyday life *within* Mexico, in contrast to both the rather abstract political science scholarship and the economic history that overwhelmingly emphasize Mexico's export sector.[4] My approach reveals how definitions of the marketplace sprang from political interests and, in particular, from class negotiation.

In the case of bread, these questions were intimately related to everyday subsistence and politics. During most of the years studied here, definitions of citizenship and legitimate political authority were vague and fraught with contention; only rarely did the ballot box sanction the relationship between the government and the governed. However, links between the public and the state appear with greater clarity when studied through controversies over access to consumer goods, and particularly bread. Government officials repeatedly expressed the view that ensuring the supply of bread was part of their public duty. As Carol Helstosky has shown for Italy under Mussolini, "Food was the most visceral connection between government and population."[5] Regardless of their sincerity or practical ability to influence urban provisioning, political leaders used bread as a tangible medium to consolidate and legitimize their authority.

To study panaderías in the country that invented tortillas may seem strange. Indeed, maize, not wheat, has always been the staff of life for the majority of Mexicans. During his visit to New Spain in 1803, Alexander von Humboldt observed "a great number of Indians who eat maize bread... and few populous cities inhabited by whites in easy circumstances."[6] A century later, Andrés Molina Enríquez stated that "wheat is not a grain of general consumption, only foreigners and some Criollos consume it as the foundation of their sustenance; most Criollos eat more maize than wheat; the indigenous consume wheat only by exception. The population lives essentially on maize."[7] A Mexican-born Frenchman similarly wrote that "Mexicans of the wealthy classes eat as much bread as foreigners. But those of the more modest categories, and the Indians, eat instead tortillas."[8] The agricultural engineer Ramón Fernández y Fernández echoed the idea thirty years later: "Wheaten bread in Mexico is a luxury item destined exclusively for the middle and upper classes; in the urban centers, only a small proportion of the working sector consumes it."[9]

Maize was the foundation of most Mexicans' diet, but these authors overlooked the importance of wheat in the subsistence and politics of Mexico City. The divide between maize and wheat was not so much one of class and race, as these observers believed, but rather rural and urban. During the eighteenth and nineteenth centuries, the city consistently consumed roughly fifteen thousand tons of wheat a year, while the rest of the country consumed but eight thousand tons.[10] Humboldt calculated that "the consumption of bread in Mexico City equals that of the cities in Europe"—an overstatement that nonetheless highlights the importance of wheat to the city's subsistence.[11] Although urban Europeans and their descendants ate the bulk of the bread, the variety of types and the prices of bread in eighteenth-century Mexico City show that bread consumption ran through the social hierarchy. Historian Virginia García Acosta points out that "practically the whole population [of Mexico City] had incorporated bread into its diet, be it as the base or as a complement."[12] The wealthy began and ended their days by sipping chocolate and eating fine sweet breads (*bizcochos*) made with the highest quality white flour, lard, eggs, and milk.[13] The poet Guillermo Prieto remembered "a mountain of *puchas, rodeos, soletas, mostachones*," and other sweet breads upon the table of the president.[14] The 1871 novel *Chucho el ninfo* describes how every evening, "carefully placed platters of warm bizcochos rose from the white tablecloth."[15]

The poor family's bread was coarse, dense, and made with low-grade flour, water of questionable quality, bran husks, and sometimes even hay.[16] It was sometimes adulterated with substances such as lead chromate, which whitened the bread, giving the appearance of high-quality flour; health officials warned that such adulteration would "attack the organism, weighing upon the cerebellum until memory loss sets in."[17] To be sure, sweet breads were usually out of the reach of working-class families. However, they did buy *cemitas* and *pambazos* as well as the day-old bread known as *pan frío* that panaderías passed on to market vendors at the end of the day. At the end of the nineteenth century a newspaper could proclaim that "bread is the main sustenance of the working people in the capital; it is the base of their nutrition"—another exaggeration, but still indicative of the importance of bread to urban workers.[18] Bread was central to urban identities that crossed class lines. As late as 1940, the population census included eating bread as a marker of urban assimilation, along with wearing shoes and sleeping in a bed. In contrast, tortillas—along with sandals and woven sleeping mats—were signs of rural backwardness.[19]

Since bread was an essential part of the everyday diet, scarcities caused significant disturbances in the city. When the price of bread increased or its size diminished, consumers blamed producers and merchants but also held government officials responsible. People did not expect their government to feed them, but they did expect leaders to prevent abuse and make sure that food was available and accessible. Failure to fulfill this duty signaled either negligence or complicity.[20] Throughout the periods studied here, the state in Mexico assumed (though not always successfully) the paternal role of regulating the market in order to protect consumers from abusive practices, such as adulteration and underweight bread. This paternalism in the marketplace for consumer goods also allowed the state to assert its authority in several related dynamics—agriculture, manufacturing, currency flow, labor, demography, and health and sanitation, among others—that were crucial to the broader functioning of society.

The state's oversight of the bread market sometimes pitted the interests of regulators against those of the regulated. But collaboration between officials and owners was more prevalent. A fairly small, cohesive group of owners facilitated the regulation and thus helped consolidate state authority. Accordingly, officials were either indifferent or outright hostile to small producers who complained that dominant actors pushed them to the margins of the marketplace, even when the law and official rhetoric opposed monopolization.

Government authorities were equally unsympathetic to the plight of workers, who toiled in conditions that were, even by the standards of the time, deplorable. Long after most trades had abandoned such practices, debt tied workers to panaderías, and bolted doors kept them inside. Conditions worsened as the Spanish monopoly consolidated its dominance in the late nineteenth century. In 1895 the bakers literally broke down the workroom doors and launched a series of strikes that lasted thirty-five years. Striking bakers challenged owners' control and, in contrast to the elite representations of them as alcohol-crazed, barbarous children, used the language of citizenship and sovereignty to articulate their labor demands and to show that their employers—as well as the government officials who supported them—were acting outside the rule of law.

The panadería strikes also inverted the common perception of Basque immigrant entrepreneurs as a force of industrial progress and of Mexican workers as backward and resistant to change. This history of panaderías thus sharply differs from much scholarship on Basques and other Spanish immigrants, which emphasizes their collective contributions to economic development in Latin America. Explicitly or implicitly, scholars celebrate characteristics such as industriousness, frugality, and entrepreneurial acumen as inherent to a Basque mystique, the roots of which they locate in their inscrutable language, geographic isolation, and unique family socialization.[21]

Part of the Basques' success undoubtedly rested on these factors, as well as their adventurous entrepreneurialism, their ability to identify profitable trades, and their cohesive sense of ethnic identity. At the same time, though, the studies that highlight these characteristics narrowly focus on the immigrants' contributions in isolation from other actors. A wider panorama that incorporates the relationships between the immigrant entrepreneurs, their native workers, and the local authorities reveals how the panadería owners embedded themselves into, and benefited from, political and social structures of inequality that granted them cheap labor and preferential treatment by the state. In most cases, the immigrant owners did not modernize panaderías at all; in fact, in terms of labor relations, they moved backward. Archaic conditions appeared to be more profitable and more conducive to incorporating the constant stream of immigrants. Instead, the workers—pressing for regular wages, shifts measured in hours, and freedom of movement—led a "modernizing" effort that fought to bring panaderías into line with the capitalist conditions that had already long existed in other industries in Mexico.

Twentieth-century mobilization among bakery workers also added a new element to the government's responsibility to ensure the food supply. During the colonial and early republican periods, authorities saw themselves as mediators between the greed of producers and the rights of the "public," which they understood to mean consumers but not necessarily workers.[22] The people who actually made the city's food were pariahs—"outcasts in their own land"—whose degraded circumstances barred them from exercising their rights as subjects and citizens.[23] This interpretation, of course, involved a convenient kind of slippage, for what was a worker when he or she made purchases at the market if not a consumer? Mobilization changed this view as workers demanded higher wages in order to maintain their families. After the Mexican Revolution, the government increasingly geared consumer policies to meet the needs of the working class. By the 1930s the slippage had been inverted and *consumer* became synonymous with *worker*. As historian Eduardo Elena writes for the case of Peronist Argentina, "Officials often treated 'consumer' and 'worker' as overlapping categories."[24] This shift is clear in the intersection of bread, strikes, and politics in Mexico.

Since panadería strikes threatened to sever a crucial nexus between the state and the public, ensuring the supply of bread required addressing strife. Porfirio Díaz, Mexico's autocratic ruler from 1876 to 1910 who opened the way to foreign immigration and investment, had few qualms about sending horses and batons against striking workers in order to ensure the bread supply. Attracting foreign capital and suppressing disorderliness were, after all, explicit elements of his administration. For the nominally pro-labor, nationalist revolutionaries who arose in the wake of Díaz's defeat, strikebreaking was a different matter. The new leaders often followed the old dictator's approach but needed to justify their actions in strained terms of social justice. Under Díaz, bread had been symbol of urban civility and social modernization; afterward, it became a sign of the revolutionary government's commitment to the well-being of the proletariat. In the rhetoric of the state, therefore, strikebreaking in panaderías became somehow "revolutionary."

Still, repressing Mexican workers who pursued legitimate rights against foreign bosses proved to be practically ineffective and politically awkward. Bakers were among the largest and most radical contingent of the postrevolutionary labor movement. Their demands emphasized hours and wages, but in a deeper sense they made claims to citizenship as active and significant members of the Mexican nation. They sought to overturn a long heritage of exploitation, repression, and disdain. In the 1920s, their strikes were capable of paralyzing the supply of bread in the city, and consequences rippled through the urban food market. This leverage, together with shifting alliances between the state and different sectors of organized labor, meant that strikebreaking was no longer an effective strategy. Instead, the state sought to incorporate organized bakers, along with leagues of other workers, as constituents of the populist regime.

The move from strikebreaking to negotiations, in turn, yielded new laws that formed the foundation of state involvement in markets that became official policy until the neoliberal reforms of the 1980s.[25] Promulgated in 1929, bread regulations aimed to ensure that owners and workers adhered to their newly signed collective contract. In practice, the new definitions of the formal market strengthened the Basque bread cartel by marginalizing the Mexican-owned small bakeries that relied on nonunionized, mostly family labor. Unionist bakery workers were de facto enforcers of the regulation and their employers' unwitting shock troops. The irony is not only that the interests of the original antagonists came to overlap, but that a nationalist government allegedly committed to tempering the brutalities and indignities of foreign-led capitalism supported the interests of immigrant entrepreneurs by marginalizing Mexican producers. In a broader sense, the regulations turned markets into mechanisms with which to negotiate class conflict, forge state constituencies, and marginalize political threats.

In this book I approach the intersection of bread, politics, and labor strife by taking a long view of Mexico City panaderías. Chapter 1 discusses the late colonial bread monopoly, its contradictory relationship with the colonial government, and the free-trade reforms spurred by the outbreak of the war of independence in 1810. Chapter 2 argues that these reforms, together with the turbulence that characterized the first decades after independence, contributed to a relatively democratic marketplace in which small producers took center stage. This period of openness waned, however, with the arrival of wealthier, mostly foreign, entrepreneurs after 1850, which provoked debates around the meaning of "free commerce." Chapter 3 traces how Basque immigrants were able to capitalize on the gains of earlier immigrant entrepreneurs in order to ensconce themselves into the bread and flour markets and build a tight network of family and ethnic solidarity. Chapter 4 reconstructs the everyday violence that bakery workers experienced as the number of shops rapidly increased. Although the press presented this violence as proof of workers' barbarity, the ensuing strikes revealed bakers' capacity to mobilize effective protests and draw on national discourses of citizenship. Chapter 5 discusses the famine that the revolution brought upon Mexico City and shows how the government that emerged from the revolution relied on the Basques to pull the city from hunger and chaos. The resulting alliance helps explain why, as chapter 6 details, the revolutionary government repressed the frequent strikes in

Spanish-owned bakeries from 1915 to 1929. Finally, chapter 7 analyzes how, after 1929, owners, union leaders, and officials redefined the formal market in such a way that codified the "Spanish monopoly" and forced small Mexican producers into the informal economy.

CHAPTER ONE

"Zelo y desvelo"

The Bread Monopoly and Late Colonial Market Reforms

※ A BLACK SLAVE, OWNED BY HERNÁN CORTÉS, ALLEGEDLY PLANTED Mexico's first wheat after he found three grains at the bottom of a rice sack. A single grain yielded 180; soon, wrote the sixteenth-century chronicler Francisco López de Gómara, "there was infinite wheat." Cortés established the Santo Domingo Mill on the banks of the Tacubaya River on the outskirts of Mexico City, the capital of what the Spaniards called New Spain, not far from where another conquistador, Antonio Nuño de Guzmán, had erected the first flour mill.[1] Streams flowing down the mountains that surrounded the city pushed the millstones as the water irrigated the newly planted wheat fields.

Bread was part of the Spaniards' mission to civilize the Native Americans. Friar Bernardino de Sahagún urged the Indians to "eat that which the Castilian people eat" in order to become "the same as them, strong and pure and wise."[2] Bread soon became central to the diet of urban residents, although Mexicans (and many Spaniards) continued to subsist on maize, and wheat was a rarity in the countryside. By the eighteenth century, bread was so important that Alexander von Humboldt, during his tour of Spanish America, estimated that Mexico City consumed as much wheat as many European cities. He assumed that the Spaniards and their Mexican-born descendants consumed the bulk, but this would have been practically impossible. In reality, the majority of the city's population ate bread either as a base or as a complement.[3]

Privately owned panaderías made all of the city's bread. However, since bread fulfilled what consumers and the Spanish Crown considered to be a public function of nurturing residents, it was subject to close supervision by authorities. This supervision was based on the assumption that the Crown and its colonial representatives were the only forces capable of protecting consumers from the intrinsic tendency toward fraud among producers and merchants. Without government restraint, they feared, entrepreneurs would form oligopolies, or business cartels, that could wield disproportionate influence over the everyday life of the city at great cost to both consumers and civil officials. The Crown elaborated a complex series of regulations that aimed to assert royal authority, repress the private sector's tendency toward abuse, and create a stable, static marketplace that reliably produced bread of predicable quality and weight.[4]

These laws addressed virtually every detail of the business, and generally, bread was of reasonable quality and price. Yet for all their thoroughness they did not prevent the formation of entrenched elite groups who defrauded the public and the royal treasury. A powerful cartel—organized within an owners' guild, or *gremio*—dominated the related wheat, flour, and bread businesses from the early eighteenth century, and probably earlier, until the end of the colonial era. The gremio emerged both despite and because of colonial laws. This chapter explores this contradiction as well as the even more marked contrast that existed between official policy and actual practice. These tensions came to a breaking point during the deep crisis within the Spanish empire in the early nineteenth century. Under the threat of an insurgency, authorities abandoned the model of a static, regulated marketplace in favor of the "absolute liberty" of commerce. They hoped that free-market reforms would encourage competition and bring an abundance of cheap, quality foods to the city. They were partially successful, but the same vicissitudes that sparked the free-market reforms also ended colonial rule.

Markets and Colonial Paternalism

The Crown enacted laws governing the grain and bread trades after a horrific decade of pestilence and hunger, from 1575 to 1585, ravaged much of Mexico and convinced authorities of the need for close supervision of the urban food supply.[5] The Fiel Ejecutoría—the Office of the Faithful Executor—was in charge of enforcing these and other regulations related to the production and sale of consumer goods. Bread regulations specified who could purchase how much wheat or flour of what type, from whom, where, and when. They also limited what types of bread bakers could make, and they set prices. Bakers could not sell before seven in the morning, and they had to offer their goods only in certain plazas and streets or in licensed stores. Vending sites were distributed around the city, such that each one would supply a certain neighborhood.[6] In theory, since all panaderías provided bread at the same price and complied with the same norms, there was no need for shops to compete with each other. Equilibrium and stability, not competition, was the goal for both the economy and the social order.

For owners or managers, these regulations entailed onerous bureaucracy. Every four months, they had to declare to the Fiel Ejecutoría how much wheat they bought, from whom, when, and at what price. Inspectors corroborated these declarations using those given by the wheat growers. Then, based on the price of wheat, plus bakers' other expenses such as milling fees, officials set the official weight of bread, known as the *postura*. The price of bread was permanently fixed at one *medio real* (one-sixteenth of a peso). What varied over time were the ounces. In good times, a medio real bought eighteen ounces of fine white bread (*pan floreado*). In slim times, bread could weigh as little as fourteen ounces. The cheaper pambazo (literally "low bread"), made with coarse unsifted flour, usually weighed around forty ounces but could drop to sixteen.[7]

Officials known as faithful re-weighers (*fieles repesadores*) regularly checked the weight and quality of bread. To make the inspectors' job easier, bakeries could only sell at determined spots and had to mark each piece with distinctive registered insignia. Punishment for noncompliance could be severe. Unbranded bread could cost an owner ten pesos for the first offense, four years' suspension from the trade and two years' banishment for the second, and "definite suspension, public shame, and perpetual banishment" for the third. Selling underweight bread could land an owner in jail for two years.[8]

This vigilance sprang from the well-founded assumption that, given the opportunity, panaderías would defraud the public with underweight or poor quality bread. It also provided the colonial state with a platform from which to declare its responsibility to protect subjects from malfeasance and thus reaffirm the paternal relationship between the Crown and its vassals. In declaration after declaration, viceroys, the highest royal authority in the colony, pronounced and celebrated the *zelo y desvelo*—zealous vigilance—with which they safeguarded the people's well-being.[9]

The opposing concept, championed by liberal economists and philosophers of the eighteenth century, posited that an unregulated free market encouraged competition and, in turn, lowered prices and improved the quality of consumer goods.[10] The solution to fraud, in this view, was not severe regulation and government control but exactly the contrary, the withdrawal of restrictions on commerce. France and Britain had removed many government controls on food markets, and the free market had influential advocates in Spain, such as the Enlightenment polymath Gaspar de Jovellanos who, like Adam Smith, advocated the removal of regulations that limited the individual's pursuit of economic self-interest.[11] In the Spanish empire movement toward free trade focused on international, and especially transatlantic, commerce and culminated in the broadening of exports and imports in 1778.[12] Easing regulations on production and commerce within domestic markets, however, lagged; even Jovellanos recommended continued state regulation of grain prices out of fear of public unrest.

In Mexico colonial authorities similarly distrusted the ability of the free market to produce a positive impact. In their view, they were the only forces capable of protecting consumers from inherently greedy merchants. Without official oversight—the government's zelo y desvelo—consumers would become victims of all kinds of fraud. If panaderías cheated the public even when inspectors were watching, what would they do without government regulations? Also at stake, of course, were the interests of the influential group of owners who were hardly advocates of opening *their* business to anyone who happened to have an oven, some flour, and leaven.

The attorney general (*procurador general*) of the Fiel Ejecutoría clearly articulated this philosophy of a paternal state that oversaw a static, regulated market when in 1779 he rejected the bakery owners' proposition that the "free market," the unfettered interplay between diverse buyers and sellers, set prices instead of the government. He responded that if Mexico had not seen the "revolutions over a lack of bread that are so common in the most cultured countries of Europe, where bread production is entirely free," it was because price fixing had "ensured the public's peace and tranquility." Indeed, following the release of bread from strict government oversight in London, Paris, and other cities, bakeries raised prices, and residents rose in revolt.[13] Modern ideas and inventions were fine, he said, for "physics, chemistry, shipping, and other sciences." But to trust the "tranquility of the vassals" to anything beyond the "known rules of economics and prudence" was to court disaster.[14]

In addition to protecting consumers, colonial regulations aimed to prevent producers and merchants from establishing what the Crown viewed as improper combinations of objects and activities.[15] As part of the ideal of static markets, each producer or merchant was to remain within his specific niche. Millers, for example, could not grind wheat of poor quality together with wheat of high quality; likewise, bakers could not mix different flours in their bread. Bakers of sweet breads (*bizcocheros*) could not make salted bread, under penalty of permanent banishment from the profession. Another law decreed that "bakers cannot be storekeepers and storekeepers cannot be candle makers."[16] The most significant of these regulations prohibited the simultaneous ownership of panaderías and mills. The underlying logic was that businesses gained unfair advantages over other businesses when they mixed things of different natures and bridged distinct trades because these combinations gave them the control of too many economic levers with which they could unduly influence the market, marginalize competitors, and form monopolies. Monopolies could cheat the public by hoarding, speculating, and otherwise manipulating the entire wheat-flour-bread chain. In doing so, they threatened to erode the royal zelo y desvelo, one of the Crown's key claims to legitimate authority.

If inspectors were generally successful in protecting consumers from the most egregious acts of bakers' deceit, they completely failed in their goal to prevent improper combinations within the bread trade and, consequently, the formation of a bread cartel. This failure came, in large measure, because all colonial officials in Mexico did not agree with the notion that the interests of monopolies were contradictory to those of inspectors. Many officials, especially those born in Mexico whose charge it was to enforce the laws, saw the bread monopoly as an ally and an asset to their paternalism.[17]

This tension between law and practice, between Madrid and the streets of Mexico City, came to a head in the mideighteenth century, when the Bourbon monarchs, rulers of the Spanish empire since 1700, set out to centralize authority in the colonies and increase the flow of revenue to the mother country. To this end, they passed more meticulous regulations that aimed to undermine the power of entrenched local elite groups, such as the bread gremio, and to restrict their ability to make illicit profits through abuse and fraud.

The Bread Gremio

Patriarchs of some of the wealthiest families and holders of honorific military and aristocratic titles, panadería owners often served on the city's governing council and were therefore close to the very authorities in charge of overseeing them.[18] They secured their dominance through a gremio, an owners' guild, whose membership was restricted to a dozen or so major owners who collectively controlled the city's fifty-odd shops as well as the nearby mills. Such groups of wealthy mill and panadería owners may have dominated the flour and bread trades since the sixteenth century, but the bread trade seems to have been somewhat more open to small producers before the gremio constituted itself as a legal entity in 1742. That year, the Count of Fuenclara became viceroy of New Spain armed with plans to make local government efficient, centralized, and solvent. The dominant owners persuaded Fuenclara that an official gremio strengthened his broader plan to make commerce more reliable and profitable.[19] The viceroy ratified the gremio's bylaws, which allowed members to elect their first legal representative.[20]

The bakers' gremio was not a traditional trade guild that brought together skilled artisans. Membership depended on wealth, not skill. Around four thousand pesos were required to contribute to the group's "administrative and juridical costs." The bylaws were openly elitist and excluded members of the lower classes—"those whose only possession is the will to be bakers"—because the poor were more inclined to "resort to trickery that would harm the business and the public."[21] According to this self-flattering and deeply deluded vision, the rich had little motivation to defraud the public.

The gremio was an association of owners, most of whom rarely baked or cared to spend much time at all in the workrooms they owned. Most panaderías were sharply divided between owners and administrators, on the one hand, and mostly indigenous workers, on the other. Working conditions in these shops were deplorable, even by colonial standards. In the practice known as *empeño*, workers literally pawned themselves to employers through loans that they had to work off.[22] Bakers typically received a thirty-peso loan. Earning around three and a half *reales* a day, a baker could spend at least three years working it off. In one shop, on San Pablo y San Pedro Street, an unspecified number of workers owed 271 pesos that the administrator included as "assets" in his ledger.[23] Any illness, death, or baptism of a family member only deepened the debt. "We are almost always in debt," complained a bakery worker. "Otherwise, we could not maintain our families."[24] In 1805 Viceroy Iturrigaray noted with concern that "once workers accept debts, they cannot undo them, and they remain locked up for periods that vary according to the sum of the loan."[25] The empeño system generated a vicious cycle of ingrained antagonism between worker and employers. Fearful that they would run off without working off their loans, employers treated bakers like prisoners, locking them up and regularly whipping them. Workers, in turn, were wont to flee from such brutal treatment.[26]

Concerns such as these voiced by high authorities were signs of the deeply contradictory relationship between the gremio and the colonial government. On the one hand, Bourbon high authorities regarded the gremio as a threat. This position sprang from a *political* concern that the Crown needed to weaken local elites in the colonies in order to centralize its authority. But it also sprang from a *fiscal* concern that, given the costly wars between European dynasties, was even more pressing. When mill and bakery owners speculated with grain, they generated profits that eluded the tax collector. On the other hand, local officials in Mexico City tended to support the gremio. Even through its members violated certain laws, the gremio facilitated the overall regulatory structure by providing cohesion to what otherwise would have been a fragmented market of individual actors difficult to govern. In a deeper sense, though, the ideal model of a static, balanced marketplace favored the formation of cartels over modest producers. If the overall objective was not to foster competition but rather dependability, local officials believed that a cartel was best equipped to deliver bread and orderliness.

In 1765 the Bourbon king Charles III sent José de Gálvez as inspector general (*visitador general*) to Spanish America to investigate these contradictions and recommend reforms that would tie the economic and political affairs of the colonies more closely to Madrid.[27] The bakers' gremio was precisely the kind of group that the Bourbons saw as a threat. Nonetheless, owners convinced Gálvez, as they had Fuenclara, that the monopoly ensured inexpensive, quality bread for the public, and they pledged to provide steady tax revenue for the government. They also offered to contribute three thousand pesos annually for the construction and maintenance of a public granary (*pósito*) that would further guarantee the supply and price of bread. In their favor, they likely drew on the view, articulated by an esteemed Franciscan scholar, that unlike in Europe, in Mexico "the price, the weight, and the quality of bread are never arbitrary because the business is organized in the way of a gremio."[28] The gremio, they argued, was perfectly compatible with the strict regulations. The king agreed. He approved Gálvez's recommendation in 1771 and ratified the gremio's bylaws.[29]

Yet soon after, a flood of complaints accusing the gremio of cheating wheat growers, consumers, and the royal tax collectors led the king to reconsider. He recalled that since its official institution, the gremio had pushed several small producers from the trade, with few benefits to the royal treasury or to consumers. Since the most powerful of the gremio's members owned both mills and panaderías, they were in a privileged position to speculate with grain. They bought wheat at low prices while it was still in the ground, thus providing planters with much-needed cash but preventing them from fetching higher prices after harvest. They then ground the flour for use in their own panaderías and sold it at inflated prices to other shops when supplies became scarce. Moreover, the king decided that the much-touted granary was of little use. The king stormed that the gremio had "deceived" the visitador Gálvez, and he revoked the gremio's official status.[30]

In practice, the order did little to restrict the gremio's ability to profitably manipulate the bread market. The group continued much as it had before. Madrid was far from Mexico, and the gremio had many friends in the local government. Moreover, local officials chafed at what they viewed as the Bourbons' arrogant encroachment on their authority and pursued their own agendas despite the orders of the Crown and its viceroys.[31] Punishment records reveal that local officials were strict with unmarked, underweight, and poor-quality bread but turned a blind eye to larger offenses such as the simultaneous ownership or lease of panaderías and mills, as well as millers' common practice of buying and selling wheat.[32] One royal official railed against inspectors, whose "lazy hands have not moved to punish transgressors."[33] Corruption was certainly a factor, but local authorities had good reasons to be complacent or negligent with the gremio. The organization produced significant revenue for the local government, paying special taxes that financed the city's lighting and a local militia, and provided a steady supply of bread.

What mattered to Madrid was not always important to local authorities, most of whom were born in Mexico. The Crown hoped that the regulations would undermine the power of the gremio, prevent millers and bakers from cheating the public and the royal tax collectors, and ensure inexpensive, quality bread. In contrast, local officials were much more concerned with bread itself than with the broader structural context in which it was produced. As the bakery owners were able to convince Gálvez, the gremio facilitated the regulatory efforts of inspectors who were more easily able to supervise a bread market dominated by a dozen prestigious businessmen visible and accountable to the local government than a market composed of hundreds of small producers who could elude the inspector's gaze and the tax collector's hand. The gremio's representative regularly met with the Fiel Ejecutoría to agree on the postura, and authorities certainly found it easier to enforce its meticulous laws when owners formed a cohesive group that inspectors could hold accountable. That fraud happened despite these controls suggested that worse abuses could occur in a more open market.

Yet this divergence between law and practice, between the will of the mother country and that of the colony, was exactly what the Bourbons had set out to correct. In 1789 the Crown appointed as viceroy the Second Count of Revillagigedo, a fervent reformer eager to impose order in the city and undermine the power of entrenched local elites. He took on the battle with the gremio with particular vigor. A week after arriving in Mexico City, he reiterated the old laws and enacted new ones that ordered the separation of dealings between wheat haciendas, mills, and panaderías in order to "justly prevent monopolies and usury." Bakery owners were to buy wheat only from planters. Millers were only allowed to grind that wheat, for a fee they charged to the bakers. Millers could grind and sell wheat they cultivated on their own estates, but they could not own or lease bakeries. Bakery owners, likewise, were barred from running their own mills. Revillagigedo promised to banish transgressors ten leagues from the city and confiscate all the wheat and bread implicated in illegal transactions.[34]

As revealed by the increasingly exasperated tone of Revillagigedo's subsequent decrees, the gremio members continued to run mills and panaderías simultaneously, speculate with grain, and cheat consumers. "Despite the official prices, which should allow for but moderate profits," the viceroy wrote angrily, "bakery owners live with ostentation and more than a few have made huge fortunes." Certain that such wealth came from speculation and fraud, he pledged to "make an example of their greed."[35]

By the end of his term in 1794, the viceroy came to question the entire premise of the regulations as well as the ideal of a market based on order instead of competition. He concluded that both of these pillars of the colonial economy tended to strengthen, not weaken, the gremio. Regulations alone did not cause the formation of the gremio—the transactions between wheat fields, mills, and panaderías were at the heart of the group's dominance— but they did stifle competition from smaller producers. Indeed, colonial rulers did not want to foment competition but rather a predictable, controllable supply of bread. Revillagigedo now wanted to overturn this ideal altogether.

He wrote his successor that "as long as bread production is linked to certain restrictions that can only be overcome with considerable wealth, this and other types of monopolies will continue." The solution he suggested was to encourage free trade by removing "so many government policies and provisions" and make the bread trade "absolutely free, so that any individual of medium wealth could take it up."[36] A deregulated free market, the viceroy believed, would open the bread trade to the salutary airs of competition and allow smaller producers—"individuals of medium wealth"—to take the place of elite groups like the gremio.

Revillagigedo's suggestion went beyond a mere shift in the model that governed commerce. He envisioned a transformation of the relationships between consumers, producers, and the state. For years he had stubbornly worked within the paternalist system in which the state assumed the responsibility of protecting the public's well-being through strict regulation of structures of production and commerce that were dominated by economic elites. For authorities, the "public" meant consumers, not producers; the government's responsibility was to ensure that the public had food, not access to the means of production.

Now the viceroy embraced the liberal notion that an unregulated market would allow non-elite producers greater access to the market and provide the public with quality goods without government intervention. The proposal was hardly democratic in the political sense: the viceroy hoped that this proposal would consolidate Madrid's authoritarianism by weakening local government and removing powerful merchant groups who stood between the Crown and its vassals. But it did have the potential to make the market into a more even playing field on which small producers and vendors could operate. In any case, Revillagigedo came to these conclusions only on his way out, as he looked backed on his exasperating stint as viceroy. He left the implementation to his successors, most of whom did not share his free-market enthusiasm.

Imperial Crisis and Free-Market Reforms

Crisis finally broke the old-regime model. In 1808 Napoleon invaded Spain and sent Fernando VII into exile. A regency met in the city of Cádiz to govern the empire until the king returned and instituted wide-ranging changes that limited the power of the Crown and eased some restrictions on commerce. Two years later, Mexican provincial elites and peasants responded to Miguel Hidalgo's Grito de Dolores and rose up against the colonial regime, thus beginning the decade-long insurrection that led to independence. The fighting severed Mexico City from its hinterland. Consumer goods became scarce, prices shot up, and authorities struggled to find ways to bring food to the capital. In 1811 Viceroy Venegas sent out dozens of letters to neighboring provinces, urging them to send wheat to the capital. None of the responses were positive. The intendant in nearby Toluca wrote that "rebels have taken the surrounding roads, they've threatened to kill anyone who tries to transport grain to the capital." From Querétaro the intendant responded that growers were too afraid of "insurgent bandits" to venture onto the roads. All the rest wrote that they had no wheat to send to the capital. [37] In 1812 drought made grain even scarcer, forcing the Fiel Ejecutoría to drop the postura to a historic low of ten ounces for white bread and thirteen and a half for pambazos.[38] Maize, meat, and vegetables were similarly scarce and expensive.

Mexico was experiencing the calamitous and yet inspiring clash between the new possibilities represented by the reforms from Cádiz and the threats of violence and hunger. The failure of the old system forced authorities to consider new ideas and to reconsider ones that their predecessors had rejected. Given the inability of the conventional suppliers to bring food to the city, the viceroy's advisers recommended removing all of the commercial restrictions. The *síndico de lo común*, the government's attorney for civil affairs, was a particularly enthusiastic proponent of free trade. He insisted that releasing bread prices from the postura would encourage competition among growers, which in turn would "infallibly bring lower prices."[39] From bread, the government moved to other foodstuffs. Advisers encouraged lifting the taxes on cattle and allowing the slaughter and sale of meat outside the official abattoirs. After taking these small steps, the viceroy declared "absolute liberty of commerce," allowing anyone to sell bread, meat, candles, and maize anywhere in the city, at any price.[40] Free trade quickly transformed from a controversial, risky, and "modern" notion into an urgent imperative whose superior ability to attract abundance and lower prices suddenly appeared self-evident. "As everyone now knows," wrote the attorney for fiscal affairs, citing the Spanish philosopher Jovellanos, "it is in vain to expect abundance to emerge from any principle other than the free sale of goods."[41]

At the same time, officials also tried quickly to modernize the archaic labor regime, though they were more eager to liberate panaderías from Indian workers than vice versa. Taken up by winds of the free market, Mexico City councilmen argued that the empeño system had caused everyone problems. Workers, forced to live in the workrooms, slept badly next to the dough troughs, contaminating the public's bread with their filth. Owners lost money when bakers fled before working off their debts. Even God suffered because bakers got drunk and committed "infinite sins" with women while they were cloistered inside. In sum, the empeño system encouraged the "vile sentiments of the Indians," whose only food was any "strip of cow," whose only drink was "*chinguirito, pulque*, or other infernal brews," and whose only clothing was "ragged loincloths [*pobres taparrabos*]." "There is no religion among them; they know neither God, nor his sacred law. They have no feelings; they receive gifts just as they do blows." The goal was not to ameliorate the wretched lives of such a lot but rather to "exterminate" them.[42] Presumably, "exterminate" meant replace the current workforce with clean, sober, polite, and industrious bakers who would appear, somehow, if employers simply stopped advancing loans and instead paid wages for work completed.

Authorities did not attack labor conditions with nearly the same urgency with which they restructured the retail food market. Nor did they lift controls on other areas of commerce such as mining and tobacco, held by royal monopolies, as many wealthy Mexicans were demanding. As historian Michael Costeloe stresses, the colonial government's "main criterion" for considering economic reforms "was the balance of benefits in respect for stopping the insurrections."[43] Feeding Mexico City, which had so far not joined the insurrection, was vital. Authorities' immediate objective was to bring more food to the city; shifts in working conditions would not have accomplished this goal in the short term. In a broader sense, though, the reforms in the food market show how the threat of insurgency forced the authorities to release some of the Crown's control over everyday life in the colony.[44] An influx of bread, meat, and maize did alleviate hunger in the city, and despite some warnings to the contrary, prices remained stable.

The colonial government maintained its free-trade convictions even when unexpected negative consequences led authorities to readjust the absoluteness of the *libertad absoluta*. Among the sudden proliferation of food producers and sellers, several makeshift butcheries appeared, many of which allegedly sold meat from stolen cattle. Customers unwittingly ate "unusual" meat from mules and dogs. On its way to slaughter, a bull ran off and trampled an Indian water seller to death. The overwhelmed faithful re-weighers found that butchers did not sell at the rates they advertised. The viceroy consequently decreed, among other provisions, that cowboys could bring bulls to the city only at dawn and that butchers had to slaughter cattle inside the city limits (to ensure that the meat came from healthy and "usual" animals).[45] The decrees asserted that the colonial government had not relinquished its authority over the market nor neglected its responsibility to protect consumers.

These were adjustments to the free-market experiment, in which officials persisted despite tempting offers by wealthy suppliers to monopolize the market.[46] The síndico de lo común insisted that the problems did not arise from the free market itself, but rather from the momentary dislocations caused by the insurgency. Once the war was over, and the colonial state had reasserted its authority in New Spain, bandits would no longer prevent the abundant and profitable flow of goods. The long-term result would be a more efficient and democratic marketplace.[47] Of course, the colonial state lost the war, and Mexico became independent from Spain in 1821, but these reforms and considerations constituted the foundation of the market policies of the new nation.

CHAPTER TWO

"A system that offends the hands of brothers"

Small Bakers and the Free Market in Independent Mexico

☙

☩ THE LEADERS OF INDEPENDENT MEXICO EXPLICITLY FOLLOWED THE late Bourbon model of free market with limited government oversight. They continued the search for a balance between releasing the supposedly innate dynamism of competition and curbing the equally innate greed of merchants and producers. During the first thirty-five years or so of independence, though, they found little success on either count. Panaderías, like many businesses in Mexico, suffered a decline that led most of the old owners to leave the trade. Authorities, despite their ideological faith in the free market, repeatedly attempted to intervene during times of scarcity and when panaderías committed fraud. Yet they failed to impact the market significantly. As a result, they saw neither the abundance promised by free-market advocates nor the controlled stability of the earlier colonial paternalism. The food crises that periodically fell upon Mexico City between the 1820s and 1840s threatened not only the physical well-being of residents but also the legitimacy of the political leaders.

However difficult the period was for the government and consumers, the first three decades after independence offered some advantages for small bread producers who were able to take center stage in a trade previously dominated by the colonial gremio and restricted by burdensome regulations.[1] In a period of frequent coups, civil war, and foreign invasions, political and economic turbulence acted as a barrier that prevented more leveraged entrepreneurs from entering the volatile market. Likewise, panadería workers also made important gains during these years; though they remained impoverished, they freed themselves from the debt and violence that had tied them to employers. These barriers of turbulence receded when Mexico began to experience a degree of tranquility and growth in the 1850s. Immigrant entrepreneurs moved into the bread trade and began to marginalize small producers and reinstate mechanisms of labor coercion. The period of weak state and egalitarian market waned as a stronger state and monopolies began to rise.

"Ocean of uncertainty": Instability and Opportunity After Independence

Mexico's new leaders expressed a practical and ideological commitment to the freedom of commerce. However, volatility in the food market threatened to erode their political legitimacy among a population still accustomed to the paternalistic zelo y desvelo. Inflation of food prices invariably coincided with moments of political instability, when officials had the least authority over producers and merchants. Institutions such as the Fiel Ejecutoría, which the colonial government had used to regulate markets, no longer existed, and the cohesive gremio had given way to dozens of small producers who eluded government control. Unable to lower prices and improve quality by decree, the new leaders instead loudly echoed consumers' indignation in an attempt to identify themselves with the public instead of with the alleged greedy speculators. Still, when the price of bread rose, citizens accused officials of complicity with unscrupulous merchants and of indifference to the public's suffering.[2]

The ties between governance and food were most crucial during instances of political crisis. What was most apparent in these moments, however, was how tenuous these ties had become. Leaders could do little to regulate the market. For instance, an 1828 riot in Mexico City over disputed presidential elections, known as the Acordada Revolt, sent bakers and other food providers to raise their already high prices. The governor of Mexico City, struggling to assert his authority, tried to pressure bakers into selling at fixed prices, but they refused to comply. The governor then ordered them at least to mark prices on their bread.[3] Owners balked at this decree as well, convincing authorities that some bread types did not lend themselves to such markings. A new law ordered them merely to advertise their prices on signs inside bakeries. But owners resisted even this law, claiming that it was impossible to "calculate the exact weight of bread."[4] When the governor inspected bakeries in 1834, he criticized the "scandalous abuses in detriment to the public" and reminded owners of the requirement to place signs with the prices and weights of bread.[5]

In 1837, in the midst of Texas's war of secession, inflation again caused what the Mexico City governor called "times of calamity and misery." In a decree, he called upon the "principal merchants in the areas of bread, meat, candles, etc." to lower their prices.[6] He stressed, however, that this was a voluntary "invitation," a clarification that reflected the state's impotence as least as much as its stated adherence to the free market.[7] Scarcity and fraud in panaderías rose together with political instability, which revealed authorities' inability to fulfill one of the public's most fundamental expectations of government—to ensure the food supply. This failing, in turn, further eroded the legitimacy of new leaders.

Links between political instability and food crisis were particularly evident under Antonio López de Santa Anna, the on-again, off-again president and war hero. Santa Anna lost the war with Texas but recovered his national prestige by repelling a French invasion in 1838. During the so-called Pastry War, French gunboats blockaded and bombarded the Atlantic port city of Veracruz, demanding reparations for bread taken from a French bakery during the Acordada Revolt, among other alleged damages.[8] Redeemed by victory and his sacrifice to the nation—he lost his leg to French cannon fire and ceremoniously buried it—Santa Anna then sought to overthrow the presidency of Anastasio Bustamante.[9] In the winter of 1841, Santa Anna held Mexico City in a state of siege until Bustamante capitulated. Even when the victorious Santa Anna lifted the blockade, merchants were wary of selling what little stock they had. As a contemporary editorialist put it, "Society is thrust back and forth in an ocean of uncertainty and fear; no one feels safe in their home ... the industrious man, Mexican or foreigner, does not dare to invest in such precarious soil."[10] The district governor Luis Gonzaga Vieyra tried to pressure owners to sell bread at a fixed weight (twenty-two ounces) per real, but the latter countered that flour was too scarce and expensive to comply. Bakery owners hired police to prevent hungry customers from rioting over the ever-rising prices of the ever-shrinking pieces.[11]

The press accused the "heartless merchants" of "dictating laws as they see fit, speculating with the misery of the hopeless consumers."[12] Many doubtlessly sought to exploit the crisis, but the desperate, erratic fiscal policy of the increasingly dictatorial Santa Anna government was at least as much to blame for the dislocations and hunger that ravaged commerce and households in the city. Bankrupt from the defeat in Texas and the French bombardment of Veracruz, the government turned out a surfeit of copper coins, provoking exorbitant inflation. When officials discovered that the coins were easily counterfeited, they ordered merchants to give them over to the government, with the pledge to replace them with new ones six months later.[13] Meanwhile, to the indignation of workers, whose wages were still paid in copper, shopkeepers refused to receive the soon-to-be-useless coins and demanded payment in silver. The government ordered bakeries not only to receive copper but also to pay a third of their taxes in silver.[14]

In response, most bakeries simply closed. According to historian Carlos María de Bustamante, a firsthand witness to these events, other shops "tripled or quadrupled their prices." Desperate residents appealed for bread "with deafening screams" and struggled to get past guards stationed in bakeries "to prevent disorderliness." The streets of Mexico City "were awash in the tears of the hungry."[15] The governor of Mexico City ordered all bakeries to open, but officials acknowledged that forcing businesses to operate in such a climate was unjust and futile. Councilmen asked the Mexican president, "What authority could possibly force commercial interests to run their businesses into ruin? There is no police, no force strong enough, to achieve obedience." The situation, the councilmen concluded, would soon lead to civil unrest. "Soon the people will ask for bread. Hungry, they will scream. Finally, they will become furious. Nothing will be sacred. Nothing will contain their irresistible force."[16]

The food crisis turned even worse the next winter. Civil war raged, hailstorms decimated wheat fields, and peasants took to the hills to avoid conscription. Winds blew away the few grains that had survived. The per capita consumption of wheat bread in the capital fell from a daily average of 811 to 242 grams.[17] Inflation and scarcities continued, garbage piled up in streets, and a drought hit the central plateau in 1843. Not only was wheat scarce, there was barely enough water to move the grinding stones.[18] The leaseholder of the Santo Domingo Mill requested permission to dig a new well because the explosion of a nearby gunpowder factory had destroyed the aqueducts.[19] According to Niceto de Zamacois, another contemporary historian critical of Santa Anna, "The government could have gained in popularity and prestige by gathering grain in order to help the people, as any good leader should do." Instead, it focused on conscripting more soldiers and increasing taxes, actions that further "inclined the people to revolt."[20]

In effect, Mexico City residents grew increasingly desperate and indignant as Santa Anna and his close followers grew wealthier. When Santa Anna organized a New Year's "banquet of unprecedented splendor of food and delicate wine," he may as well have told the masses to eat cake. In the streets, an "infinity of poor anxiously searched for bread, maize, and meat; the bakeries were under guard to contain the excesses of the unfortunate tormented by misery."[21] When Santa Anna fell from power, a crowd of hungry, angry citizens disinterred his leg and dragged it through the streets of Mexico City. Previous leaders' failures to regulate the bread market had revealed their impotence, but at least they had tried to conjure the paternal allure of the colonial state. In the view of the common people, Santa Anna had cynically displayed his indifference to the public's hunger.

This turbulence notwithstanding, some planters still grew wheat, some millers still ground it, and bakers still baked. The difference was that the dominant owners no longer remained, and the nodes of agriculture, manufacturing, and commerce were no longer integrated by overlapping ownership and cohesion among owners. Notably, the power of the millers, the centerpieces of the whole wheat-flour-bread complex, was the first to deteriorate. Periodic scarcities of wheat led some to refit their mills for textiles. The owners of the formerly prestigious Santa Mónica mill sold off their properties in 1833; the surrounding wheat fields lay fallow, and the mill fell into disrepair. Four other mill-owning families followed suit.[22] In 1826 Guillermo Pollard, who leased the Molino del Rey, asked the city council for permission to use the mill's water rights not to move the grinding stone but to irrigate the surrounding fields. The owner of the Santo Domingo Mill, founded by Hernán Cortés, used her water rights to wash clothes.[23] A French entrepreneur approached the municipal government in 1840 with a plan to build a steam-powered flour mill inside the city limits. Officials eagerly approved the project, but the mill was never built.[24]

Old panadería owners also left the business. By the early 1830s, the vast majority of the owners who dominated the business had disappeared from the record.[25] The writer Guillermo Prieto lamented that his Mexican middle-class peers had abandoned the commercial and manufacturing ventures of their fathers, preferring instead to be "senators, generals, lawyers, doctors, or, at least, engineers."[26] Prieto himself was no exception. Born into a family of millers and bakers, he became a lawyer, senator, and poet. Given the lack of interest among the sons of former owners, in 1830 Mexico's city council tried to tap into the "*gran comercio del Universo*" by repealing the "barbarous legislation" from the colonial period that prohibited foreign ownership of businesses.[27] A handful of mostly French and Italian immigrants who listed their occupation as bakers arrived between 1824 and 1840; most, however, settled in cities away from the capital.[28]

Spaniards, who had dominated panaderías during colonialism and again at the end of the nineteenth century, were largely absent from the trade, mostly because Spain and Mexico remained in conflict for decades after independence. Spanish troops, driven from the rest of the country, continued to control an enclave of Veracruz until 1825, which prevented the foundling Mexican government from collecting customs revenue from its most important port. Spain even launched an invasion in 1828; poorly executed, it only exacerbated tensions and intensified anti-Hispanic sentiment. These continued conflicts and intrigues put the "old" Spaniards—those who had arrived during the colonial period—at the center of the early republic's constant discord. Resentment over the colonial past, suspicion over lingering imperialist ambitions, and grievances over land and commerce ignited *anti-gachupinismo*, or hatred of Spaniards (whom Mexicans pejoratively called *gachupines*).[29] Madrid only recognized Mexico's independence in 1836, when it sent the first of its ambassadors. However, these emissaries, together with Mexican monarchists, continually devised plots to bring a Spanish prince to Mexico.[30] Expulsion orders forced out of Mexico thousands of Spaniards in the late 1820s.[31] Many who remained became targets of retribution and looting during the civil wars of the 1840s and 1850s, when groups of armed peasants terrified owners with the threat of a "caste war that could lead to the extermination of all the whites."[32]

This picture of war, riots, and instability generally coincides with the general impression drawn by historians who characterize the first decades after independence as a period of political upheaval and economic depression. Markets were fragmented, transportation was underdeveloped and expensive, capital was scarce, and the weak, beleaguered state was unable to enforce laws that could have encouraged and protected investments. Mexico's major industries—mining and agriculture—were slow to recover from the decade-long war of independence.[33] Yet there has been little research into internal markets, domestic production, and labor for the early republican period largely because of the spotty archival record for that period.[34] Unlike that of previous and successive periods, for which historians are often able to reconstruct the day-by-day development of certain tendencies, the historical record for these years contains major gaps. Not surprisingly, moments of crisis produced the most documentation, which gives the impression that the entire period was an unbroken series of epidemics and violent clashes.

Nonetheless, there are also strong indications that the late colonial free-trade reforms, the war of independence, and the subsequent political instability opened up the way for smaller producers, those whom Revillagigedo called "individuals of medium wealth." Wheat, flour, and bread no longer flowed along closely guarded circuits but rather through multiple routes that formed an ungovernable sieve. The bread oligopoly embodied in the gremio ceded to a volatile, uncertain market of disconnected, opportunistic owners of small businesses who bet that the payoffs of inflation would outweigh the occasional threat of riots and unpredictable fiscal policies. One of the most complete lists of owners, from 1834, includes twenty-one names, only two of which appeared in earlier records.[35]

This occupation by small producers of what had been a business of the rich lowered the prestige of the bread and flour trades. A Panamanian investor refused an opportunity to buy the Santa Mónica mill because it involved dealing with "bakers, planters, and other riffraff."[36] Despite the risks, this "riffraff" enjoyed a fairly egalitarian market, free of oligarchs and an overbearing state. Indeed, as the failed attempts to force panaderías to sell at determined prices suggest, authorities wielded very little influence over shops at all. The new bakery owners lacked status, but, because of the inability of local authorities to regulate, they had a great deal of freedom to determine how to run their businesses.

Similarly, the colonial-era empeño system, in which workers pawned themselves to employers through debt, fell after independence, together with the attendant violence with which employers had coerced workers into bakeries. Workers subsequently asserted themselves with unprecedented boldness. Bakers staged what was probably their first collective protest during the 1828 Acordada Revolt when they refused to work and ran out on their debts. The Mexico City governor, desperate to contain the restive population, called on police and even ordinary citizens "to detain the bakers who used to work by empeño."[37] The old system had collapsed, and authorities had little means by which to force workers back into panaderías.

To be sure, the lives of poor workers in Mexico City were still fairly wretched. The average life span of the city's general population was just short of thirty-seven years, and about half of the city's residents lacked steady employment.[38] An 1844 workers' magazine noted that panaderías still drained the "glowing health characteristic of adolescence," and the dust, filth, and smoke caused tuberculosis, eye diseases, and rashes that turned into gruesome ulcers.[39]

Nonetheless, new owners who emerged after independence were most likely bakers themselves and therefore relied more on family labor than their oligarchic predecessors. They did not need to attract and retain labor through debt and coercion. Even if employers, or their workers, wanted to continue the old empeño system, most lacked the capital necessary to pay workers in advance.

These favorable developments for small producers and workers attracted less attention from leaders than the vicissitudes in which they unfolded. Viceroy Revillagigedo and his pro-free-market successors had hoped that market reforms would undermine monopolies, encourage abundance, and stave off crisis. The bread gremio had disappeared, and a relatively democratic marketplace free of oligarchic domination and overbearing regulations had in fact emerged. Workers were no longer tied by debt and locked in bakery workrooms. But scarcity, inflation, and political instability overshadowed these accomplishments. Although free trade was not the cause of Mexico's political and economic ills, the removal of controls on the food trade occurred amid recurrent crises that revealed the political leadership's inability to effectively attend to the everyday needs of residents. In this context, the result of the free market was not abundance and prosperity, but rather periodic scarcity and chaos. In the absence of formal institutions that could effectively regulate the bread market, and without alliances between the state and a cohesive group of bakery and mill owners, official food policy amounted to little more than finger-wagging decrees. For government authorities, these circumstances gave new credence to the old-regime authoritarian model of the gremio.

"The most iniquitous greed"

The most compelling evidence that small producers and workers experienced some progress amid the vicissitudes that shook the country after independence is that both groups began to complain of reverses in the 1850s. Since 1848, small producers had already been under pressure from the government, which desperately sought out new revenue after the devastating war with the United States by imposing steep taxes on panaderías and ordering the immediate closure of unlicensed shops.[40] Another more structural shift occurred in mills, the crucial central node of the wheat-flour-bread complex.

New owners, Mexican and foreign (particularly French), began repairing aqueducts, ordering famed grinding stones from the French town La Ferté-sous-Jouarre, and installing new turbines with which to move them.[41] Official trade policies encouraged these innovations by placing high tariffs on foreign flour and low tariffs on foreign wheat. This selective protectionism ensured millers a high profit by granting them access to cheap wheat from the United States and sparing them competition from cheaper American flour that flowed along the Mississippi and around the Gulf of Mexico. The Santa Anna regime went as far as to prohibit any importation of flour in the early 1850s. Liberals, who took power in 1855, replaced the ban with high tariffs.[42]

The tariffs were particularly burdensome for regions on the Atlantic coast that could purchase flour and other goods from the United States at lower prices. In 1852 the city council of the port of Veracruz requested permission to import flour from New Orleans since the flour sent by mills in Mexico City and Puebla was "of poor quality and very expensive." The cost of shipping flour from central Mexico to the coast put bread beyond the reach of "the proletarian class," which led to "poverty and hunger, a constant danger for society and no small obstacle to tranquility." Still the Federal Chamber of Deputies denied the request, probably because the tariffs were part of an arrangement between the millers of central Mexico and the federal government.[43] In addition to supporting industrial development (at the expense of wheat planters and consumers far from the center), the tariffs increased the government's revenue. In addition to collecting import taxes, the government charged *alcabalas* (internal tariffs) on flour, which constituted a quarter of the internal customs revenue.[44]

This closeness between the government and millers in central Mexico was merely an initial step toward consolidation of the industry under wealthy businessmen supported by the state. The Mexican government remained poor, fragmented, and debilitated by conflict. The U.S. invasion and seizure of half the country in 1847–1848 exacerbated the antagonisms that had plagued Mexican politics since independence. The mercurial Santa Anna, back from his exile following the U.S. victory, took power in 1853 from the moderate president Mariano Arista. In his subsequent dictatorship he exiled opponents, banned books, and formed a secret police. Santa Anna dedicated much of the national treasury's funds—wrested from the population through taxes on pets, windows, and doors—to strengthening the military. But he also moved to improve the formal channels of commerce by launching important infrastructure projects (telegraph lines, stagecoach lines, waterworks, and gas lights) and mercilessly pursuing bandits.[45] Leveraged capitalists entered with new vigor into not only flour and bread markets, but also mining, agriculture, and land speculation.

If these businessmen equated Santa Anna's despotism with political stability, they were mistaken. In 1854 the liberals launched the Revolution of Ayutla, which overthrew Santa Anna and sent him back into exile the next year. Still, in the early 1850s, millers acquired and maintained new leverage that impinged upon the autonomy small bakers and retailers had enjoyed for the previous decades. The ensuing conflicts revealed palpable shifts in the flour and bread trades as well as contested meanings of *free market*. The question that emerged was for *whom* was the market *free*.

The first sign of conflict occurred when a group of small-bakery owners objected to the decision in 1853 of millers to raise grinding fees. The bakers—Manuel Ortíz de Montellano, Leandro Cuevas, Francisco Javier Y., Rodrigo Marañón, and Julián García—complained to the Mexico City governing council that the fees violated their "freedom of commerce." At the center of the debate were the meanings and consequences of *comercio libre*, or free trade. The millers—Benito Muriel, Aquilino Mendieta, and Manuel de Castro—argued that their action was an expression of "the exercise of property," which was guaranteed to "all men who live in freedom." They cited the views of Viceroy Revillagigedo, as well as the progress of Britain, the United States, and France, and embraced "the new spirit that animates modern societies [which] has shot down the rotten edifice of the old doctrines that condemned commerce for so long." For the bakers, in contrast, "comercio libre" signaled unrestricted, destructive selfishness. They proposed instead "freedom of commerce" (*libertad de comercio*), by which they meant freedom from cartels that restricted their access to the marketplace, a freedom that justified and required governmental intervention. The millers' fee increase would only lead to "more and more," and if the government did not curb the millers now, nothing would stop them from taking over the business. "Under the spurious pretext of the free market," the bakers warned, "society will become a chaos, leading even to its annihilation."

Underlying this overwrought rhetoric was the bakers' fear of a reemerging bread gremio that could undermine their recently acquired position. What the millers really planned, the bakers insisted, was to open their own bakeries and ruin the smaller shops. Raising fees was merely the first step. Once the millers added bread to the flour business, no one would be able to compete. If the millers could "own the grains we buy and set arbitrary prices on grinding," and also establish panaderías, "Who would be strong enough to resist them?" With such vertical integration, the bakers pointed out, the mill-and-bakery owners could make cheaper bread. This seemed patently unjust. "If this is not an attack on the freedom of commerce, then truth as we know it no longer exists. The millers . . . will form a privileged class of veritable despots."[46]

The councilmen saw the matter differently. Given the continuing threat of civil war, scarcity, and inflation, the bakers' arguments made no sense. What the bakers regarded as the seed of chaos and despotism, the councilmen saw as the undisputable advantage of the free market. That vertical integration could lower prices, they noted, "is precisely what we should encourage instead of hinder." It was "one of the objectives to which the authority should effectively dedicate its protective efforts."[47] Protecting the marketplace for small producers, as a matter of principle, was considerably less important.

An Invasion of Pastry Chefs

The bakers' claim that in an unrestricted market the millers would dominate the trade proved premature. However, their general fear that competitors would displace them was correct. This competition came from European bakery owners who arrived during the French invasion and subsequent rule of Maximilian of Hapsburg between 1862 and 1867. The dozen or so French and Austrian bakers and pastry chefs acquired many of the city's downtown bakeries, likely paying good money to lease the shops from their beleaguered owners.

French, German, Austrian, and Spanish immigrants owned the majority of the twenty-seven downtown bakeries listed in the 1867 *Commercial Directory of the Mexican Empire* (table 1).[48] Santiago Schewey opened a shop on Alconedo Street, not far from the bakery owned by María Dietrich on 16 Zuleta Street and Jorge Steiert's shop on Revillagigedo Street. The Aragonese immigrant Antonio Buerba had three shops. His countryman and business partner Gerónimo Galnares had two. Titus Vaast, owner of the "renowned Panadería Francesa on 13 Espíritu Santo Street," announced to the readership of the French-language daily *Le Trait d'Union* that he was opening another shop, on Santo Domingo Street, where consumers could find "fresh bread in the morning and at noon, in addition to pastries and warm Brioches every day."[49]

Table 1. Mexico City panadería owners, 1867.

OWNER	BAKERY AND ADDRESS
Agesta (Testamentaria de)	Mesones (2nd Block) 14
Aldana y Cía	Manzanares
	Monserrate
Antonio Buerba	Calle Ancha
	San Fernando
	San Juan (3rd Block)
Antonio Vallejo	San Andrés 8
Enrique Neve	Factor
Félix Chassin	Olmedo
Francisco Gual	Damas (2nd Block)
Francisco Prieto	Santa Catarina (1st Block)
	Tacuba 25
	Tacuba 5
Francisco Verni	Medinas 24
Gavino Caballeros	San Pedro y San Pablo
Gerónimo Galnares	Alhóndiga
	San Juan (3rd Block)
Gorostiaga y Besares	Vanegas (2nd Block)
Gregorio Lasa	Esclavo
	San Lorenzo 10
	Santa María 4
Jorge Steiert	Revillagigedo 1
Josefa Esnaurrizar	Joya
Juan Hugues	Calle Nueva
Juan Perrot	Espírituo Santo
Justo de la Lama	Puente de Aduana
María Dietrich	Zuleta 16
Nicolás de la Rosa	Merced
Ramón Gamez	Damas (1st Block)
Ramón Gavino	Portillo de San Diego
Raymundo Mora	Santa Clara (corner of Manrique)
Santiago Schewey	Alconedo
Tiburcio Amavisca	Puente Jesús Nazareno
	Rastro (3rd Block)
Tomás Bueno	Jesús María
Vega y Cía	Sepulcros de Santo Domingo

Source: *Directorio del comercio del imperio mexicano para el año de 1867.*

Although most of these Europeans left, some rather hurriedly, after the liberal victory and Maximilian's execution in 1867, others remained through the decade. Teodoro Weis remained through the early 1870s. Víctor Monteaut, a "French subject," told authorities that he was unaware of the requirement to advertise his prices because he did not speak Spanish. He was fined by municipal inspectors in 1869, as were Francisco Veniy, Paulina Aubery de Huques, José Schurey, Celestino Hommel, and other foreign owners.[50]

These owners introduced a variety of modifications to Mexican bakeries. Austrians and the French introduced an array of new breads and pastries whose names—*vienés, francés, mollete*—bespeak their origin. The introduction of new, smaller bread types like those listed in table 2 represented a broader shift from large pieces that weighed between one or two pounds to individual rolls and buns (bolillos).[51] Some owners, such as Angel de la Lama, one of the few wealthy Mexicans among the emerging group, relinked mills and bakeries. Lama owned five bakeries 1871 while he was leasing the Valdés Mill.[52] These owners renewed the bread trade's air of respectability. Unlike the "riffraff" of earlier times, these bakers wore suits, not aprons. They were gentlemen entrepreneurs, peers of the "decent people" who enjoyed their goods and of the government officials who were eager to see the reliable bread supply reestablished.

These new owners also moved to restructure the retail operations in bakeries by initiating in-store sales in place of the old system of selling through small grocery stores and street vendors. Petty retailers, seeing their livelihood threatened, sent a drastically worded letter to Mexico City governor Juan José Baz in July 1869 that denounced "the most iniquitous greed of the monopoly of foreign bakery owners." These petty retailers, fifty-eight men and thirty-two women, stressed that they had built a modest but decent livelihood, going to bakeries "before dawn, shivering in the cold," and taking fresh bread "practically to consumers' homes." Since it saved residents time and the bother of going downtown where bakeries were concentrated, their labor was "humanitarian and economical." Indeed, these petty merchants argued that they protected consumers from "the abusive despotism" of the bakery owners, who "would certainly raise the price of bread, or diminish its weight," if their employees distributed the bread.

"We are the victims," they continued, "of the iniquitous greed and the monopoly of bakery owners, principally three or four of the richest bakery owners, the Frenchman don Teodoro N., the Spaniard D. José Juncal, and Mr. Lama, together with four others, who own mills." These owners rescinded the

Table 2. (continued on page 38) Ounces of bread per real, 1869.

BAKERY	BREAD	OUNCES/REAL
La Merced 10	Pan de manteca	20
	Pambazo	23
	Birote	24
	Blanco	24
Puente de Jesús María	Peluca	21
	Pambazo	21
	Rosca	22
Rejas de Balbaneras	Rosca	23
	Peluca	23
	Boyo	24
	Birote	28.5
	Pambazo	29.5
Tacuba	Pan de manteca	16
	Pan blanco	20
	Birote	20
Santo Domingo	Peluca	18
	Boyo	18
	Pan de manteca	18
	Pambazo prieto	20
	Birote	22
Alhóndiga	Pan blanco	20
	Pan de manteca	20
	Pambazo blanco	24
Santa Catarina	Pan de manteca	17
	Rosca	17
	Tahona	17
	Peluca	22
	Boyo	22
	Birote	23
	Pambazo	23
San Juan	Pan de manteca	18
	Pan blanco	20
	Birote	22
	Pambazo	24
Joya 5	Mantecada	18
	Pambazo	24
	Pan floreado	43

Table 2. (continued from page 37) Ounces of bread per real, 1869.

BAKERY	BREAD	OUNCES/REAL
Santa Clara	Pan de manteca	22
	Birote	26
	Pambazo blanco	30
San Lorenzo	Rosca	14
	Tahona	14
	Mantecada	14
	Peluca and boyo	16

Source: "Estracto de las tarifas de las panaderías de esta capital," AHCM, Fondo Ayuntamiento de Mexico, Sección Panaderías, vol. 3453, exp. 94.

custom of selling to retailers at a discount. They sought to keep peddlers from selling their own bread and "pressured the other bakeries to shut down our humble stores and refuse to sell us bread so that they alone can sell it." The peddlers urged the governor to intervene, drawing on the same anti-free-trade argument that the small-bakery owners had used. While comercio libre was well suited to some industries, the peddlers insisted that it should not apply to bread. "The state still should recognize the unique *social pact* that bakeries have with the public." Given the indispensable character of bread, the baker "can never say that he is free to sell to whomever he likes, as he pleases, and at whatever time suits him."

The peddlers' letter described, in the most dramatic terms, the peril of comercio libre, the dissolution of what they called the "social pact" around bread: "Under a system that purports to adopt the progressive spirit of the century, we see a system that offends the hand of brothers." Consumed by "devouring greed," the owners not only threatened to throw the retailers' "two thousand families" into the street, "plunging the dagger of death into their hearts," they would also leave multitudes of consumers who lived in the outlying, poorer neighborhoods without any bread. Further, the peddlers conflated their misfortune with the plight of the entire nation. Now that a "foreign monopoly" wielded inordinate power, the peddlers asked, "What gigantic progress was achieved by the national independence in 1821, in which we overcame three centuries of odious distinctions?" Will the "divine democratic system" merely "cover with empty words the same oppression our fathers suffered?" The question was especially poignant given Mexico's recent "independence" from Maximilian and the French.[53]

Much like the councilmen who mediated the earlier dispute between the millers and the bakers, Governor Baz was more concerned with the supply of bread than with defending the egalitarian character of the market. Indeed, having assumed the governorship of the city after the liberal victory over Maximilian, Baz was determined to destroy the redoubts of conservatism. He forced the sale of church properties in Mexico City and ordered the demolition of monasteries and temples, supposedly in order to improve the flow of traffic.[54] As a liberal convinced of the virtues of the free market, Baz could only have regarded the peddlers' apocalyptic claims as exaggerated and anachronistic. What is more, the peddlers chided him for having "pulverized in a matter of hours temples whose solidity had defied centuries" and for persecuting nuns, "venerable old ladies preparing for their death." In contrast to his anticlerical zeal, Baz was "complacent with the wealthy bakers who have reduced us to the most frightening misery."[55]

Small wonder that these "ironic and ridiculing words" infuriated Baz, who threw the letter's primary author in jail. At the same time, however, he assembled the city's fifteen dominant bakery owners, who controlled most of the thirty downtown bakeries, and convinced them to continue to provide minimal discounts to the retailers.[56] Baz may have agreed to advocate for the retailers who had so angered him because he did not want to add the peddlers and the "two thousand families" they allegedly maintained to the city's unemployed masses. He was probably more concerned about the residents who lived far from downtown and relied on the peddlers and retailers. Furthermore, if bread was a sign of political legitimacy, which the liberals were eager to assert, then retailers were spreading a vital symbol of stability by hawking it on the street and selling it from their stores. A dyed-in-the-wool liberal, Baz was still hesitant to abandon the bread supply entirely to comercio libre, which could have eliminated the peddlers.

Like the small bakers who complained about the millers, these petty retailers were witnessing the gradual formation of a new bread cartel. However, this development did not mean that the cold capitalist laws of supply and demand now prevailed over the zelo y desvelo that under colonialism had sought to protect consumers from the greed of dishonest merchants. In the sense that the bakers and the peddlers were calling on the state to prevent powerful actors from driving them out of business and to defend a "social pact," they advocated for a "moral economy" much like consumers in eighteenth-century France and Britain who pillaged bakeries in order to enforce what they viewed as fair prices.[57] Yet their argument was disingenuous.

During the years in which these small actors enjoyed a relatively egalitarian market, effective state intervention had been absent. Indeed, state officials struggled throughout these years to force bakers to sell at accessible prices. Instead, market forces—shaped by turbulence, instability, and opportunism—set prices. Their bakeries had charged as much as consumers were willing to pay. As a result, only the wealthy could afford bread on a regular basis. These were the circumstances the small actors now yearned for. "Free trade," for them, did not refer to government intervention as much as their own ability to "freely" conduct business. The organization of the bread trade that emerged in the second half of the nineteenth century was not necessarily more capitalistic or less moral. Rather, it most resembled the gremio-dominated bread trade that existed previous to the pro-free-market reforms in the final years of the colony.

If the petty retailers' complaint caused the council members any hesitation, their concern was ephemeral. In June 1870, the city council met to discuss the "measures that should be taken in order to prevent the monopoly that the owners of mills and bakeries are attempting to establish."[58] They decided to summon the dominant owners to a meeting. The owners gave their "word of honor as businessmen" to sell at fixed, fair prices: eight pieces of bread for one real. If they strayed from this price, they promised to pay a thousand-peso fine.[59] Perhaps the councilmen failed to notice an omission that, in practice, could have rendered the heartfelt pledge meaningless: the owners did not specify how much each piece would weigh. Nonetheless, in a "secret meeting" the city council decided to test the owners' word by sending agents to check the prices (per ounce) of bread in an early morning surprise inspection. Inspectors returned with the unprecedented news that all the bakeries sold quality bread at the agreed price and even above advertised weight.[60]

Working Conditions and Reluctant Reformers

The consolidation of more powerful owners coincided with the reappearance of complaints over working conditions. A sixteen-year-old worker's mother reported to authorities in 1853 that her son labored so hard in a panadería that he repeatedly collapsed, only to have the foreman drive him back to work with the whip. The owner accused the boy of stealing bread and deducted the cost from his wages. When he and another boy tried to leave the shop, skipping out on their debt, the owner locked both of them inside. Only the mother's appeals secured their release.[61] José Mariano Gallegos, a contributor to the paper *El Siglo Diez y Nueve*, denounced violence as well as debt peonage, which he regarded as the cause of "frequent abuses, disorder, and disasters" in bakeries. He proposed that contracts should not bind bakers for more than four months and that "owners and overseers should not use lashes, whips, or any other weapons against workers, unless in self-defense."[62]

An 1861 letter to the *Monitor Republicano*, signed by "the Lincoln of the bakers," called on President Benito Juárez to follow the example of his northern counterpart and abolish "slavery."[63] In the influential 1864 book, *On the Causes of the Current Situation of the Indigenous Race in Mexico*, Francisco Pimentel regarded bakeries as Mexico City's counterpart to oppressive rural haciendas. He lamented that "a part of the indigenous race still whimpers ... in servitude.... In the very capital, the system [of indebtedness] is used with bakery workers, who never leave the workshop, if not to go to mass on feast days, and always in the company of an overseer who never lets them out of his sight."[64]

Working conditions in panaderías also figured prominently for liberal politicians assembled in 1856 to draft a new constitution. In these debates, bakeries symbolized degrading conditions in workplaces more generally. Delegates went as far as to propose a constitutional ban on "forced servitude" to "eliminate a thousand abuses committed in workshops, bakeries, and elsewhere."[65] Servitude, they argued, undermined the formation of reasoning citizens as well as workers' freedom to express their own will. Delegate Isodoro Olvera argued that direct elections should only be implemented after "the emancipation of unfortunate classes." Otherwise, "those who live like slaves in the bakeries won't have their own free will." Francisco Zarco countered that to premise the rights of citizens upon the freedoms of workers was to add political exclusion to social injustice. Zarco's view prevailed, and the constitution established universal male suffrage and direct elections of congressional representatives.[66]

A decade later, in 1867, the governor of Mexico City, Juan José Baz, decreed a series of regulations to improve working conditions. The 1871 Penal Code for Mexico City prohibited "owners of panaderías, *obrajes* or factories" from "arresting or detaining another individual in a private prison or other place, without orders from the competent authority."[67] "Bakers," he declared, "are one of society's most miserable classes. They find themselves in a type of slavery contrary not only to all humane sentiment, but also to the guarantees expressly granted by the fundamental law of the Republic." From then on, shifts could not exceed ten hours, and bakery owners were to provide workers with "healthy, well-ventilated, clean, and comfortable rooms" to sleep in or else pay a fine of "not more than twenty-five pesos." The governor also restricted the practice of retaining workers through debt. Owners could no longer give loans that exceeded a week's worth of wages nor grant new loans before the previous ones were repaid.[68]

However sincere his actual concern for workers may have been, Governor Baz's political legitimacy relied in part on a reasonably well-fed populace. The governor was no labor crusader, but he hoped that improved working conditions would put more bread on shelves. He also evinced a paternalistic strand of midcentury reformism that saw a causal link between working conditions and workers' behavior.[69] Cruel environments produced improper conduct. If the republican elites were to forge citizens out of the dissolute poor, they would have to address the brutalizing influence of working conditions. Yet, the liberals' actual commitment to rescuing bakers and other poor workers from brutal conditions was shallower than their rhetoric might suggest. Even the most insistent champions of bakers' rights did not call for a complete reform of working conditions, which could have made panaderías more humane and attractive to workers. Given a choice between forming modern citizens and ensuring the bread supply, political leaders tended toward the latter and hesitated to end coercion altogether. Indeed, they doubted whether bakers could ever become decent, respectable citizens.

Despite his defense of panadería workers, Gallegos, the editorialist for *El Siglo Diez y Nueve*, evoked a deep disdain for poor workers when his letter recommended establishing a bakery in the Santiago Tlatelolco House of Corrections for Juveniles, in order to "educate a new class of workers, free of the vices that currently exist."[70] Governor Baz's reforms were similarly tepid and contradictory. He aimed "to make the baker's trade more common than it currently is" by improving conditions. Just in case, though, he suggested keeping a degree of coercion in order to ensure the supply of bread. The ten-hour shifts he mandated could actually last quite a bit longer since managers were free to "distribute [the hours] throughout the day as needed" so as to pass over the idle moments while the dough rose and the bread baked. Also, he restricted the practice of retaining workers through debt but did not abolish it altogether. Like Gallegos, Baz stressed the advantages of using prisoners as bakers. Criminals guilty of "minor crimes that only require correctional punishment" could be "assigned as apprentices in bakeries."[71] He also invited contractors to "teach the trade to prisoners" in the infamous Belem Prison.[72]

After some thirty years of intermittent war, epidemics, and invasions, republican leaders reverted to the older model of monopoly and coercion. Although war, not free trade, had caused the periods of scarcity and hunger, the governing classes of Mexico preferred to entrust the bread industry to wealthy entrepreneurs even if this meant a displacement of smaller shops and the re-introduction of archaic mechanisms of debt peonage and physical punishment to control workers. As the small producers unwittingly made clear in 1853, businessmen who could integrate the wheat trade, the grinding and sale of flour, and the production and retail of bread could make cheaper bread and more of it. In the government's words, "this is precisely what we should encourage instead of hinder."[73]

CHAPTER THREE

"An uncle in America"

Chain Migration and the Spanish Monopoly

❧ FEW SPANIARDS TOOK PART IN THE "INVASION OF PASTRY CHEFS" OF the 1850s. But a decade later, immigrants from northern Spain, particularly the Basque province of Navarre, slowly began to arrive in Mexico City and venture into the bread trade. By the 1890s, they had become owners of most of the city's panaderías. These Spaniards built upon the efforts of the mill and panadería owners who in the 1850s had begun to dominate these trades. Yet this earlier group of mostly European owners lacked the cohesion necessary to integrate the still fragmented businesses of wheat, flour, and bread. Furthermore, having appeared under the umbrella of Maximilian's ill-fated empire, they were unable to benefit from the long-term stability and support of the state. The Basques, by contrast, had two advantages. Able to build networks based on the steady influx of family members and neighbors, they had much greater unity. They also operated in a more favorable political and social milieu under the dictatorship of Porfirio Díaz, who imposed an unprecedented degree of political stability and encouraged foreign entrepreneurs to exploit native labor. This change, in turn, stimulated more Spanish immigration, which further strengthened the "Spanish monopoly."

Gachupines, Old and New

For many Mexican conservatives, as well as "old" Spaniards who had lived in Mexico before independence, the disorder that characterized the early decades of independence confirmed their view of Mexico's inability to govern itself as an independent republic. They argued that monarchy, the Spanish language, and Catholicism had held Mexico together during three centuries of colonialism. The coups, revolts, civil wars, invasions, and economic disasters that plagued independent Mexico were consequences of the assaults that liberals and their plebian followers had launched on the Hispanic legacy. The civilization Mexico had achieved was due to Spain, which had freed Mexicans from idolatry and human sacrifice. In the minds of conservatives, the violence that followed independence showed that without the restraint of colonial institutions, the indigenous and mixed-race masses had reverted to barbarism.[1]

Mexico's political and spiritual salvation, conservatives insisted, lay in *hispanismo*, the "superior apostolate" that the Spanish legacy of hierarchy, religion, and culture had exercised over Mexico. Otherwise, the country would disintegrate—if not out of internal discord then from the external threat of the expansionist United States. They pointed out how the weakened Mexican state had allowed the United States to seize half of the nation's territory in 1847 and 1848. Hispanists feared that the Americans also would supplant Spain's "spiritual guidance" with Anglo-Saxon materialism.[2]

Only strong, centralist leadership (preferably monarchist), a strong church, and Spanish immigration could restrain the masses and the Protestant threat. After the liberal attack on the Catholic Church and the defeat of monarchism, Spanish immigration remained a crucial source of hope. According to Hispanist Ricardo de Alcázar, Spaniards were "the only *testicular* people, creators of peoples." In contrast to racially prejudiced North Americans, Spaniards formed families with Mexican women. And unlike Jews and Arabs, who, Alcázar insisted, were only interested in commerce, Spaniards worked "plows not shop counters."[3] Though the other pillars of colonial order had been destroyed or weakened, Spanish immigrants were still called upon to bring prosperity to Mexico through their superior industriousness and lineage.

Many Latin America elites agreed and sought to attract Spanish immigrants with subsidized ship fares, employment, and land grants. From the northern regions of Cantabria and the Basque provinces, young men (and some women) headed to Buenos Aires, Havana, Mexico City, and the open pampas in the southern cone of South America. Many governments specifically worked to attract Basques, on account of their "undisputed aptitude ... for jobs of the field and mountain."[4] For the underpopulated, undercapitalized parts of Latin America, the Basques, with their conservative Catholicism, rustic families, and storied entrepreneurial acumen, seemed to be the ideal immigrants to exploit the untapped resources of the newly independent nations.

To the disappointment of Mexican Hispanists, political instability, recurrent violence, and anti-gachupinismo kept most immigrants from choosing their country. In 1842 the Spanish ambassador to Mexico Pedro Pascual de Oliver discouraged immigration to Mexico. He wrote that before independence his countrymen had been able to find work easily in textile shops, groceries, panaderías, and other trades dominated by Spaniards, but these businesses had "declined considerably in recent years." Now newly arrived Spaniards found only poverty, "presenting a sad spectacle to their countrymen." He called on officials in Spain to "inform the inhabitants of our provinces of these facts so that they will consider them before sending their children to America to harvest tears and disappointment instead of riches."[5]

Spanish immigrants to Mexico were accordingly far fewer and arrived later than their counterparts elsewhere in America. Even when immigration to Mexico increased in the mid-1870s, the numbers of immigrants remained low. Unlike Argentina, Mexico had a large, cheap native workforce, and the fertile, irrigated areas in the countryside did not want for population. Immigrants to Mexico were mostly adventurers, entrepreneurs, and professionals—or hoped to become as much—not manual laborers. Unlike Basque immigrants who pursued the traditional livelihood of shepherding in the Sierra Nevada of California and in Uruguay, their counterparts in Mexico left their hamlets to find success—or, as the saying went, "hacer la América"—in urban commerce.[6] They were not interested in the "field and mountain." Contrary to Alcázar's ideal, they wanted to trade their plows for countertops.

Few moved collectively from the rural world to that of urban commerce with the success of the Navarrese Basques from the Baztán Valley who settled in Mexico City. The Baztán Valley consists of fourteen towns and several hamlets scattered between Pamplona and the Pyrenees, primarily dedicated to agriculture and raising sheep. It is a beautiful, rugged country, isolated from the bustling port cities to the north. "A journey to Navarre," noted one historian in 1961, was "still an expedition to the Middle Ages."[7] Their geographic isolation, compounded by their singularly difficult language, made the Navarrese fiercely loyal to their *echea*, the household lineage embedded in surnames such as Benguechea or Goseascoechea. Navarre's juridical autonomy and extensive communal lands kept capitalism at bay long after other Spanish regions were enmeshed in global trade.[8]

But if Navarre had escaped some disruptions of modernity, its youth increasingly sought opportunities overseas and contracted themselves to the several emigration agencies that ship captains and Latin American governments commissioned in the Basque provinces.[9] By the end of the nineteenth century, so many had left that a Basque novelist wrote, "To be a true Basque, you must have a sonorous surname that speaks of one's origin, speak the tongue of the sons of Aitor [the mythical patriarch of the Basques], and have an uncle in America."[10]

Young Baztanese left their sheep, the isolation of their inland villages, and the confines of their inscrutable language in droves.[11] Primogeniture, the custom in which the first-born male inherited the family land, forced many younger siblings to seek prospects beyond home. Basque specialists have argued that parents socialized non-heirs to become immigrant entrepreneurs.[12] Others attribute emigration to the Carlista Wars of succession (1833–1839 and 1872–1876), which were particularly disruptive in Navarre, from where many young men emigrated in order to escape military service.[13] These regional factors pushed the young to join the general wave of emigration that swept over Europe in the nineteenth century. Like emigrants elsewhere, they took advantage of the technological innovations—railroads, telegraphs, and steamships—that allowed them to embrace what historian José Moya calls the novel "right to go where one pleased."[14]

The Basques who arrived in Mexico City from the Baztán Valley did not turn to bread out of love for baking. If any had experience in the trade before arriving in Mexico, they did not work as manual laborers once they arrived. They became administrators, overseers, and clerks. Connected to each other through networks of family and regional identity, the owners of these panaderías formed what Mexican competitors soon came to call the "Spanish monopoly." However, they did not put a distinguishable culinary stamp on bread in Mexico. They were businessmen, not bakers, and had come to Mexico in order to leave behind the shepherding of their hamlets and enter into urban commerce in the New World. Rarely did they touch flour in the workroom, where the Mexican bakers carried out the tiresome labor of kneading and baking. The Basques came into the bread trade simply because one of their own had already established an important position in the trade.

Among the first of them was Pedro Albaitero. In the 1850s, Albaitero appeared before civil authorities near his hometown of Errazu in the Baztán Valley to request his passport. If he followed the customary procedure, he presented permission from his father to emigrate, a certificate of good character from the Errazu mayor, and documentation that his family was "clean" of Jewish or African blood. He was around twenty when he boarded a sailing ship in the port of Bayonne and headed across the Atlantic.[15]

The voyage was uncomfortable and treacherous. Passengers without the means to bribe the captain crammed into the ship "like bundles." Food was often "scarce and detestable," consisting of "one raw sardine per person and a sip of horrible wine for breakfast."[16] After some two months at sea, Cuba, still a Spanish colony, shined like paradise to the seasick, lice-ridden passengers. Albaitero continued on to Veracruz, where Spaniards still dominated trade with Cuba, New Orleans, and London, before making the ten-day trip along bandit-ridden roads to Mexico City upon a bone-jarring litter or the more expensive but quicker trip in a coach.[17] Mexico was still reeling from the war with the United States, deep in the Reform War between liberals and conservatives, and soon to be occupied by the French. With some 130,000 residents, Mexico City was beginning to outgrow its colonial *traza*, the quadrangular grid of streets built around the central plaza. The two-story mansions, plazas, and cathedral continued to give the city an air of elegance, but it suffered from the damages of war, filth, and street noise.

Albaitero must have had some connections among the two thousand Spaniards ("old" and "new") in the city, for it would have been bold for a lone immigrant without connections to travel so far into the general insecurity of everyday life in Mexico.[18] The Royal Basque Society of the Friends of the Country—the social and religious civic association for Basque immigrants—was still active, though much humbled since its late colonial zenith, and may have linked Albaitero to local social circles.

He first appears as a panadería owner in 1869. What he had been doing since his arrival some fifteen years before is unknown. Whatever they were, his early ventures gave him a dash of respectability—and discomfort in his feet. An 1864 newspaper advertisement for Mr. Schlosser, a "callus surgeon," referred to Albaitero with the double honorific "Señor Don" and clearly valued his testimony that Schlosser had "removed seven corns from [his] feet with the greatest skill and without causing . . . any pain."[19]

Albaitero married a Mexican woman, Luisa García Rejón y Piñón, and in 1865 their first child, Mercedes, was born in San Luis Potosí. Their next child, Cipriana, received baptism in the Mexico City suburb of Tacubaya in 1868. Later, Cristina and Bernardo were born.[20] Since Spanish entrepreneurs tended to defer marriage until they had secured a patrimony, Albaitero was likely a man of means by then. Luisa's grandfather Joaquín García Rejón was a prominent landowner and general who served in the first Yucatán state congress in 1823. In the late 1840s, Luisa's father, Manuel García Rejón, moved the family, perhaps driven from the Yucatán by the Caste War in which Maya Indians routed whites from much of the region.[21] Though their fortunes had declined, they settled in Tacubaya on the southwestern edge of Mexico City, among flour mills, olive orchards, and the villas of the wealthy.

Pedro and Luisa may have fallen deeply in love, but marriage was more a business venture than a pact of affection. As a Panamanian entrepreneur complained, "In Mexico, the best arbiter for everything is personal influence," which only came from family connections. "In this country one cannot do anything by the straight road," agreed his brother. "The only way for us to make a good business is to find ourselves a good *compadre* or *padrino*."[22] Marriage into Mexican families gave foreigners access to capital. In the absence of banks (which only appeared in the 1880s), family connections provided means to secure loans, protect investments, and consolidate capital.[23] As a result, kinship was a carefully monitored institution, with restricted membership. To marry into the García Rejón family, Albaitero must have had some prospects to offer in return.

Luisa's father likely helped Albaitero establish residence in Tacubaya and may have introduced him to the owners of the flour mills that he soon began to lease. Luisa's dowry doubtlessly helped him to buy his first two downtown panaderías in 1869 and acquire one of Mexico's oldest mills, Molino Santo Domingo in Tacubaya, which Hernán Cortés had established in 1533. Like many aristocratic families whose fortunes waned during the civil wars after independence, Luisa's family relied on a Spanish immigrant to link them to emerging enterprises.

Hence, while the García Rejón y Piñóns maintained their stakes in the more prestigious endeavors of land and the military (Luisa's brother Andrés continued the family tradition of belonging to the officer corps, becoming a brigadier general by 1913), the family also joined its lot with the promising commercial ventures of a Spanish immigrant who was willing to take on work in risky and somewhat demeaning sectors of the economy.[24] The Basques' particular and widely touted mystique of frugality, business acumen, family loyalty, and conservative Catholicism made Albaitero an attractive son-in-law.

This reciprocity burgeoned when Luisa's sister María de la Luz married Albaitero's countryman and business partner, José Arrache, at La Candelaria Church in Tacubaya in 1874.[25] The joining of families, together with a second dowry, must have strengthened Albaitero and Arrache's prospects. By the mid-1870s, the partners had added four downtown shops to the two Albaitero already owned. They solidified their position in 1874 when they beat out rival bids for the lucrative concession to supply bread to Mexico City's public hospitals and asylums.[26] Together with a handful of Mexicans and the few remaining French and Austrian owners, Albaitero and Arrache dominated the bread trade. They were far from forming a Basque-dominated monopoly, simply because there were few Basque immigrants. This circumstance changed sharply after 1876.

Porfirio Díaz and the Consolidation of the "Spanish Monopoly"

Politics in Mexico became increasingly stable, and authoritarian, in ways that helped Albaitero and Arrache extend their dominance in the bread trade. General Porfirio Díaz, a war hero in battles against the French, launched a failed rebellion in 1871 against Benito Juárez, who had just assumed his fourth presidential term. The next year, Juárez died of a heart attack, leaving the Supreme Court chief justice Sebastián Lerdo de Tejada in the presidential seat. In 1876, when Lerdo de Tejada announced his plans to seek reelection, Díaz again rebelled, this time successfully. Coming into power pledging effective suffrage and federalism, Díaz gradually accomplished exactly the opposite—a centralist autocracy.

Over the following thirty-five years, Díaz imposed a degree of political and social stability that in turn ushered in an era of economic development unprecedented in Mexico. Combining capitalist boosterism with the earlier hispanismo, Díaz urged foreigners to exploit the country's bountiful natural resources and to inject European blood and their supposedly more vigorous entrepreneurial spirit into Mexico. "Immigration," he stated in his first annual address in September 1877, "is one of our most imperious needs."[27] He attracted foreigners with the promise of paid passage, land grants, and tools. He also enacted legal reforms that eased restrictions on foreign investment and ownership. Spanish immigration to Mexico, still modest compared to the massive waves to other American nations, grew sharply from 6,400 in 1877 to 29,500 in 1910.[28]

With new immigrants, the numbers of panaderías quickly grew. The thirty-five or so shops in the 1850s had increased to sixty-eight by 1877.[29] The 1898 census did not record how many panaderías there were, but it did count 2,538 workers—a threefold increase from 1877.[30] Spaniards, and particularly Basques, dominated the bread trade. In 1895 the Spanish immigrant newspaper *El Correo Español* published a list of donators to Spain's military campaign in Cuba. It included 130 Spanish panadería owners, over half of whom had Basque surnames.[31] Of the thirty-four panaderías that paid their municipal taxes in 1896, Basques owned twenty-three, and Spaniards from other provinces owned nine. The rest belonged to other non-Spanish foreigners (Barles, Begnous, Cailat, Delfonty, Delon, and Honel).[32]

At the center of this growth, Pedro Albaitero quickly expanded his reach. He drew on his own family back in the Baztán Valley and brought over his nephew Juan Irigoyen Echartea, who arrived in Mexico in 1884 and soon occupied a vital position in his uncle's business.[33] Less than a year after arriving, he married Albaitero's oldest daughter, Mercedes, at La Candelaria Church in Tacubaya. They moved into the house inside the Santo Domingo mill, which Juan immediately began to manage.[34] Albaitero followed a common immigrant pattern, particularly engrained among Basques.[35] Nephews were more likely to offer hard work and loyalty than, say, Albaitero's Mexican brothers-in-law, for whom working in a panadería—as clerks, no less—would have been unthinkable. Nephews were a logical choice also because Spanish entrepreneurs often married in their late thirties or forties (Albaitero, for instance, did not have a son until he was forty-one).[36] Their sons grew up in relative wealth and, much like their bourgeois Mexican peers, showed little interest in the penny-pushing routine of panaderías. Nephews, in contrast, lacked prospects. Often second or third sons, blocked from inheritance by primogeniture, they relied on their uncles' sponsorship to cross the ocean and come into the future prospect of entrepreneurship. In exchange, nephews provided entrepreneurs with trustworthy labor and the means to keep capital within the family circle.

In 1887 Albaitero and Arrache constructed La Florida, the first flour mill located inside the city. La Florida was a technological and logistical innovation unprecedented in Mexico. While most mills in Mexico were "inferior to those Don Quixote battled," La Florida incorporated the most recent developments of the milling industry in Europe and the United States.[37] "The mill is a true novelty in Mexico," glowed the press.[38] Cylindrical steel rollers from

Budapest allowed for higher yields of better quality flour than the traditional millstones. Steam-powered motors allowed the mill to function virtually anywhere.[39] With La Florida's massive capacity, Albaitero and Arrache supplied their own panaderías and others at an enormous profit. Typical mills ground at a cost of two to four pesos per *carga* (approximately 178 tons). La Florida, in contrast, expended merely "twelve to fifteen cents" per carga—that is, approximately $0.0009 per kilogram of wheat that cost $0.06 wholesale. They allegedly sold the resulting flour at $0.21 a kilo.[40] The reported markup is certainly an exaggeration (in 1899, the closest year with somewhat reliable data, flour retailed at ten cents a kilo), but whether the partners sold flour to other panaderías or kept it for their own, La Florida was a good business.[41]

A year later, Albaitero and Arrache opened Mexico's first mechanized panadería, Los Gallos. Compared to the rudimentary operations in most shops, the imported machinery in Los Gallos was impressive. Careful measurements of flour, water, and yeast traveled from repositories through tubes into steam-powered mixing machines; pulleys raised and tilted the mixing bowls so that the dough poured onto the worktables; and stoves outside the building sent heat to the ovens through metallic tubes, making much more efficient use of fuel.[42] Seventy-nine workers baked "day and night."[43] Members of the Factory and Industry Commission of the Superior Health Council believed they were witnessing the solution to panaderías' notorious lack of hygiene.[44]

Fellow owners were less enthusiastic. The French baker-owner Joseph Bagnouls wrote that in Mexico, as in Paris, "only handmade bread fulfills all the appetizing conditions. That is why it is the only accepted bread." The new ovens "leave the dough half-cooked and dense [*apelmazada*], rendering the bread difficult to digest." The bread tasted bad, Bagnouls argued, and absorbed dangerous iron oxide from the tubes. Otherwise, he concluded, "those of us who have the constant desire to improve our business would have adopted this system long ago since it is faster, easier, and makes production cheaper." Yet, two months later, Bagnouls visited Los Gallos and ate his words. His public apology noted that the machinery worked fine and the bread was "delicious."[45]

The panadería supplied grocery stores, small bread outlets, and even mules that carried bread to outlying villages, risking occasional attack from thieves.[46] Los Gallos also joined the growing venues that catered to the wealthy. When Los Gallos opened, the city still struck many as humble and dirty—animals still roamed muddy streets—but Albaitero and Arrache were at the forefront of Mexico City's rapid gentrification. Porfirio Díaz inaugurated a modern sewage system, broad avenues, monuments, hospitals, penitentiaries, and opulent buildings like the Palace of Fine Arts and the Postal Palace.[47] Sanitation and luxury consumer goods were symbols of Mexico's deliverance from instability and discord, of its arrival into modern, cultured urbanism. Old neighborhoods were rebuilt, and new ones emerged as the "respectable" segments of the population increasingly pushed the poor to the margins of the city.[48]

Albaitero was able to pass his legacy to his nephew upon his death in 1900.[49] Although José Arrache maintained control of Los Gallos and La Florida, under a new partnership with Florencio Córdoba (from Elizondo in the Baztán Valley), Irigoyen took on his uncle's other panaderías, under the name of Albaitero y Compañía Sucesores. By then he also owned haciendas in El Bajío, the fertile crescent-shaped region northwest of Mexico City.[50] Together with his younger brothers, Pedro, José, and Francisco, he expanded the agricultural production to include sugarcane, maize, and cattle. They built the Molino del Carmen in Celaya, as well as a rum distillery.[51] In 1907 Irigoyen cofounded the Centro Vasco, the business and social hub of the Basque community that occupied three floors in the luxurious palace known as the Casa de Azulejos (House of Tiles), the gathering point for wealthy businessmen and politicians, a short walk from the main plaza in Mexico City.[52]

Soon the brothers had made sufficient fortunes in Mexico to contribute donations to their town back in Navarre. They had a public clotheswashing facility built in their old neighborhood, the local cemetery beautified, and the church bell recast.[53] By the outbreak of the revolution in 1910, Pedro Irigoyen was Mexico City's principal grain trader, bringing in wheat from his brothers' estates in the Bajío, as well as from Europe, the United States, and South America. The Irigoyens did not, however, pass their fortune on to a subsequent generation. Juan Irigoyen and Mercedes Albaitero had seven children, but none of these seem to have entered the bread or grain trades.[54] José and Pedro both died single after returning to Errazu. Francisco also returned to Errazu where he married a local woman but never returned to Mexico. Their nephew, who had gone to Mexico to administer their mills, also died single in Navarre.[55]

Albaitero, however, laid the foundation for the more enduring success of another immigrant from the Baztán Valley, Braulio Iriarte Goyeneche, whose memory owners still celebrate. Born in the town of Elizondo in 1860, he arrived in Mexico in 1877, a year after Porfirio Díaz took power. He began working in the bread trade in Mexico City, reportedly distributing bread for Albaitero before finding work at the Molino Blanco in San Bartolo Naucalpan, on the edge of the city.⁵⁶ Through these jobs, he became familiar with the business and enmeshed in the Basque circles. By 1890, he owned some of the most important panaderías, including El Factor, which, according to an 1899 tourist guidebook, boasted "all the technological advances seen in other great capital cities of the world."⁵⁷ Iriarte also bought the Panadería Venegas from Pedro Albaitero and came to own La Vasconia (the ancient name for the Basque lands), the elegant downtown shop still located on Tacuba Street.

In 1903 Iriarte opened another flour mill inside the city, along with Baztanese immigrants Fermín Echandi and Juan Oteiza, who each owned at least one major panadería (on Ancha Street and Corpus Christi Street, respectively).⁵⁸ He named it El Eúskaro (The Basque). In 1912 he joined with Pablo Díez Fernández, a Spanish immigrant from León, to found Mexico's first industrial yeast factory, Leviatán y Flor.⁵⁹ With yeast, grain, and considerable capital, he led a group of Baztanese owners in opening the Modelo Beer Factory, maker of Corona, in 1925. When he established a new El Eúskaro mill in 1929, he was grinding the lion's share of Mexico's wheat.⁶⁰

Iriarte lived with a Mexican woman, Angela Moreno, who gave birth to several children, mostly girls.⁶¹ His daughters became a crucial mechanism to build family and business cohesion. Sons were certainly valued, but daughters afforded other advantages. Sons could turn out profligate and unreliable, as Iriarte's son reportedly did, or simply be uninterested in the family business. But fathers could choose their sons-in-law, in principle at least. Iriarte's daughter Leonor married Andrés Barberena Urrutia, who was born in Garralda, Navarre, in 1880 and arrived in Mexico around 1900.⁶² Barberena started out as an administrator at La Vasconia and then took up the ownership of the panaderías on San Juan de Letrán Street and El Factor sometime around 1920. In 1907 Iriarte brought over his nineteen-year-old nephew Segundo Minondo Rota, also from Garralda. By 1915, Minondo had taken his place among the dominant owners and sat on the Centro Vasco's board of directors, together with Albaitero's son and Irigoyen's nephew.⁶³

Another nephew, Agustín Jáuregui Iriarte, son of Iriarte's sister, arrived in 1909 when he was nineteen years old. By 1915, he owned the panadería on Santa María la Redonda Street and worked as an administrator at El Eúskaro.⁶⁴ He also served on the Centro Vasco's board of directors (1916–1917, 1935–1937). Jáuregui married Iriarte's daughter Esperanza. In the 1930s, shortly after Iriarte's death, he bought the flour mill El Carmen from the Irigoyen brothers, probably with the help of his uncle's inheritance. The children of Iriarte's other sister also came to Mexico and profited under their uncle's guidance.

In 1915 José Larregui Iriarte arrived, and his brothers Bautista and Miguel followed in 1919 and 1923, respectively. Together the three established the Compañía Molinera de Toluca, a flour mill in the agricultural and industrial zone west of Mexico City.[65]

With control of the most productive flour mills, the largest panaderías, and several wheat fields, Albaitero and Iriarte after him had tremendous leverage over the entire wheat-flour-bread complex. Wheat constituted up to 93 percent of millers' total costs, and the largest, most productive mills like La Florida and El Eúskaro reduced prices by cultivating their own wheat and purchasing large amounts of grain directly from growers. Growers preferred to sell to the Basque millers because they bought large amounts and provided credit. These sales could be "ruinous" for cash-hungry small and medium growers since they agreed to sell for "one or two pesos" per carga below the post-harvest market price while the wheat was still in the ground. Growers sold the rest of their wheat to merchants like Irigoyen, who then sold it to the smaller mills that had neither the capital to purchase large quantities of grain nor the facilities to store and conserve it.[66]

The largest mills also sold wheat to the smaller ones, especially in the months between harvests when they could fetch higher prices for their excess wheat than for their flour.[67] The largest mills, then, bought wheat when it was cheap and sold it when it was expensive. Furthermore, since they could grind the grain at a cheaper rate than the smaller mills, their margin of profit was even higher when they sold the flour and higher still when their panaderías kneaded their flour. The Basques' "monopoly" emerged not from exclusive control of a market, but rather from unequal competition that they could dominate.

The greatest single decade for Navarrese immigration was the 1920s, when two hundred Navarrese, most from towns and villages in the Baztán Valley, arrived to work in the bread trade.[68] While insignificant compared to the thousands of Europeans who moved to the New World during the same period, these numbers still highlight the Navarrese Basques' continued over-representation in the bread trade. Of the 192 non-manual-labor employees listed in a 1922 survey, 121 were "foreigners"—that is, Spanish—and this was just when the small wave of migrants began to arrive.[69] They offered services and qualities that were essential to profitable operation: low-cost clerical labor, long hours, and loyalty, or at least obedience.[70] A French traveler at the turn of the century observed that Spanish businessmen "habitually recruit employees from the region of Spain that borders with France.... Of all the foreigners residing in Mexico, they do the most thankless work."[71] Later, a Spanish writer admonished young men in Spain not to be fooled by those who returned from Mexico "with half a dozen suits and hats, three pairs of silk socks, a pearl-studded tie clip, and a six-karat 'rock' on their pinky." Even these petty luxuries, he warned, "cost them assiduous, constant work over many, many years."[72]

Still, many clerks expected to earn enough money to establish their own businesses. In 1922 the Department of Labor estimated that a worker needed to earn eighty-four pesos a month as the minimum to provide basic necessities for a family of four.[73] A survey from the same year showed that most non-manual-labor panadería employees earned between $100 and $160 a month. The vast majority were single, and many received room and board in addition to their pay. Furthermore, their years of work amounted to an extended apprenticeship, and after some ten or fifteen years many struck out on their own, often with credit, loans, and even machinery from their former employers. Clerical workers handled accounts, ordered raw materials, gave the daily orders to the bakers, dealt with the peddlers, and handed out the daily wages.

What they did not do was knead dough half naked in the hot, grimy workrooms with Mexican bakers whose wages were generally far too low for upward mobility. A sharp racial segregation continued to run through panaderías and generated antagonism between Mexican workers and the Spanish overseers and owners. Mexican workers rarely were able to set up their own shops, so they often complemented their paltry wages by pilfering ingredients. Drinking was also a common way to numb the fatigue of drudgery and to retain a sense of autonomy within an exploitative environment.[74] As a result, the rationale for segregation must have appeared self-evident to Spanish owners. Whereas relations between Spanish owners and Mexican workers were filled with class and ethnic animosity, the immigrant employee offered loyal submission.

This cycle of chain migration—in which newcomers provided cheap clerical labor, amassed capital, established their own businesses, and then hired other immigrants fresh off the boats—depended on the capacity of panaderías to expand. Basque immigrants worked in many different businesses, including hotels, cantinas, pawnshops, soap factories, banks, and in agriculture.[75] But bakeries were unique in their ability to support chain migration. Factory owners brought in nephews as managers, but factories could not multiply and spread through the city like panaderías. Other immigrants opened shops that catered to their countrymen. The Galician-owned Alpargatería Española (Spanish Espadrille Shop), for instance, offered "espadrilles, balls from Pamplona, berets, and jai-alai baskets." The American Grocery likewise sold

Grape-Nuts and Shredded Wheat to expatriates in Mexico. But the growth of these businesses was restricted by limited demand.[76] Panaderías, by contrast, literally fed a growing demand, and their numbers grew apace with the influx of immigrants.

The new shops sold increasingly more bread to more consumers as the city expanded beyond its colonial core. All of the city was eating considerably more bread: panaderías increased by 121 percent between 1877 and 1900 (from 68 to 150), while the population of the city increased only 45 percent in the same period (from 327,500 to 476,000).[77] The middle and upper classes, long accustomed to eating bread, were now dipping more and more pieces into their frothy chocolate. The working class, which increased threefold between the 1860s and 1900, settled into the dense new neighborhoods, such as La Bolsa and Santa Julia in the northern part of the city.[78] For them, bread was a novelty, a sign of their urbanization. This expansive demand allowed immigrants to open new shops once they had gathered sufficient capital and experience working as clerks and managers.

Figure 2. "El Vizcaíno," Mexico City, ca. 1920. Courtesy of the Fototeca Constantino Reyes-Valerio of the Coordinación Nacional de Monumentos Históricos–INAH.

The bread trade inserted Spanish immigrants deep into the cityscape and the everyday lives of ordinary Mexicans. Since consumers walked daily (and often twice a day) to get their bread, shops proliferated over the city, instead of concentrating around certain locations.

To expand their reach even further, owners relied on peddlers who sold in the street and door-to-door. Typically, peddlers arrived at panaderías early in the morning and filled their own baskets with bread. They were not employees but independent workers who kept a percentage of the sale price. After breakfast hours, they returned to pay for the bread they had sold and to return the leftover pieces, which panaderías sold at half price the following day at public markets. Most owners would have preferred not to accept leftover pieces, and instead make peddlers "eat" the bread they could not sell, but peddlers insisted that excess bread was crucial to their sales. Once consumers became accustomed to a variety of sweet and savory breads, they demanded selection. By late morning peddlers also had a hard time selling the few remaining pieces at the bottom of the basket because customers did not want the bread that their neighbors had already fingered and passed over. Peddlers argued that it was not fair for them to take the loss, especially since, in theory, the value of the unsold bread could exceed that of the pieces sold.[79]

With small shops scattered around the city, owners found that it was not economical to invest in expensive machinery. So overhead costs remained low, which allowed immigrant employees to eventually become proprietors. Unlike other businesses—textiles, for instance—panaderías did not require huge initial outlays. Although Albaitero and Iriarte concentrated production at their flagship panaderías and distributed to branches, most owners kept separate units where bread was both baked and sold. Most were small and simple—a ground-level retail area over a basement workroom equipped with a table, a kneading trough, and an oven. These were shops with few capital expenses. According to the 1922 census, most employed fewer than ten workers.[80]

The growth of panaderías diverged from the broader trend in turn-of-the-century Mexico City in which large mechanized workshops and factories pushed out smaller artisan shops.[81] The Spanish owners may have marginalized small Mexican owners, but they did not undermine them with industrial production. Indeed, this dispersion of small panaderías owned by Spaniards, instead of a concentration of large ones, precluded significant mechanization. Less than a third of shops had any machinery at all, and those that did had mostly simple mixers and manual cutting machines.[82]

None were entirely mechanized and, even with machinery, the multiple steps involved in the production of bread relied on the manual labor and artisan knowledge of Mexican bakers.

"Mexico for Mexicans"

By the end of the century, Telésforo García, a prominent Spanish banker and publicist in Mexico, could brag that "on every corner in the capital there is a store and in every store, three or four Spaniards. . . . We are owners of the food market, a good part of the cloth trade belongs to us, and we have almost monopolized the banks."[83] But many Mexicans were uncomfortable with the rapidly growing presence of Spaniards, especially in bakeries. "There are insistent murmurs," reported the conservative newspaper *La Voz de Mexico*, "that panadería owners regularly meet to discuss how to raise their profits." Owners rented shops and kept them closed, allegedly in order to "exclude any speculator alien to their league."[84] Likewise, the liberal daily *El Siglo Diez y Nueve* inveighed against a "despicable bread monopoly formed to exploit the people."[85] The working-class press was, not surprisingly, the most critical of the new bread barons. *El Popular* specifically complained about Spaniards who were buying up mills and panaderías in order to bankrupt the "poor Mexican baker" with "ruinous competition." Confident of their command of the market, these "kings of commerce" had become "exploiters of the people's hunger" who shirked at nothing that could yield them "illicit and excessive profits." The indifference or complicity of the authorities only further "excited their ambition [and] encourage[d] their greed." The editorial in *El Popular* warned that the "monopoly is exasperating the poor worker, the poor people."[86]

El Hijo del Ahuizote echoed this angry tone and denounced the "Spaniards [who] have monopolized all the panaderías and all the flour mills." The paper decried the Spaniards who, like the sixteenth-century conquistadores, cavalierly renamed Mexico's geography. They "NEVER give Mexican names to their businesses and factories. They erase the indigenous name and invariably replace it with the name of some saint, some bullfighter, or some jai alai player." The paper further rejected the notion that Spaniards embraced Mexican society through marriage: "Rarely do they marry Mexican women, and when they do, it is generally in pursuit of their wretched, greedy interests." Instead, they formed closed cabals that hoarded resources. "It is time," the article concluded, "to openly wage the economic struggle toward the patriotic goal: MEXICO FOR MEXICANS!"[87]

These accusations reflected a growing resentment over the inequalities that emerged from the late-century capitalist development. Nationalists used the term *monopoly* to denounce foreign dominance and the complicity of government authorities. It was a freighted term, implying chicanery and greed, but one that was used rather loosely. The networks that arose from the Basque panadería barons like Albaitero, Irigoyen, and Iriarte exerted considerable influence over the bread trade, but the accusations overstated the degree to which they had monopolized it. These men were never the sole producers; competition was fierce, even among the Basque-owned shops; and the same relatively low entrance barriers that allowed immigrant clerks to move on to proprietorship also allowed Mexicans of modest means to set up panaderías—be they legally licensed shops or clandestine ones hidden in tenements and patios.

Other foreign capitalists operated businesses that were much closer to becoming monopolies but did not inspire the same degree of animosity. An American traveler observed what he termed an "invasion of foreigners" in Mexico City.[88] The French-owned El Buen Tono overwhelmingly dominated cigarette production. Its only competition came from La Tabacalera Mexicana, owned by the Basque financier Antonio Basagoiti y Arteta.[89] The Franco-Mexican Compañía Mexicana de Dinamita y Explosivos, founded in 1901, made exclusive deals with the Díaz government that exempted the company from exorbitant taxes, effectively preventing any competition.[90] Immigrants from the Barcelonnette region of the French Alps dominated textiles and monopolized department stores, including El Palacio de Hierro, the emblem of Parisian modernity that had arrived in Porfirio Díaz's Mexico City.[91]

The foreign domination of key sectors of the economy in Mexico City and elsewhere in the country provoked suspicion, but nationalists directed these sentiments at the panadería owners with particular vehemence.[92] This was, in part, because they were Spanish, and accusations against them grew from the heritage of anti-gachupinismo. Yet the Spaniards who sold jai alai balls, salted cod, and wine from Rioja did not provoke such Hispanophobia. Bread, more than any other product made by foreigners, embedded Spaniards into everyday life in Mexico, for as a workers' paper stated, "Everyone, from the millionaire to the beggar, eats bread."[93] Unlike distant proprietors of factories and department stores, panadería owners and their clerks were visible, palpable features in neighborhoods throughout the city.

Despite criticisms of the "Spanish monopoly," the continued expansion of the Basques and other Spaniards into Mexico City's panaderías did not unleash a nationalist backlash that went beyond heated rhetoric. For one, if "everyone" ate bread, it was thanks to the immigrants who had doubled the number of shops and extended their reach through the city. The nationalists in the press inveighed against them, but the bread they ate may well have come from Spanish-owned shops. Moreover, the turn of the century was an era of economic expansion driven by foreign capital and defended by the Díaz dictatorship. In the state's view, control of the bread trade by a dominant group of owners was advantageous. That they were foreigners, even Spaniards, was not a concern, as foreigners appeared to be the only entrepreneurs willing to modernize the country's commercial and manufacturing sectors. The hispanismo of earlier decades had developed into a broader embrace of the capital, industriousness, and know-how that foreigners brought to Mexico. The view from the top continued to undervalue the efforts of Mexican businesses and discount the potential of Mexican workers. Most officials did not share the view that domination by foreign entrepreneurs was an affront to national sovereignty. For them, the cry of "Mexico for Mexicans" was tantamount to clinging to backwardness and instability.

CHAPTER FOUR

"Dough Kneaded with Blood"

GENDARME NO. 905 WAS AT HIS DOWNTOWN POST NEAR THE PLAZUELA Aguilita around 11:30 p.m. when he heard a tremendous crash and a voice calling for help. He ran down the street and entered La Florida, the flour mill that Pedro Albaitero and José Arrache had established the year before. In a corner of the mill grounds was a rundown room with a collapsed roof. The owners told the press that they had been "rebuilding" the room so that workers could sleep in it. Meanwhile, nine people were already living there. Among them were Marcelo Iniestra, his wife, Rita Flores, and their four children, who died under the weight of the roof. "The proprietors of La Florida were in no way guilty" of the deaths, the press opined. "Although the house was in ruins, the owners had asked the family long ago to abandon the room it was occupying at no charge."[1]

The building's collapse in September 1889 was indicative of how working conditions deteriorated as the position of Albaitero, Arrache, and other recent owners improved. During the first thirty-five years or so after independence, panadería workers had enjoyed significant autonomy and improved working conditions. This declined with the arrival of European owners—mostly French, German, and Austrian—beginning in the 1850s. Following them, the

Basques and other Spaniards imposed and enforced even more archaic conditions at the same time that they mobilized ethnic and family solidarity to integrate and expand the organizational structures of the wheat-flour-bread complex. The development of Mexico City's panaderías, then, differed sharply from that of London's bakeries, as observed by Karl Marx just a few decades earlier. Marx described them as the "most archaic, pre-Christian" of all British industries. "But capital," he argued, "is at first indifferent towards the technical character of the labor process it seizes control of. At the outset, it takes it as it finds it."[2] The backwardness of Mexico City panaderías, however, was not merely a vestige of earlier eras, a condition that new capitalists encountered. Together with the absence of any reprehension from authorities over the deaths of the Iniestras, the deplorable working conditions highlighted the prevailing notion that progress could proceed despite continued hardship for workers. Indeed, low labor costs were essential to attracting immigrants who, officials hoped, would further modernize Mexico's economy.

The bakers challenged these beliefs by responding to the worsening conditions with an unprecedented capacity to organize and demand improvements as befitted citizens. Some observers regarded the ensuing protests as *escandalitos*, further evidence of workers' inherent irresponsibility. However, the gains that bakers achieved through strikes underscored the degree to which the city's collective stomach relied on the bakers' knowledge and skills.

Working Conditions and "Disorder"

Working conditions did not immediately worsen as the new owners established themselves in the bread trade. There is some indication that the Spanish immigrants initially made bakeries more attractive for workers. An 1875 ledger from the Panadería Santa Clara shows that workers once again were receiving loans, which tied them to shops, but also afforded them access to much-needed cash. Tellingly, the most specialized highest paid workers were most indebted to employers, suggesting that they were able to leverage their skills to obtain higher loans (table 3).[3]

Likewise, bakers appear to have regained their freedom of movement. In 1880 when authorities asked B. O. Montellano, owner of the panadería on San Pedro y San Pablo Street, why his shop lacked rooms designated for sleeping in accordance with Governor Baz's 1867 decree, he explained that all his workers slept "in their own houses as soon as they finish their work; there is no need to have a special place for them [to sleep]."[4] Bakers also seem to have

Table 3. Workers and wages, 1875.

NAME	POSITION	EARNS (PESOS/DAY)	OWES
Julián	Calero (oven heater)	0.30	0
José 2	Maquinista (machinist)	0.30	0
Matilde	Atajador (sheet cleaner?)	0.40	1.20
José	Calero	0.40	3.70
Rafael	Calero	0.40	0.20
Dimas	Cernidor (flour sifter)	0.40	0
Alverto	Operario (unskilled worker)	0.60	3.40
Macario	Operario	0.60	0.40
Rodriguez	Operario	0.60	4.50
Guadalupe	Operario	0.60	0
Vestas	Pambazero (pambazo baker)	1.00	0
Gregorio	Mayordomo (overseer)	1.20	0
Napoles	Sopero (dough mixer)	1.20	3.40
Lázaro	Hornero (oven worker)	1.60	14.00

Source: Ayuntamiento, June 1, 1875, Policía en General, vol. 3635, exp. 743.

overcome their status as the poorest and most forsaken of urban workers. In 1884 when the bakers joined with tailors, carpenters, and bricklayers to form the Bakers' Union and Friendship Mutualist Society (which provided financial support for members in case of sickness or death), they took their place among artisans in more prestigious skilled trades.[5] Improved conditions may explain one historian's puzzlement over why bakers were slow, relative to other workers, to mobilize collective resistance to the increasingly brutal demands of capitalist factories and workshops.[6]

These are mere hints, however, for sources do not definitively show that conditions were universally improved. In 1874 when the Mexico City *ayuntamiento* (city council) called for bids to supply municipal hospitals and asylums with bread, one official proposed that prisoners in the National Jail bake the bread instead of private shops. After all, he noted, "there are continually a rising number of bakers" in jail.[7] Albaitero and Arrache's bid won out because their panaderías could produce bread more than 5 percent cheaper than the prison, and this was long before they opened the mechanized Los Gallos.

If their "free" workers could outbid convict labor, they were either more efficient and motivated (a reasonable assumption given the lamentable conditions in prison) or they earned even less than prisoners.

Whether or not conditions improved when the Basques began to establish themselves, they definitely got worse in the early 1890s. By then the immigrants had firmly secured their dominance of the bread trade, and Porfirio Díaz had consolidated his control as president of Mexico. Díaz predicated his dictatorial rule on the promise of a modern, dynamic economy. While technology and infrastructure were broadly progressing in the form of railroads, telegraphs, and smoke stacks, labor conditions in panaderías were moving backward.

During the colonial era, the textile workshops known as obrajes were among the few sites that rivaled bakeries for the dread they inspired. Employers routinely ensnared obraje workers in perpetual indebtedness and even shackled them to prevent flight. But the influx of imported textiles and the arrival of mechanized factories made obrajes obsolete in the early nineteenth century. Mechanisms of naked force had ceded to voluntary wage labor. In the early twentieth century, textile factories resolutely refused to lend money to workers.[8] Cigar rollers similarly complained that their "abject poverty" was a "phenomenon of supply and demand." "Since there is a lack of work and an abundance of workers the value of the human merchandise is minimal."[9] To be sure, workers in textile factories and other occupations continued to live a mostly thankless existence. The workers' newspaper, appropriately titled *El Desheredado* (*The Disinherited*), noted that work shifts in Mexico City lasted sixteen to eighteen hours, and still many workers could barely feed their families.[10] But the root cause of grievances for workers in these fields was not direct coercion; instead it was the surplus of unemployed workers that allowed bosses to lower wages. Although panadería owners similarly undervalued their "human merchandise," bread was not subject to the same pressures from the global market. Unlike cloth, it could not be imported, nor was machinery diminishing the need for labor. Instead of modernizing labor-capital relations, panadería owners reverted to archaic mechanisms of coercion.

Infrastructure similarly remained backward and dangerous. The collapse of La Florida's roof onto sleeping mill workers was just one of many tragedies. Workers were threatened by insecure buildings such as those in which the "overhead wooden beams were so dry that the mere heat of the ovens caused them to burst into flames" and collapse. Bakers also suffered burns produced by the petroleum lamps that illuminated workrooms. One "unfortunate" worker was "bathed with the burning liquid," and "the poor burning man ran about trying to rip his clothing off."[11]

Bakers continued to suffer from work-related diseases. Particles of flour, smoke, and ash that permeated the air caused tuberculosis, chronic colds, and inflamed eyes, ears, noses, and throats. Moreover, exposure to the heat of the ovens brought on another host of ailments including "anemia, general weakness, rigid joints, lumbago, Bright's disease, rashes, rheumatism, cystic fibrosis, premature aging, cataracts, retinitis, and conjunctivitis."[12] Few workrooms had running water or toilets. Workers defecated into holes cracked in the floor, the stench somewhat covered by the smells of rising yeast, burning sugar, and cinnamon. Popular lore had it that the perspiration streaming from bakers' half-naked bodies gave bread its salty taste. Other flavors may have come from the bakers' custom of kneading dough in large troughs with their feet—which they called *bailar la masa*, "dancing the dough." A decree prohibited the practice in 1893, but a newspaper reporter, sent to verify compliance, alleged that he could see "traces of dough through [the bakers'] sandals."[13]

Instead of criticizing owners and government officials, many commentators increasingly came to see workers as the cause of these deplorable conditions. By contrast, earlier liberals in the 1850s posited that working conditions engendered vice and other social ills. But by the time that the roof collapsed upon Marcelo Iniestra and his family, this liberal paternalism—ineffectual and ambivalent as it was—had unabashedly hardened into support for the exigencies of production at the expense of workers. Díaz, who surrounded himself with advisers who adhered to the positivist teachings of the French philosopher Auguste Comte, purported to govern "scientifically" according to actual circumstances, not idealist aspirations. Positivist critics of "doctrinaire liberalism," with its faith that societal transformation could spring from legislation, argued that "metaphysical" beliefs had created a legal fiction that bore little relevance to Mexico's social reality. In this view, civil rights and democratic rule could only take root in Mexico after political stability and economic progress had created a more mature population and solid institutions.[14]

Inculcating modernity in a populace ill disposed to its virtues would require years of education and reform. Campaigns to "improve" the lower classes through charity became more vigorous. But concerns over working conditions ceded to an emphasis on deficiencies and faults that were supposedly inherent to the habits and beliefs of the poor.[15] In 1877 *El Monitor Republicano*, the same paper that in 1861 had published the letter from the

Figure 3. Bakers kneading, Mexico City, ca. 1935. Fondo Casasola, Inventory No. 877. Courtesy of the Fototeca Nacional of the Instituto Nacional de Antropología e Historia.

self-proclaimed "Lincoln of the Bakers," asserted that "it was not fatigue that prompted the workers to demand reductions in their working hours but their devotion to vice in their free hours."[16] Drinking, filth, and ignorance were the causes, not the consequences, of poverty. Accordingly, workers who called for changes in conditions were manifesting not social problems related to the exploitation they suffered under employers, but rather their own deficiencies.

Though perhaps not hopelessly innate, these deficiencies were certainly too ingrained for any high-minded republican legislation to extirpate any time soon. Meanwhile, strong-arm tactics were necessary to restrain the poor. In the 1890s, the Díaz regime began to enact what historian John Lear calls "a flurry of city ordinances regulating public appearances . . . clearly aimed at the poor."[17] New laws prohibited public drunkenness, sleeping in the streets, begging, and traditional fiestas. Others required that Indian men wear trousers instead of the traditional cotton *calzones*.

In order to enforce these laws, Díaz increased the police vigilance. As many as 422 policemen patrolled the streets on horseback. Another 1,872 gendarmes seemed to be on every corner.[18] At the same time, migrants from towns and villages in Mexico were arriving to the city in numbers that confounded effective enforcement of the laws. By 1900, 66 percent of Mexico City's residents had been born elsewhere.[19] In his famous mural *Sueño de una tarde dominical en la Alameda Central*, Diego Rivera painted police keeping the poor away from the Alameda Park a few blocks west of the central plaza, but in the view of "respectable citizens," the park, as well as the plaza itself, had become the lair of pickpockets, prostitutes, vagrants, and hucksters. Much milder disturbances sufficed to bother elites who felt that the riffraff had taken over their city. One resident pleaded with police to crack down on the errand boys who caused an "infernal racket and roughhoused" in the street as they transported bread from panaderías to the groceries.[20] Although new laws endeavored to regulate, if not eliminate, the places were the poor walked, slept, drank, ate, and danced, the city's factories drew growing numbers of workers who frequented these very streets, flophouses, cantinas, and dance halls.

Proof of workers' barbarism was on display almost daily in Mexico City newspapers' *nota roja* sections, which published news that was "red" with blood. Bakers became standard characters in these depictions of the city's underbelly. One article described how Angel Castro and José Castro, bakers at Vanegas, began to fight over "personal issues" just as the night shift began around 6:00 p.m. Angel stabbed a hook into José's chest. Gravely injured, José was still able to crash a piece of firewood over his adversary's head.[21] In another case, Manuel Ruiz had grown tired of the way other bakers mocked him and preferred José Ugalde's work to his. So when Ugalde was asleep, Ruiz covered a strip of paper with lard, placed it over Ugalde's body, and lit it on fire, leaving him with serious burns.[22]

At the Tompeate Street panadería, someone tossed a ball of dough at Pedro García. Certain that the perpetrator was Luis García, Pedro stabbed him seventeen times with his baker's knife.[23] Adelaido Ramos and Antonio Terán, at the Estanco Street panadería, "had been enemies for some time on account of matters of their trade." Ramos teasingly launched an innuendo (*indirecta*) at Terán, and when the latter responded "insolently," Ramos smashed his face with a piece of firewood.[24] Another article, luridly titled "DOUGH KNEADED WITH BLOOD," reported that Eustaquio Suárez and Manuel Franco were working in the *bizcochería* on Arcos de Belem Street when, "for a trifle," Franco stabbed Suárez to death. Suárez's blood "gushed into the dough."[25]

The concentration of violent incidents and reports about them in the 1890s is striking. Similar incidents may have occurred in previous decades, but if so they went unreported. The sensationalist descriptions in the nota roja reflected newspaper readers' morbid fascination with the underworld in a city whose rapid growth was transforming such ordinary places as the corner bakeries into menaces. There was a discursive change in how the literate, nonproletarian population perceived and described workers. But this violence was not merely a product of new attention. Actual changes occurred in the concrete, everyday lives of panadería workers. Brutality signaled deep tensions in the bread trade, in which retrograde working conditions coexisted with elites' desire for the products of fin de siècle modernity. But the changes in actual circumstances and in perception moved together. Their coincidence was not accidental. As working conditions grew ever more backward, new interpretations emerged (and old ideas were recycled) to explain how this backwardness could coexist with the progress that Porfirio Díaz promoted and that the mostly foreign capitalists were bringing about.

The nota roja provides glimpses, however distorted, of everyday life in the workrooms and shows how the rapid expansion of panaderías affected workers. The almost threefold increase of the workforce—from 873 bakers in 1877 to 2,286 in 1895—exasperated tensions in the cramped, hot workrooms.[26] The proliferation of bakeries intensified competition among owners, provoking a "merciless war [*guerra sin cuartel*]" between shops. In their attempts to expand sales, owners sold at increasingly lower prices, losing in the process "up to two hundred pesos a day."[27] To compensate for these losses, owners demanded more of their workers.

Differentiation between panadería workers had also grown more pronounced. In the eighteenth century, there was little hierarchy among workers. All received similar pay, with the exception of the few bakers who made the finest bread exclusively for the viceroy and other elites of the colonial bureaucracy.[28] The types of bread were also fairly homogeneous. Distinctions resided in the quality of ingredients (especially flour) more than in flavor, shape, or technique. As late as 1849, most panadería workers listed their position as *operarios*, the generic term for unskilled laborers.[29] Soon after, differentiation began to grow more prominent as immigrants to Mexico City, both from various European countries and from regions across Mexico, introduced new types of bread, which gradually expanded into the practically endless myriad of salted and sweet bread that panaderías offer today. The quality of flour continued to account for differences in the quality and price of bread, but the choicer ingredients now went to the more elaborate pieces. For instance, bakers used flour from the cheap "long wheat" for the coarse cemitas of the poor and from *candial* wheat for more expensive pieces that also contained eggs, milk, and lard.[30]

Bread production became more complicated and varied enough to require specialization. This specialization also led to a guildlike hierarchy with *maestros* at the top followed by *oficiales* (journeymen), *medio-oficiales* (sub-journeymen), and apprentices who were usually young boys. Despite these titles, the bakers' "guild" was informal (bakers, unlike other artisans, did not have an official guild during the colonial period, and, in any case, legislation in the late eighteenth century prohibited guilds).[31] There were no bylaws, membership fees, or even protocol to evaluate craftsmanship and determine ascension. Most maestros were also the oven workers (*horneros*). Other titles, such as *soperos*, *caleros*, and *atafadores*, referred less to rank than to the duties of those who, respectively, mixed dough, brought firewood, and removed bread from the oven. Since these jobs required specific skills they fetched higher wages. In 1868 horneros and soperos, at least those with the misfortune of being convicts in the Belem Prison, each collected one peso per day, more than twice as much as oficiales and some five times more than medio-oficiales, who earned forty and twenty cents per day, respectively.[32]

Maestros who had worked their way up in the trade over decades no doubt felt their higher wages were well deserved. Their knowledge of formulas, command of techniques, and ability to gauge the heat of the oven and the time for baking constituted the foundation of production. Their subalterns, who arrived in panaderías at precisely the time when conditions were becoming more demanding and degrading, likely chafed at these distinctions within the Mexican workforce, not to mention the sharp racial segregation between Mexicans and Spaniards. As the nota roja pages mentioned, Adelaido Ramos and Antonio Terán, at the Estanco Street panadería, "had been enemies for some time on account of matters of their trade." Manuel Ruiz attacked José Ugalde because his coworkers preferred the work of the latter to his. The new workers had to prove their stamina and dexterity to the more experienced bakers, who mocked them and even punished them for their mistakes. In the incidents of violence I have mentioned, insecurities over the quality of work were predominant.

Although incidents of violence showed how exhausted and brutalized workers were, the crime pages provided ample evidence for elites that the behavior and vices of bakers were the causes of their misfortune. The "trifles" that allegedly provoked the violence in the workrooms underscored the pathological nature of the bakers—that playful flicking of dough, innuendos, and jealousy were enough to launch them into murderous frenzies. The drudgery of kneading and baking, onerous as it was, could not explain why

Pedro García had to stab Luis García seventeen times when one or two well-aimed thrusts would have done the trick.

Just as panaderías had joined brothels and cantinas in the scenery of the threatening urban underworld imagined and feared by the respectable, literate bourgeoisie, bakers also became regular fixtures in the cast of urban deviants. The famous turn-of-the-century criminologist Carlos Roumagnac found plenty of bakers in the jails and mental asylums. Gamblers, drunks, fathers who abandoned their children, and enraged lovers who lacerated their girlfriends' faces were all bakers. Regarding "Abraham L.," a baker accused of murder, Roumagnac wrote, "He has led a disorderly life, drinking as soon as he leaves the panadería, joining with prostitutes and frequenting all kinds of places. Naturally, he has the illnesses inherent to such an existence." Abraham insisted that "he ha[d] never done anything bad in his life." But Roumagnac had already described the baker's father (an alcoholic former soldier), his alcoholic uncles, his frail mother, and his dead sibling and determined that he is "of a hypocritical and deceitful type." Although bakers earned less than a peso a day, Roumagnac's specimens always managed to pay for pulque (fermented maguey juice) and prostitutes.[33]

Bakers' problems, then, were drunkenness and barbarity. Surely higher pay would only lead to higher levels of alcoholism. Witness, for instance, the "bloody scene" at Albaitero and Arrache's shop on the Calle de los Ciegos, in which alcohol turned men into beasts who needlessly slaughtered each other. Master baker Pedro González had invited several bakers to drink pulque after their shift. When "the white liquor . . . was producing its effects," González and an eighteen-year-old baker named Adolfo Pérez began to fight over a "work dispute." Before the fight went very far, another baker "prudently took Pérez away." González continued drinking until noon when he went back to the panadería "perfectly inebriated." There he fought with another baker before again attacking Adolfo Pérez, "who happened to be sleeping along with his companions." Provoked a second time, Pérez "refused to turn the other cheek." He grabbed a knife and "thrust himself like a wild animal upon his adversary." Pérez, stabbed in the stomach, was soon dead at González's feet. "The weapon pierced the abdominal wall and penetrated some four centimeters of the short intestine, producing a monstrous hernia." Confirming his animal nature, González "coldly confessed his crime." When the police carried the body away through the crowd of neighbors who had gathered around the scene, one "piercing scream cried out, 'That's my baby [*mi hijo de mi corazón*]!'"[34]

Solving conflicts with violence was hardly extraordinary in Mexican society, nor was it a practice limited to the poor. Dueling had become popular among wealthy men in Mexico City. The adversaries agreed upon the time and place and used single-shot pistols with smoothed barrels that hindered accuracy in order to ensure an equal match regardless of the shooters' skill. In the eyes of their peers, the observance of these rules exalted the honor of both men, regardless of the result. This was gentleman's violence that observed strict protocol.[35] This elite vision of violence differed sharply, however, from that which occurred among the lower classes. According to the depictions of bakers in the press, these spontaneous explosions of rage lacked any sense of honor or accepted norms. Victory came through surprise and deception combined with the brutish handling of dough knives, firewood, and anything else at hand that could injure or kill.

The growing violence brought new attention to circumstances within panaderías, particularly the hygiene. Alarmed at how filthy this source of the city's food was, the ayuntamiento in 1901 named a commission to study the state of bakeries. The commission described lamentable conditions; however, its concern was not the treatment of workers but rather the noxious effect that workers had on the city they fed. "Bakers never bathe or change their clothes," the commission wrote. "They sleep right there with the dough." They commonly had "infectious diseases" and "mix their medicine with the tools to make bread."[36] Panadería workrooms engendered vice and dissolution and attracted the lowest deviants and outcasts. Criminals found them an ideal place to hide, for the police never ventured inside. Furthermore, many minors worked in panaderías where they "inevitably acquire immoral habits," such as "playing cards" and other "bad habits that bakers almost always have."

Tellingly, the commission blamed the conditions on the workers' filthy habits and filthy bodies—not the conditions created by the owners. The committee deplored the workrooms, but its underlying concern was for "the public," who unknowingly ate bread made by such nefarious characters.[37] The commission's report recalls the disdain that colonial officials had for what they called the "vile sentiments of the Indian bakers."[38]

"In the name of the law we must act": Panadería Strikes

As long as the violence erupted from "trifles" and remained within the workrooms, the barbarism was self-explanatory—workers acted like animals because their nature was bestial. However, workers had their own interpretations of social strife, and they defied this tautology, as well as the class hierarchy on which it stood. The ephemeral newspapers and broadsheets written by and for proletarians countered that the scorn heaped upon them reflected not workers' vices as much as employers' exploitation. What a coincidence, wrote *La Cagarruta* in 1906, that "those who wear shirts and have calloused hands" were inevitably "called drunkards," whereas "those who wear suits and frock coats, whose artistic heads are well combed and perfumed, were decent people." Another paper, *Don Cucfate*, opposed the stereotype of the indolence with a more heroic vision: "[The worker is] the Herculean arm of the arts and sciences who builds statues and immortal temples; he is the one who founds cities and makes them powerful with the strong beat of his hammer." In this view, the Porfirian gendarmes, not workers, provoked disorder in the street, for they "embodied the antithesis of Law and Order, the negation of Justice, and the rule of Force."[39] These alternative visions contributed to a positive worker identity and provided workers with a vocabulary with which to articulate their grievances and mobilize resistance.

Struggles between workers and employers drew on these competing visions of workers—as hardworking citizens unjustly denied their rights or as childish, violent brutes. This discursive clash was common to the labor conflicts that erupted in many sectors at the end of the century. What distinguished the bakers' struggle from that of other workers was its immediate impact. In addition to challenging the dominant interpretation of workers, bakers' resistance threatened to leave the city without its bread. Striking textile workers, who were probably the most organized and militant of the turn-of-the-century laborers, compromised their employers' interests, but they did not force the rest of the population to go around naked.[40] The importance of bread to the daily functions of the city also meant that, in the view of authorities, bakers had a *civic duty* to bake, a responsibility that transcended their individual rights. Consequently, owners and politicians also had an obligation to make sure that bakers fulfilled their labors, using force if necessary.

Soon after Pedro González killed Adolfo Pérez in 1894, owners began to lock bakers inside the workrooms, a practice that panaderías had abandoned since independence. It is not clear if owners were reacting to this particular incident, but they did overtly validate this step backward by pointing to bakers' propensity to drink, fight, and flee with their pay, taking with them all the flour, sugar, eggs, and lard they could sneak out as well. Bakers' deviant behavior not only explained the poor circumstances of their lives, now it even justified virtual prison terms.

Owners insisted that workers' brutishness—their penchant to drink, brawl, and steal—required the imposition of disciplinary measures. They drew on the same rationale by which the political elite justified limiting the lower classes' participation in the political process. Dissolute, uneducated, and immature, workers could no more complete their work without the firm hand of employers than they could elect political leaders.

Owners also couched the lockups, known as *encierros*, in more generous terms. Encierros were part of a paternal duty to ensure that workers did not "squander the product of their labor." They also kept bakers' disorderliness from spilling out on the street. "Order is disturbed enough when they are locked inside," owners argued. "Out on the street they get so drunk that they are incapable of fulfilling their duty to the public."[41] Encierros, in sum, were part of employers' responsibility to ensure that panaderías completed their duty of providing the city with bread. The increase of violence and drunkenness alone could have convinced owners that they needed to restrict bakers' mobility in order to run more orderly and productive shops. By 1895, though, the bread market had reached a saturation point, and owners were struggling to extract as much labor as possible out of their workers in order to outproduce and undersell competitors.

Encierros successfully constrained bakers, for a while. Protests only arose after one owner allowed the bakers to leave "during their rest hours." Braulio Iriarte, by then the kingpin of the bread and flour trades, had also "experimented" with such an open-door policy, but after "the few bakers who returned to work were entirely drunk," he changed his mind.[42] This second time, instead of getting drunk or disappearing, the bakers went from shop to shop calling on bosses to release their workers. A gendarme quickly approached them on the street and whistled for reinforcements to help disperse the unruly group. The bakers threw mud at the police, and the whole group spent five days in the Belem Prison.[43]

The rest of the workers returned to work and it seemed that the conflict had ended. The following week, though, workers locked inside of La Moderna and the Aldama Street panadería kicked down the doors and joined other bakers at the San Dimas Street panadería. San Dimas's manager, faced with a group of eighty workers, acquiesced to their (quite civil) demand to go the police station and negotiate with the maestros from the three shops, whose owners were Albaitero and Arrache. They agreed to twelve-hour shifts—from 6:00 p.m. to 6:00 a.m.—and daily wages of $3.00 for maestros, $1.75 for oficiales, and $1.50 for medio-oficiales.[44] Their first concerted protests yielded important results.

However, the deal was limited to these three shops since there were no links between panaderías or bakers that would require any general application.

But by then most bakers had decided to leave their workrooms and go on strike. Only a few shops remained open: the Calle Real panadería paid its workers double in hopes of compensating with huge sales, and La Alameda sent clerks back to the workroom to bumble through the degrading manual labor. Bakers at San Pedro y San Pablo had initially joined the strike, but owner Antonio Buerba managed to "dissuade" them by having three of the supposed instigators arrested for "introducing disorder." Another owner "invited" bakers to continue working if they accepted the encierros. If not, "they were free to act as they pleased." However, he warned, "bad things could happen" to those who left. When the workers took their chances out on the street, the owner sent employees as far away as Puebla and Veracruz to look for replacements.[45]

Echoing the view that workers were brutish children, the conservative paper *El Universal* made light of the strike. "This matter, which has given rise to so much alarm, lacks the importance it has been given. The cloistered bakers wanted out and, when they were refused, they banged down the door. Once in the street, they caused some little scandals [escandalitos], but nothing serious."[46] Other observers recognized that the strike had disrupted city life. *El Siglo Diez y Nueve* reported, "Today the city awoke to the news that there was no bread, and where there was, it was expensive and of bad quality."[47] Long before the 6:00 a.m. opening time, customers waited in lines that wound around the block at the few open panaderías and fought over day-old bread. When families compensated by buying more tortillas, tortilla sellers in the market promptly raised their prices, thus harming the poorest urban consumers who rarely could afford to buy bread.[48]

The striking bakers complained of "being kept like prisoners, watched over even when [we] speak and eat with [our] families." Locked in the workrooms, they "lack[ed] the comforts of home."[49] In a deeper sense, they demanded regular shifts and salaries because the laws of the republic had granted them these rights. In an anonymous letter signed by "several workers," they demanded that the governor of Mexico City, General Pedro Rincón Gallardo, give the workers freedom from slavery and equal treatment under the law—in other words, recognition of their citizenship. They appealed to the "exalted sentiments of patriotism that are manifest in the law and the care of the citizens; today before the world a glorious second independence from slavery is rising." "The good name of the Nation will never allow . . . the unequal application of the law, because we bakers are enslaved and in name of the law we must act. Before the Governor we have a single sentiment and objective, to realize the Fundamental Law as it was written by Benito Juárez."⁵⁰

The government alleged that the real author of the anonymous letter was a lawyer from San Luis Potosí, Narciso Zermeño.⁵¹ This may have been true, for most panadería workers were illiterate. Whoever Zermeño was—a demagogic agitator as the government suggested, a straw man fabricated to discredit the strike, or a sympathetic intellectual associated with the small but increasingly vocal opposition—the letter expressed ideas that had been prominent in the contentious public arena since independence. The bakers may not have written the letter themselves, but as residents of the capital, they would have only had to hear the frequent proclamations of liberals and radicals in order to soak in the florid prose that criticized the despotism they lived under.

Anarchism had influenced some circles of workers, but the bakers followed the majority of organized workers in embracing the doctrines of liberal republicanism, which offered worker vindication and national progress, universal dignity, rationality, and human potential regardless of social standing.⁵² As the hatmakers' union celebrated, "Today the worker thinks, discusses, analyzes, he educates himself and others." When the hatters went on strike in 1875, they called on their companions to renounce "revenge and reprisals." Instead, they insisted, "Our weapons will be reason and persuasion; our gunpowder for the charge will be the fact that capital will always need labor, just as much as labor needs capital."⁵³ Though not a call for social revolution, popular liberalism was radical in that it countered the vision of workers as barbarous drunkards and called for the realization of what Porfirio Díaz himself, during his failed revolt of 1871, had called "the highest principles of democracy."⁵⁴

Díaz had brought foreign capital into Mexico, but bakers and other workers who protested their deplorable conditions with increasing vehemence and organization called on him to fulfill his pledge to make Mexico more prosperous and democratic. Díaz responded with a paternalistic mix of conciliation and chastisement. The police did not arrest bakers for their labor protests per se but rather for the disorderly behavior—throwing mud, writing threatening letters, attacking private property—that was, in a sense, incidental to the strikes. Gendarmes and mounted police were on hand to make arrests and protect the few shops that continued to function, but they did not directly use violence to break the strikes. During the 1890s, when strikes became increasingly common, Porfirian labor policy shied from outright repression. For Díaz, violent strikebreaking was a sign of administrative failure.⁵⁵

The strikers still experienced intimidation and incarceration, but the administration's approach was more adroit than outright oppression would have been. The police contained the bakers without causing other sectors of the inchoate labor movement to rally to their defense. By avoiding a head-on clash between strikers and police, Díaz maintained a regal aloofness that allowed him to purport to be the nation's able guide and a father to the poor.

Workers appealed to the president to intercede on their behalf instead of calling for an end to Díaz's regime. But actual events strained this connection between workers and Díaz. The conservative *El Tiempo* echoed the impression of most "respectable" sectors of society when it asserted that the bakers' declaration had "neither head nor tail and only further discredits the strike." It contrasted the strikers' "pretensions" with the owners' "demands," ignoring that bakers had made the demands. The reporter further doubted that bakers had the capacity to mobilize consciously for specific objectives. "Perhaps the vast majority of the strikers are unaware of the damage they are doing to themselves and ignore the motivations of this senseless, inconsequential movement, in which only envy and selfish ambition are at stake. We are certain that . . . the bakers will soon reverse their steps and all will be over." Behind the "unjust strike," wrote the reporter, hid "scandalous instigators" whose secret motives belied the bakers' "exalted sentiments of patriotism."[56]

During the strike's first day, General Rincón Gallardo and the police inspector met with the city's principal owners—José Arrache, Braulio Iriarte, Juan Oteiza, Fermín Echandi, Gerónimo Galnares, Bernardo Ortiz Montellano, Alfonso Mancebo, J. Zabalburu, and Antonio Buerba—at Buerba's shop on Tacuba Street. The meeting, which lasted for most of the day, represented a uniting of forces against the workers' insubordination. Rincón Gallardo declared that "the proprietors of panaderías have the most perfect right to demand that their employees remain in their establishments, just like private individuals have with their servants, and no one would think to claim such an absurd liberty."[57] Bakers were not "free" modern workers, much less full citizens. They were servants duty-bound to feed the city.

On the second day of the strike, the bakers tried to extend the strike into the few shops that remained open. Unable to convince the nonstriking bakers to join them, they turned to threats. The police arrested five strikers for allegedly writing anonymous death threats to the "miserable cowards."[58] The strikers persuaded (or intimidated) some more bakers to join and then went to the panadería on the Calle Real, where workers were earning double. Just before the 6:00 a.m. opening, the strikers tried to enter by banging down the door, but the police repelled them.[59]

Owners refused to meet with the strikers directly and instead gathered at Los Gallos three days later and proposed their own terms to end the conflict. They agreed to stop paying workers in advance and adopt a "common scale of wages" to be paid on a daily basis. "If workers are sober enough to fulfill their labor," the owners admonished, "they may return to the workroom; if not they'll be fired." With these changes, the bakers returned to work. They had won. The press, however, insisted that the strikers had damaged their own interests. With advanced payments, they had been able to "provide themselves with the objects they needed and enjoy their leisure time only once." Now, the reporter continued, referring to bakers' penchant to drink, "they'll have the occasion to do so every day."[60] Owners similarly tried to conceal their bitterness by portraying the resolution as a Pyrrhic victory that the bakers would regret. Such contrition never came: three months later, when the owners together decided to lower wages and reinstate lockups, some one hundred bakers immediately declared a strike.[61]

Conflicts continued to erupt as employers tried to increase production and assert greater control over bakers in the workrooms. In 1897 workers at Iriarte's El Factor attempted to leave the workroom between tasks. The manager "opposed this tenaciously." Together with his clerks, he kept the door closed long enough for police to arrive and "calm the belligerent bakers."[62] A year later, "a formidable scandal" with similar motivations occurred at the Tompeate Street panadería. "It seems," the press reported, "that workers were upset because of an increase in their work." At the beginning of the shift, one reportedly drunk baker, Crispín González, "refused to work and tried to jump over the front counter and leave the panadería." The manager, Simón Ganastachua, and a clerk tried to "reduce him to order" by slapping his face. The other bakers reacted by shattering the windows with firewood. Gendarmes Nos. 878 and 865 arrived, followed by twelve more. One of these, No. 987, "known as 'la Liebre' [the Hare], penetrated the workroom alone, perhaps to prove how unfair his nickname was." When the bakers received him with a beating, he shot his pistol into the air, and a detachment of mounted police hauled the thirty-four bakers to the Belem Prison.[63]

Employers also tried to crack down on bakers' customary drinking in the workroom. In 1902 when the manager of Los Gallos refused to allow a worker to bring in a "bucket of pulque," the whole crew walked out, "dragging with them the clerks who tried to stop them." Outside, they "screamed insults against their bosses," José Arrache and his partner, Florencio Córdoba. The latter two went out, hoping to convince the spontaneous strikers to return to work, but quickly ran back to safety inside. The bakers then went to a hardware store and grabbed a "great number of canes," with which to threaten their bosses, and "several bunches of fireworks" that they ignited in front of the panadería. Again, the police arrived and arrested the "scandalous bakers."[64]

Despite employers' perception of bakers as immoderate drinkers unable to submit to the rigors of modern production, there was clearly order to their riot. When denied the customary prerogative of drinking pulque, they asserted their right to leave. They did not mindlessly raid the hardware store but rather took specific items in order to fight the clerks who had physically challenged them and to engage the panadería itself in a symbolic battle.

The two precipitating factors for this sudden protest—the refusal to allow workers to introduce pulque and the clerks' thankless efforts to physically restrain them—may show how, in the words of one historian, the bakers, like most other workers in nineteenth-century Mexico City, "clung to traditional moral norms concerning authority."[65] In this view, workers, many of whom were recent arrivals to the city, were accustomed to the peasant rhythm of the countryside in which they alternated between work and leisure.[66] The peasants' ability to determine how and when to work ran counter to the rhythm imposed by industrial capitalism, in which workers commenced their labors, took their breaks, and left the factory according to the abstract notion of "clock time."[67] Thus, when workers drank, gambled, and even walked out of the workrooms, they were resisting their employers' efforts to control their time and hence their labor. They were often successful—once, when Spanish clerks ordered workers to stop playing cards, the latter shooed them away with a barrage of firewood.[68] But the relationship between workers and owners was particularly antagonistic in panaderías since workrooms had been significantly freer before 1890.

The clash between rhythms and priorities was not as neat as this division between traditional and industrial suggests. First, bread production did not follow the impersonal, mechanized movement of the clock as closely as other products did. Baking times could vary according to temperature, humidity, and the quality of ingredients. There were many lapses of time during production when bakers had little to do except rest, drink, and play cards. What marked the duration of shifts was volume, measured in sacks of flour rather than time. After the Revolution of 1910, workers called for shifts measured in precise clock time, and employers resisted making this change. Furthermore, although the bakers drew on their own sense of what was right and fair in order to defend their interests and to resist those of their employers, it is not clear that these norms were necessarily "traditional." The intensifying exigencies in the workrooms, starting with the captivity of the encierros, gave rise to the bakers' ideas and actions of resistance at least as much as any lingering precapitalist rural habits.

Not by accident, conflicts erupted first in the largest semi-mechanized shops owned by wealthy immigrants like Albaitero and Braulio Iriarte, not because workers at these shops were more traditional, but rather because the demands upon them were more intensive. Earlier customs and beliefs were doubtless important, but now they took on novel meanings inseparable from a struggle that was increasingly uniting workers (who until recently had directed their animosity mostly at each other) against their mostly Spanish employers.

The bakers' combativeness emerged from their common grievances and their accumulative experiences with strikes and other, more spontaneous, protests. Like other workers, they were also emboldened by the growing national opposition to Díaz and the privileged cohort of investors and politicians who surrounded him. Since Díaz had taken power in 1876, a new generation of workers, intellectuals, and progressive elites had come into its own but found its aspirations blocked by the elderly president and other "mummies who clung to political and economic power."[69] Along with the unfulfilled promises of electoral democracy, the opposition criticized Díaz's preference for foreign capitalists over Mexican workers. This preference was manifested not only in bread but also in several other key sectors of the economy such as textiles, ranching, mining, and banking. Díaz's sterling accomplishments—the extension of rail lines, the establishment of new factories, the construction of luxurious buildings—all showed that Mexico was progressing. But just as the political process excluded the majority of citizens, the country's resources—land, water, and labor—also seemed to benefit a small, largely foreign, elite.

Together, the economy and politics underscored the exclusion of Mexicans from full participation in their country's affairs, and at the turn of the century workers joined middle-class intellectuals such as the anarchist Flores Magón brothers and the more moderate Francisco I. Madero in their anti-Díaz agitation. There is no indication that bakers joined associations of workers in other trades or the "Anti-Reelection Clubs" that called for a democratic opening. However, the presence of such organizations, and the ideas that they espoused, reaffirmed the justice of their own struggle. Indeed, after the mid-1890s, strikes were no longer anomalies but practically the conventional means by which workers leveraged for improved conditions.

The bakers' demands grew bolder, more organized, and "modern." They no longer focused on traditional prerogatives such as drinking or the liberty to leave the panaderías but on wages. Owners, in turn, dug in their heels. In July 1907 oficiales at Los Gallos demanded a raise from $2.00 to $2.25. Arrache and Córdoba refused, arguing, "If we acquiesce to this, workers will have new demands two or three months from now." The strike began at the end of the day shift. The dough prepared for the night workers rotted in the troughs, and the firewood in the ovens burned up, causing "significant losses to the proprietors."

Following a now familiar pattern, the strikers assembled in the downtown Alameda Park and then marched from shop to shop, calling on the bakers to demand higher wages. The gendarmes rushed in to "exercise strict vigilance around panaderías, to protect them if necessary, and prevent the workers who wish to work from being mistreated by the others." Workers from El Factor, Tacuba Street, San Dimas Street, and others seconded the strike. Other bakers who did not join contributed funds that allowed the strikers to persist for seven days. Backed by the police presence, employers nonetheless wore the strikers down by hiring temporary replacements brought from surrounding rural areas.[70]

Bakers, though, were not nearly as replaceable as owners wished. Any person with strong arms (or, as was often the case, feet) could knead dough. But knowing how to bring leaven to life; how much firewood to place in the ovens; when to remove it once the oven reached the right temperature; what flours were best for what types of bread; what flour was "hot" or "cold"; whether to use white sugar or brown, water or milk, oil or lard; how much anise, cinnamon, and vanilla to add to what pieces when—these were skills learned only from years of experience. Not surprisingly, then, Florencio Córdoba did not simply replace all the striking bakers with scabs. Instead, he "invited his old workers to lay down their hostile attitude" and return to the workroom, "assuring them that in his house they would be treated with all types of considerations." Most of the strikers supposedly "showed repentance for their violence" and returned to work.[71] They did not achieve a wage raise, but they did manage to mobilize and sustain their longest strike to date. They also made clear the indispensable nature of their expertise.

During another strike in 1911, employers again hired inexperienced workers—in this case, women and children—in order to break the strike. They paid them a third of the going wages. When the strikers protested, the owners, suddenly illuminated with a feminist consciousness, defended "a woman's right to make a living." "These workers," employers argued, "could become maestros after just four days."[72] However, when the bakers cancelled the strike, owners immediately welcomed them back, allegedly because they did not wish to leave "their old workers without a means of subsistence."[73]

As much as they used language that emphasized their own paternal generosity, and therefore the workers' dependence, owners acknowledged the depth of their reliance on the bakers' skilled labor. After several bread strikes, workers, owners, and politicians all understood not only the political importance of supplying the city with bread, but the degree to which production rested on workers' knowledge, dexterity, and drudgery.

The bread struggles went beyond workers and employers. They touched all city residents, especially the growing working class, for whom bread had become an expected part of their everyday diet. Bakers opposed the vision, articulated by Rincón Gallardo, that they were servants. If bakers had a "duty" to make bread, then it was the owners' duty to pay them well and treat them with respect. Paternalism, which had never characterized owners' actual treatment, could hardly address the deep grievances of the workers—much less contain the repercussions that extended from the panaderías throughout the city.

Díaz's own paternalism had also failed to convince workers that they could gain much by appealing to his authority. After strikes at the Cananea Mine in Sonora and Río Blanco textile factory in Veracruz ended in brutal violence, many workers listened instead to dissidents such as Francisco Madero, leader of the Anti-Reelectionist movement, who told them that "neither increases in wages nor decreases in working hours depend upon the government." Workers could gain these accomplishments only through organization. In Madero's vision, the government should defend workers' right to form "powerful associations" that would allow them to pursue their interests. "You do not want bread," he famously declared, "you want only freedom because freedom will enable you to win your bread."[74] When Madero called on Mexicans to rise up in arms against Díaz in 1910, thousands responded and forced Díaz to resign. The victory was only momentary, though. In the ensuing decade of bloodshed, Madero's vision that freedom from Díaz and from oppressive bosses would yield more bread—in both the figurative and literal meanings of the word—proved tragically optimistic.

CHAPTER FIVE

"We have no bread"

Hunger, Opportunity, and War

❧ AT THE HIGH POINT OF THE REVOLUTION'S VIOLENCE, IN FALL OF 1915, Coronel Ignacio C. Enríquez, interim president of Mexico City, ordered his subaltern Pablo des Georges to take the next day's train to San Andrés Chalchicomula, Puebla, where he was to pick up four thousand cargas (around 710 tons) of wheat that the Constitutionalist government had recently purchased. Once he weighed and sealed the sacks, he was to load them on the train and deposit them in the municipal warehouse in Mexico City. Enríquez told Georges to telegram him "if any difficulties arise in the fulfillment of your assignment." Enríquez concluded the memo by reiterating his "attentive consideration and particular appreciation" and signed "El Coronel."[1]

Mexico City residents, and the fledgling government, urgently needed the wheat that Pablo des Georges was to retrieve. During the previous winter, women in Mexico City had been sacking panaderías in desperate attempts to keep their families from joining the famished who lay dead on the streets. Hunger hit the capital long after other regions that were ravaged by the revolution, where people ate no more than weeds and prickly pears or succumbed to starvation.[2] The capital, the privileged consumer hub where producers brought their best goods, had managed to delay the food crisis. But when it crashed suddenly upon the city in early 1915, hunger left no doubt that the old political order had collapsed. If hunger was the most poignant sign of disorder and suffering, food was among the most important signs of political legitimacy. Pablo des Georges's mission, then, was as much about building the new government as it was about feeding the people.

Georges's task seemed simple, especially to the *coronel*, who had only recently arrived from the northern state of Chihuahua to occupy the municipal presidency of Mexico City. He had little understanding of the complications of the food supply in the capital. The numerous obstacles that Pablo des Georges encountered, and dutifully noted in his diary, revealed how limited the emerging revolutionary government was in its efforts to provide basic public needs and how dependent it remained on the businessmen who had achieved their dominance under Porfirio Díaz.

Revolution and the City

After three decades of rule, Díaz was swiftly forced from power by peasants and provincial elites. The octogenarian dictator conceded to a dignified exile in France after a brief period of battles in northern Mexico in 1910. When Francisco I. Madero won presidential elections in 1911, Mexico appeared to have embarked on a peaceful, moderate transition to electoral democracy. But the new president soon found himself squeezed between the lower classes, who demanded deeper social reforms, and the elites, who defended the status quo.[3] In February 1913, Madero's general Victoriano Huerta joined a counter-revolutionary coup that ended in the murder of Madero. For the subsequent year and a half, Huerta controlled the capital but struggled against the armies of Emiliano Zapata in the south and Pancho Villa and Venustiano Carranza in the north.

Under Huerta, the capital became a recalcitrant island of nostalgia where the wealthy seemed mostly unruffled. In January 1914, the Centro Vasco held the annual Three Kings Day party for their children in the Palacio de los Azulejos. The social pages announced that "all the principal Basque families were in attendance." The event was "elegant, as expected."[4] In March, the panadería owners raised money for Spaniards fleeing from Chihuahua, where Villa threatened to execute them and expropriate their estates, but the owners felt secure enough to stay with their businesses in Mexico City.[5] The Spanish government sent the steamship *Carlos V* (named for the monarch who reigned during the conquest) to give them passage back to Europe. Few in the city accepted the offer and instead honored the sailors with a banquet at the exclusive Casino Español. "The Spaniards in Mexico today," toasted Telésforo García, spokesman of the Spanish immigrant community, "are as industrious conquistadores as those of yesteryear.⁶ As if to prove it, several months later Braulio Iriarte and Pablo Díez inaugurated their compressed yeast factory.

However, this confident air of tranquility in the capital was shattered as united factions of revolutionaries forced Huerta's surrender. Constitutionalists led by General Álvaro Obregón occupied the capital in August 1914. One of their first tasks was to stave off a food crisis. The disruption of agriculture and transportation, the conscription of peasants, and the fiscal chaos caused by the coinage of factional currencies had drastically reduced the year's wheat harvest from 326 million to 34 million tons.[7]

In late 1914, women took bread from overwhelmed clerks, and rumors circulated that unscrupulous food merchants had "raised prices in order to earn a little bit more money."[8] Constitutionalists understood that a food crisis could undermine their efforts to gain political legitimacy in the capital. The concern was all the more pressing since the armies of Villa and Zapata had recently rejected the Constitutionalists' claim of national leadership at the Convention of Aguascalientes. Villa and Zapata loosely joined their forces into the Conventionist Army and declared war on the Constitutionalists.[9]

There was little the Constitutionalists in Mexico City could do to supply more food. Carranza and Obregón preferred to move precious resources to the battlefields, and their local leaders' hold on power was tenuous. The city governor, Alfredo Robles Domínguez, prohibited merchants from selling food out of the city, fixed the prices of basic foods, and ordered stores to declare their stock. He also sent envoys to the countryside for grain. However, his initiatives floundered. Inflation rose, and residents grew ever more panicked. *El Diario del Hogar*, a Constitutionalist newspaper, noted that "false rumors" of food scarcity had led to panicked purchases that only worsened the situation. Although it acknowledged that "lack of wheat was growing more visible every day," the paper stressed that "large quantities of wheat" were arriving to the city daily.[10] Yet the food situation continued to disintegrate, and Robles Domínguez resigned in frustration a month after receiving his post. At the end of November, the Constitutionalists left altogether, abandoning the city before the advancing Conventionists.[11]

As Villa and Zapata approached the city, the Spanish owners changed their customary arrangements with the peddlers, lowering the percentage that the latter could take from the purchase price from 20 to 15 percent and refusing to take back unsold pieces.[12] Forty-five peddlers, who had recently formed a union, turned to the Department of Labor, where the Conventionists had installed their people only days before.[13] Labor Chief José Colado and his inspector Eloy Armenta were both Spanish immigrants (from Asturias and Catalonia, respectively) and labor activists who were among the handful of European and American radicals drawn to Mexico by the revolution. They were organizers of the anarchist group Casa del Obrero Mundial (House of World Workers), founded in 1912, with which the peddlers' union had just affiliated. Huerta had deported both of them for being "assiduous propagandists of dissolution and pernicious ideas contrary to order, government, and property," but they returned during the Zapatista occupation.[14]

After hearing the peddlers' grievances, Colado met with sixteen owners led by José Arrache and Pedro Laguna (a Mexican owner whom competitors accused of being "Hispanicized").[15] Colado first proposed reinstating the 20 percent discount. Arrache instead offered to sell peddlers twenty *manos* for one peso. One mano (hand) equaled six cents worth of bread, regardless of the price of the individual pieces, which typically cost one, three, and six cents. Under this arrangement, the peddlers would make twenty cents for every twenty manos they sold. This seemed fair to Colado, and he urged the peddlers not be "so intransigent in these difficult times."

The peddlers insisted. "We want earnings in money, not in bread," for if owners refused to buy back leftover bread, the peddlers risked not making any money at all. "Understand, we are poor," they said, and "all our families will have to eat" is bread. Still confused over why owners should buy back what the peddlers could not sell—"such is the struggle of commerce," he reasoned—Colado suggested that the peddlers simply mix the leftover bread with fresh and sell it at full price the next day. "Day-old bread," he argued, "is healthier and more hygienic." He may not have understood that this practice would have prevented the poor from buying the cheaper day-old bread (clearly, his department was not consumer protection), and neither did this anarchist, known for fiery speeches against capitalist exploiters, defend the well-being of labor against what he called, in a memo to superiors, the owners' "hunger for greater profits" and the consequent "increase in bread prices."[16]

Colado favored the owners' claims, first, because he probably did not understand how the bread trade operated. "Hands" of bread, for instance, were hardly universal measurements. More importantly, he was keenly aware of the Conventionists' weakness in the capital. The appointed city governor,

Manuel Chao, had recently set the price of flour and announced "severe punishments" for "merchants possessed by greed." But inspectors fined only one panadería (Las Tres Colonias, owned by Baztanese immigrants Victoriano Loperena Ilarregui and Pedro Alemán Oteiza) five hundred pesos for selling "microscopic" bolillos for two cents, twice the normal price.[17]

Like their adversaries who occupied the city before them, the hastily established interim Conventionist authorities had little support from the leadership. Villa and Zapata were neither willing nor able to permanently occupy the city. They were dedicated to their own regional struggles and only tepidly supported administrators in the capital, including the convention-appointed national president, Eulalio Gutiérrez. Colado's position was also shaky. He had only been the labor chief for weeks, and his employment in the government had earned him the scorn of his comrades in the Casa del Obrero Mundial who expelled him for having violated anarchist principles by accepting a position within the government.[18] As a result, Colado had scarce political capital with which to challenge the bread barons. He was not going to exhaust it in the futile defense of the peddlers' archaic arrangements.

The revolutionary factions' weak attempts to govern encouraged the owners to take steps to further their dominance of the bread trade at a time when scarcities threatened to put them all out of business. Their next move was to marginalize smaller Mexican competitors; in fact, the circumstances practically compelled them to do so. Given the shortage of grain and reliable currency, millers restricted the supply of flour to their own shops and to those of their relatives and countrymen whose credit they could trust. Everyone else had to pay up front. Suddenly, the forty-five or so small Mexican owners had no flour.

"The Iberian potentate forces us to pay in cash at such elevated prices," complained one Mexican baker. "It is impossible for us to continue."[19] The Mexican owners insisted that the "terrible monopoly" had created an artificial scarcity in order to get rich and drive competitors into ruin. They pointed to one Spanish owner who had just received over three hundred tons of wheat and was selling sacks at twice the normal rate. Such maneuvers, they argued, threatened not only the small owners, their workers, and their customers, but also the very ideals of the revolution. As long as the "monopoly of hoarders" continued, they argued, "our brothers will have soaked the fatherland with blood in vain, the sacrifices that you, our valiant warriors, have made for peace, will be but sterile efforts."[20]

José Segura, leader of the recently formed Association of Mexican Bakery Owners, met with the Conventionist-appointed national president Gutiérrez and proposed that the government seize all the wheat and flour and put a group of businessmen—"Mexicans, not Spaniards"—in charge of administering the sale of flour at a fixed price. To avoid hoarding, each shop would only be able to purchase enough for its own production.[21] Gutiérrez agreed with Segura that the "Union of Hoarders of Wheat and Flour" was a threat to the populace, but he delegated the bread matter to the city government, suggesting that "a commission of honest people" set a "reasonable" retail price based on how much wheat flour mills had in stock.[22] Instead, the city government passed the matter on to the secretary of the interior, who met with Braulio Iriarte, Pedro Irigoyen, and José Arrache. With remarkable cynicism, they, too, criticized the "lucrative speculation by the many unscrupulous wheat and flour merchants who are causing this lamentable situation that could perturb public order and peace."[23]

They agreed to sell the Mexican owners eight hundred sacks of flour at thirty cents a kilo. But they only provided six hundred, and much of the flour was rotten. Again, the small Mexican bakers faced ruin.[24] "We don't have any flour," Aniseto Martínez wrote to Segura. "We used it all up and I and those who work in my house will have to stop working if you do not send us the means to keep working."[25] Another baker wrote, "The flour that they sold us is so bad that I had to throw part of it away." Moreover, he said the Spanish millers had threatened to cut him off altogether: "Those evil octopuses are willing to never sell us another grain. They say that they are willing to continue hurting us and take revenge if we seek refuge with the Government, since they are too rich and powerful for a few poor Indians to kick their feet."[26]

The members of the city council understood that the Spanish owners effectively controlled the flow of wheat and flour in the city. They also knew that Segura's proposal to seize all the flour in the city was impractical and would exacerbate the already precarious food situation. Instead, the council simply named a Special Commission on Food Items, which summoned the mill owners and the Mexican bakers to another meeting. The millers again agreed to sell flour at thirty cents a kilo, but on the condition that the government provided enough railroad cars to get wheat to the capital.[27] Soon after, they declared that their wheat was almost gone and that they would not be able to comply if the government did not import grain.[28] In mid-January, the Henkel brothers, German millers in the neighboring city of Toluca, agreed to provide the government with sixteen train cars of flour with twenty-two more to follow.²⁹ Officials distributed the flour directly to the Mexican-owned panaderías.³⁰ Wheat was finally flowing again, and it was hoped that bread would soon become abundant and cheap. But then the Constitutionalists drove the Conventionists from the city.

The Year of Hunger, Filth, and Pestilence

The goal of the second Constitutionalist occupation, which lasted just over a month, was to recruit workers and levy taxes on the city's foreign merchants. Obregón accused the Spaniards of having supported antirevolutionary forces and hoarding. In practice, he had little time, desire, or ability to address the food crisis.³¹ Some accused him of deliberately shutting off food shipments from the countryside in order to punish residents for having permitted the Conventionist occupation. An anonymous Committee of Americans attributed to Obregón "a premeditated campaign to starve the people and force them to join his army."³² He then decreed that the foreign merchants make a "special contribution" of twenty million pesos and threatened to allow hungry residents to pillage. He also ordered food merchants to turn over 10 percent of their stock to the military.³³ "If my children had no bread," Obregón declared, "I would go out and look for it with a dagger in my hand. At the first attempt at riot, I will leave the city at the head of my troops in order that they may not fire a single shot against the hungry multitude."³⁴

Obregón's bluster satisfied some who had suffered high food prices, long lines, and empty shelves. Activists from the Casa del Obrero Mundial took to the streets to celebrate the measures and to pressure foreign merchants to comply. For most residents, though, the brief Constitutionalist occupation only worsened the situation.³⁵ The Committee of Americans wrote that when foreign merchants paid only five hundred thousand pesos, Obregón forced them to sweep city streets. The merchants responded by closing their shops, "paralyzing commerce in the city."³⁶ When Obregón threatened to force them open, foreign consulates placed official seals on their citizens' doors, and breaking them would have exposed the Constitutionalists to diplomatic conflicts.³⁷ According to local authorities, food prices had shot up 400 percent; the American Red Cross estimated the increase at 900 percent.³⁸ American resident Leone Moats described the winter of 1915 as "a time of filth and pestilence. The city was full of lice, and there was a terrific epidemic of typhus fever . . . the poor people were absolutely starving. Even foreign colonies suffered for lack of white bread."³⁹

As winter turned to spring, food grew even scarcer. The *Mexican Herald* reported that markets had only "meager quantities" of maize; there were "no tortillas in the city."[40] The Superior Health Council denounced bakers who adulterated bread with "bran and hay."[41] German immigrant Luisa Bröker wrote home that "our life here has been going downhill." "We have no bread," she wrote, and "vegetables are virtually unavailable; only carrots and cabbage and, every once in a while, artichokes. The quality of the meat has become so poor that one does better without it, and everything that is still available costs a fortune. Tortillas are almost unaffordable when one is lucky enough to find them."[42]

Residents took to sacking the panaderías and grocery stores in March after Obregón and his troops left and the Conventionists marched back in. "Very large crowds, mostly women," gathered menacingly in front of bakeries. The police, stationed in front, "had considerable difficulty in maintaining order," and an "indignant crowd" took all the bread.[43] At other shops, women lined up around eight at night to wait for bread the next morning. "Caravans of women with baskets practically attacked" neighborhood stores in search of maize.[44] A child suffocated in a crowd of five hundred who had gathered at a store that rumors suggested had some maize.[45] The next day, more than 260 women fainted from hunger and suffocation in a crowd of ten thousand that was waiting to buy maize from a government outlet.[46] In June, an axe-wielding adolescent girl led residents in looting panaderías and grocery stores while chanting "We are hungry."[47] Firemen drove women away from stores with water hoses. Gendarmes who guarded bread shot dead four women and wounded six others in a crowd that had taken bread.[48]

Rumors circulated about hidden warehouses bursting with flour. The Association of Mexican Bakery Owners triumphantly burst into one warehouse that belonged to the José Cuervo distillery.[49] Flour, it seems, had become more valuable than tequila. This was the only direct evidence of hoarding, but the bread barons were hardly suffering. Andrés Barberena (Braulio Iriarte's nephew) had enough flour to donate twenty thousand bolillos to hungry residents.[50] Soon after, he and fellow Baztanese owner Marcelino Zugarramurdi celebrated their joint bachelor party at a downtown restaurant with many of the dominant Basque owners. According to the social pages, "great joy reigned" at the table, which was "tastefully adorned with fragrant flowers." The famous Lerdo Orchestra played for the guests who, during dessert, pronounced "affectionate speeches."[51] Outside, municipal sanitation workers picked up the extenuated corpses that lay in the street and burned them on the outskirts of the city.[52]

Figure 4. Women gathered in front of La Parisina, Mexico City, 1915. Fondo Casasola, Inventory No. 41472. Courtesy of the Fototeca Nacional of the Instituto Nacional de Antropología e Historia.

At the same time, Iriarte embarked on a real estate rush, purchasing with devalued currency dozens of buildings and rural estates from fallen oligarchs.[53] He felt sufficiently confident in the circumstances to take in his sister's sixteen-year-old son José Larregui Iriarte—whom Iriarte later helped to establish the Compañía Molinera de Toluca, a flour mill in the agricultural and industrial zone west of Mexico City—along with José's brothers, Bautista and Miguel.[54] Fellow Basque owner Martín Oyamburu also pursued extensive real estate purchases after calling in loans he had made to elite families whose fortunes had turned. In November 1915, Oyamburu purchased six of the largest buildings in the Mexico City suburb of Guadalupe-Hidalgo from a Luis F. Velázquez y Quiroga for the sum of $760,500, in addition to canceling the latter's $10,000 debt. The next month, Oyamburu invested in oil drilling in Tuxpam, Veracruz, further diversifying his enterprises that consisted of numerous panaderías, agriculture, and production of silk undergarments.[55] The low point for Mexico's old elite—and certainly for its old poor—was a high point for the immigrant entrepreneurs.

Aware of the contrast between those who suffered and those who benefitted from the crisis, women hurled insults at the ragged Zapatista peasant soldiers.

"This is your fault, you sandal-wearing sons of whores!" they yelled. "The gachupines are hiding the food and you don't have the *tanates* [balls] to force them to sell."[56] But these troops were already moving out. The Conventionists left the city submerged in epidemics and hunger as the Constitutionalists approached in August 1915.

The food crisis was, once again, a means by which the Constitutionalists hoped to prove that their administrative acumen and revolutionary concern for the populace could undo the disasters that plagued the city. The new municipal president, General Ignacio C. Enríquez, recently arrived from Chihuahua, began to distribute free meals and sell food at accessible prices. Yet, the task was beyond him, and he soon succumbed to corruption.[57] Soldiers and bureaucrats helped themselves to the food and sold it to wealthy families.[58] Civilians waited in long lines early in the morning, while military officers elbowed their way through to the front. Having to go to panaderías was "degrading" enough, said Constitutionalist lieutenant Luis Figueroa. "What would the foreign residents in our country think if they saw army officers in the lines of the multitude?"[59] The American Red Cross reported that three hundred people died every day in the capital and that the government was doing little to save them. The "poor creatures" survived on "alfalfa, pigweed, and parts of the century plant."[60] Yet despite the continued disorder and hunger, the Constitutionalists again strove to give the impression that they had transformed from mere military faction into the exclusive force of national government.

Carranza's consul in San Francisco, California, Ramón P. de Negri, rejected the Red Cross report as misinformed and slanderous. He criticized the report's author for including the testimonies of workers in the cemetery, where the Red Cross had gone to see how many dead were arriving. "The well known romantic proclivities of the average peon, who dearly loves to have his name written down in a big book," could hardly substantiate the Red Cross's claims, Negri argued. He insisted that government workers in charge of relief efforts were honest and compassionate and that "as soon as the Constitutionalists came into control, the situation was relieved, without a moment's delay." As for alfalfa, the Red Cross clearly ignored that "boiled 'greens' are a very palatable and nutritious food in common use" in Mexico.[61] But even Negri acknowledged that "August was the month of the worst conditions," although, he argued, *only* two thousand people died—"well within the normal rate."[62] With a hungry and restive urban populace threatening further disorder, and Red Cross busybodies marring their image abroad, the Constitutionalists were anxious to consolidate authority in the capital. To do so, they had to address the food crisis.

One tactic was to blame the Spanish owners, as Obregón had done during the previous occupation. Anti-gachupinismo certainly hovered close to the Constitutionalists. The Anti-Spanish League of Mexico, established in the summer of 1915, invited all "Conscious Mexicans" to join a "transcendental and patriotic" campaign for "the DE-HISPANICIZATION of our country."[63] Their flier railed against "the repugnant and murderous behavior that . . . the pernicious, degenerate, and rapacious Spanish Colony in Mexico has carried out." The league was short lived but planned to publish a monthly magazine dedicated to exposing the "perverted Spanish Colony" and to give conferences on the "disadvantages of Spanish immigration and the urgent need to substitute it with another, more honest and cultured one."[64] A member of Carranza's military special services, León Girón, vouched for the league's Constitutionalist sympathies in a letter to Carranza. "They are friends of mine," he wrote, who object to "gachupines with Judaic conduct."

Anti-gachupinismo, Girón argued, was a foundation of Mexican nationalism. Had not the struggle for independence begun with Hidalgo's cry of "death to the gachupines"?[65] In this view, the war of independence had not entirely freed Mexico from Spaniards. A vague Spanish-ness tainted everything that was previous or counter to the revolution. Agustín Iturbide, the colonial loyalist turned independence leader turned emperor, had been a "ridiculous puppet" of the Spanish. Porfirio Díaz had been a "Spanish King," despite his Mixtec heritage. Porfirio's nephew Félix Díaz, leader of the counterrevolutionary coup in 1912, had fought to reinstate "colonial" rule. Now, Girón wrote, "is the only opportunity that conscientious men will ever have to rid ourselves of the *gachupín* yoke that has weighed upon our destiny before and after 1810."[66]

Similarly, Eduardo Fuentes, "Advising Attorney for the Headquarters of the Constitutionalist Army," drafted an extended memo that identified, in his view, the causes of food scarcity in Mexico City. He inveighed against the "insatiable greed" of the "perverted Spanish element." He urged Carranza to "smash the head of this apocalyptic monster of our history" by prohibiting Spaniards from selling food.[67] Carranza put Gerardo Murillo, the painter, political radical, and rabid anti-gachupín better known as Dr. Atl, in charge of the Committee for the Relief of the Poor in the summer of 1915.[68] Murillo also became Carranza's spokesman for organized workers and edited semi-official newspapers filled with denunciations of Spanish owners.[69] There is little indication that these views influenced Carranza's policies, but he hardly discouraged anti-Spanish rhetoric, perhaps because it diverted attention from his own government's inability to handle the food crisis.

The Spanish immigrant paper *El Correo Español* responded to this barrage of anti-gachupinismo by insisting, "We have not come here to trick or exploit anyone. We aren't thieves or degenerates. The Germanophile Spanish immigrant brings his work, his energies, his virility."[70] The most pragmatic of government officials seemed to agree, for they entered into agreements with the same Basque mill and panadería owners whom the Constitutionalists had been denouncing as enemies of the revolution.

In September 1915, the city government agreed to take on the costs and difficulties of purchasing wheat, transporting it to mills, and distributing flour to two of the city's largest panaderías, Los Gallos and La Unión, owned by Arrache & Córdoba and Cofiño & Saracho, respectively. Officials also agreed to pay all these shops' expenses, including wages. In exchange, panaderías would produce bread for the government charity office, charging ten cents for each seventy-gram salted bolillo that less than a year before had cost only one cent.[71] These terms were already extremely favorable to owners. Arrache & Córdoba allegedly paid military leaders bribes of two thousand pesos per railroad car in order to get wheat to their mill.[72] Once panaderías produced the amount agreed, they were free to produce for their own shops, using the labor and flour paid for by the city government, and charge the public "whatever price favors the interests of the panaderías."[73] To the dismay of the Mexican owners and the anti-Spanish advocates close to Carranza, not only did the local government not persecute the Spanish bakers, it helped them increase their profits.

The Misadventures of Pablo des Georges

After making these arrangements with the panadería and mill owners, the next step for the government was to find wheat. So Coronel Enríquez dispatched Pablo des Georges, who boarded the morning train toward San Andrés Chalchicomula with fifteen hundred empty burlap sacks.[74] At 9:35 a.m. the next day, he arrived in San Andrés and found lodging at an inn in town. The hacienda was owned by the family of Antonio Couttolence, a recently deceased landowner and industrialist who had immigrated to Mexico in the 1860s.[75] He met with the hacienda manager, who was escorted by thirty soldiers and who told him that the wheat had been harvested but not yet threshed because Zapatista guerrillas had been active in the area, and the manager was afraid to expose the harvest and his workers to their pillaging. Georges's first task, then, was to request military protection from the town's *jefe de armas* (military commander). However, torrential rain kept him from finding the jefe de armas, much less a detachment of soldiers. On October 1 Coronel Enríquez sent Georges a telegraph that "showed his anger that we have not begun threshing." But, Georges comforted himself, "it's not my fault, as he will see soon enough." The rain was unrelenting. For October 2 and 3, he entered in his diary, "Raining very hard" and "Rain continues." Nine days into his mission, he had yet to see the wheat.

When the rain finally let up, Georges was able to meet with the jefe de armas, who agreed to provide him with soldiers during the threshing. Unfortunately, the soldiers' guns were still "on the way," which made them useless when seven hundred Zapatistas appeared near one of the haciendas on October 4. Georges then ran out of money, not having anticipated an extended stay. The coronel, angry at the slow pace of the mission, refused to respond to Georges's requests for more funds. When the señora at the inn raised her rates, Georges was forced to borrow money from the hacienda manager. On the bright side, threshing at one of the haciendas began on October 5. Soon, 120 or 125 of the 4,000 total cargas would be ready. Meanwhile, he hoped, wheat from the other haciendas would be dry enough for the threshing. On October 6, he had twenty-two cargas bagged, sealed, and ready to ship to Mexico City. But there were no trains. On October 8, twenty more soldiers arrived, but they, too, had no guns. And then the rains resumed. Optimistic nonetheless, Georges wrote, "I think the weather will favor us. In a few days we can load the first two freight cars."

All the while, Georges had been wrangling with the cantankerous and shady Provost Agent Lizárraga, in charge of the train station. As part of the contract between the landowner and the city government, the latter had to donate a quarter of the wheat it purchased to the state government of Puebla. This huge amount of wheat was for the state's official charity. The state government was responsible for getting the wheat from the hacienda to the state capital, but Lizárraga took it on himself to "meddle, as he does, in so many matters" related to Georges's assignment. Indeed, even before there was any wheat on the station platform, "two or three individuals from town (not partial to the Cause)" were "working close to said Agent to see that no wheat is taken away." When the first sacks were ready, Lizárraga insisted on taking a quarter of each individual sack, which Georges refused to allow, especially since the provost agent could not show any official authorization to do so. Georges later came to "understand that he is a shameless character. He just made such a proposal that only an exploiter and bad servant of the Cause could make." Now that the poor civil servant finally had some of the wheat in his hands, corruption and provincial distrust of Mexico City politicians kept him from embracing it.

For a week, the exasperated Georges made no note of his activities at all. The next week, he listed only difficulties. On October 21, the jefe de armas reported that the Zapatistas had attacked one of the haciendas. When the hacienda employees fled into town, Georges went to investigate but concluded that it was "more fuss [escándalo] than danger." Workers began threshing that same day, apparently without military escorts. The next day, there was a fiesta in honor of the local military chief, whom Georges took to calling "the accidental jefe de armas." Georges had to contribute twenty-two pesos— the equivalent of three weeks of room and board.

> October 28: More problems with Provost Agent Lizárraga.
> October 29: Another altercation with Lizárraga. There are things in his behavior that seem very strange to me.
> October 30: I fear that Lizárraga may cause problems for me with the governor of Puebla.
> October 31: Today, Sunday, impossible to bring wheat from the haciendas since no one works on Sundays.
> November 1: Town patron saint fiesta began. I telegrammed Coronel Enríquez telling him that I fear I won't be able to embark until after the fiesta because here the people don't work.

His wait slowly began to yield results. On November 3, he received forty sacks of wheat, though they were "80 kilos short." And, what's more, he had to leave a quarter of the wheat with Lizárraga. Finally, on November 9, more than a month after his departure, Pablo des Georges made it back to the capital with his wheat. From the Mexico City station, the grain went to Basque immigrant Florencio Sánchez's mill Harinera y Manufacturera Nacional, where it was ground at a rate of five cents a kilo.

In the end, the flour cost the city government $1.26 a kilo, more than four times the already profitable amount that mill owners had agreed to charge the small Mexican owners the previous year. This sum does not include Pablo des Georges's expenses, nor the shipping costs to the individual shops.

Moreover, once the panaderías received the flour, they committed a series of petty abuses in their budgets. Los Gallos delivered bread on mule-pulled coaches, but it seems unlikely that the panadería would need a leather worker, a blacksmith, and a carpenter—as well as their respective assistants and materials—every day. Other figures in the budgets are simply arbitrary. Where Los Gallos budgeted two pesos for its daily electricity, the much smaller La Unión budgeted ten and also threw in a substantial thirty pesos for daily "miscellaneous expenses" (table 4).[76]

For all their blatancy, these instances of minor malfeasance were hardly enough to raise the eyebrow of Coronel Enríquez or anyone else in the Constitutionalist government. Such was the price of doing business in revolutionary Mexico. After a month of waiting for a single shipment of wheat, and almost two years of hunger, the emerging government wanted to see bread on

Table 4. Budgets presented to the city government by Los Gallos and La Unión, 1915.

BUDGET OF LOS GALLOS		BUDGET OF LA UNIÓN	
Eight coach drivers, $3.00 each	$ 24.00	Rent	$10.00
Wages for clerks	$ 25.66	Wages for clerks	$12.00
One leather worker	$ 1.50	Cook	$ 1.00
One carpenter	$ 1.75	Food expenses for clerks	$20.00
One assistant	$ 0.75	Taxes	$ 1.00
One blacksmith	$ 2.50	Miscellaneous expenses	$30.00
One assistant	$ 0.87		
One corral keeper	$ 1.00		
One cook for the clerks	$ 1.00		
Food expenses for clerks	$ 30.00		
Coach upkeep	$ 10.00		
Horseshoes for mules	$ 10.00		
Pasture for sixteen mules, $2.00 daily each	$ 32.00		
Materials for carpenter, blacksmith, leather worker	$ 6.00		
Taxes	$ 7.00		
Electricity	$ 2.00		
Ice	$ 2.00		
Total:	$158.03	Total	$74.00

Source: AHCM, 1915, Ayuntamiento, Reguladora de Comercio, vol. 3853, exp. 14.

shelves as a first step toward bolstering its claim to authority. For all his bluster against foreign merchants, Álvaro Obregón understood the importance of the Spanish monopoly. He soon became quite close to Pedro Irigoyen, Pedro Albaitero's nephew, who by then controlled the flow of wheat into Mexico City. Obregón and Irigoyen exchanged chummy letters discussing barbecues and their wives.[77] As president, Obregón later named Irigoyen as part of an official agricultural commission in charge of "studying the general situation of the haciendas."[78] When Irigoyen died in 1925, Obregón sent condolences to his wife and personally arranged for the transport of his body from Ciudad Juárez to Mexico City.[79]

The new government's bread problems, however, were far from over. In October 1915, bakers formed a union affiliated with the Casa del Obrero Mundial. In November, as Pablo des Georges oversaw the final threshing of the wheat, the Union of Bakery Workers (Sindicato de Obreros y Obreras en el Ramo de la Panadería) published a list of demands for their Spanish employers and prepared to go on strike.[80]

The revolution severed the links between the capital and its hinterland, turning the city that had been the economic and political center into an isolated region, marginal to the battles that raged around it. The relative ease with which the rival factions occupied and abandoned the city reveal its strategic insignificance. As Obregón explained, "Mexico City has no military importance. It is not a railroad center, nor can troops find material to eat or to make war. Protecting the city, in contrast, requires the distraction of many forces needed in other points."[81] Feeding the city, he might have added, was an administrative disaster. Dealing with wheat, flour, and bread; negotiating with resentful Mexican bakers, small-time peddlers, and evasive Basque immigrants; distributing maize to hungry masses—these tasks would not make for victory. Wars are won with bullets, not bread. This view resulted in nightmarish consequences: starvation and pillage that destroyed the capital's ancien régime air of sophistication and civility. Scarcity, hoarding, inflation, and hunger were unmistakable signs of the deteriorated social contract that bound the state and the people. Indeed, during most of this period there was not much of a "state" to speak of, but rather occupying armies that haphazardly attempted to govern over circumstances whose difficulties repeatedly undermined their claims to authority.[82]

Victory required definitive control of the capital, and political legitimacy required grappling with everyday matters like bread. These calamitous months were the time for the Basque entrepreneurs to increase their power and assert it conspicuously in view of the warring factions. Partially fulfilling agreements, selling rotten flour, and shrinking the size of bread were more than strategies to deal with scarcities and rising costs. These actions were also expressions of power. As the misadventures of Pablo des Georges show, whatever faction endeavored to become the national government had to contend with the men who dominated the bread trade.

Land reform, an end to foreign dominance, effective suffrage, workers' rights: these were the overarching, long-term stated goals of the revolution. Yet in the short term, seeing that the people were fed was an urgent need, and in order to address it, authorities allied with the "shameless speculators" whom the factional leaders publically condemned. The Basque and other Spanish owners not only endured the revolution, the war conditions allowed them to tighten their dominance over the bread and flour markets. Among the most distrusted symbols of the turn-of-the-century social transformation under Porfirio Díaz, panadería owners ironically became crucial agents in the construction of the new political order. This compromise of revolutionary ideals underscores the political importance of bread as well as a broad reluctance to carry out profound social change that prefigured the revolutionary leaders' later hesitancy to fulfill other key pledges to the new society.

CHAPTER SIX

The Bakers' Revolution

❧ THE BAKERS' REVOLUTION BEGAN IN 1915, WHEN THE CIVIL WAR brought the worst misery on the city, five years after the initial outbreak of violence in other parts of the country. It was no accident that bakers formed their union while residents were suffering hunger. Workers, who felt the crisis disproportionately, demanded higher wages in order to provide for their families. Compelled by hunger, they were also inspired by the sense of revolutionary possibility. The collapse of the state apparatus of Porfirio Díaz, together with the chaos caused by the recurrent occupations, wiped out governmental limitations on workers' mobilization. The revolution brought hunger, but it also broadened the horizon. As a result, labor activism in Mexico City exploded with massive unionization and mobilization, the publishing of a plethora of worker newspapers, and bold assertions regarding the proletariat's imminent future. This coincidence of penury and possibility was especially galvanizing for bakery workers. Just as their employers had maneuvered through the crisis to advance their own interests, the bakers had unprecedented leverage with which to assert themselves as the workers who fed the city.

Bakers were among the most radical and militant activists within the rising labor movement. They joined anarchist and communist federations that proposed to dissolve the state or transform it into a dictatorship of the proletariat. The headquarters of the bakers' union, formed in 1915, was a hub for radical organizations, a refuge for foreign and Mexican activists. They launched combative strikes and met with violence the resistance from employers, police, and rival unionists.

Despite this wave of radicalism, the demands that bakers made of their employers were consistently reformist. The bakers sought to adjust, not transform, the relationship between labor and capital. Someday, once the labor movement was more solid and mature, workers could, perhaps, carry out a deeper social transformation. Meanwhile, hunger, recalcitrant employers, and police batons directed them toward more immediate goals: higher wages, health care, and, in a broader sense, a degree of authority over their working lives. As opposed to a conscious plan, this practical approach reflected the volcanic jumble of hope and misery that was the revolution. A far cry from the destruction of capitalism, their gains had radical repercussions and, compared to the conditions that had prevailed only twenty years earlier, they represented a significant shift in power. Moreover, the support organized bakers received from agents of the state meant that after decades of marginalization as pariahs, poor workers were becoming key constituents in the new society that emerged from the revolution.

Socialist Bakeries

When the Constitutionalist forces led by Álvaro Obregón briefly occupied the city in January and February 1915, they strengthened their links with the radical labor organization the Casa del Obrero Mundial (House of World Workers). Founded in 1912 by anarchist and communist craftsmen and intellectuals, the Casa quickly became a center for worker activism and mobilization in the city. Obregón and Carranza agreed to support the Casa's organizational and educational activities in exchange for workers' enlistment in the Batallones Rojos that combated Villa and Zapata. Commanded by Ignacio C. Enríquez (who later became Pablo des Georges's boss), the Red Battalions headed off for battle in March 1915 and returned in the fall, soon after the Constitutionalists had definitively occupied the capital in August.[1]

Neither Carranza nor Obregón were labor radicals. Their pact with the Casa was political and strategic, driven by wartime pressures. But the Constitutionalists shared some fundamental ideas with the Casa leadership. They all believed that the road to workers' liberation began with moral improvement. The Spanish anarchist José Colado, Labor Department chief during the Zapatista occupation, was typical in his sermon to peddlers. The worker, he insisted, "will reach no social, moral or economic improvement until he personally begins to moralize himself. In order to demand good wages, you must first have culture, and work honestly, this way you soon see that you'll reach your desires, through reason, logic, and justice."[2] The Casa leadership also shared the Constitutionalists' anticlericalism. For the radicals, priests were as responsible for workers' exploitation as bosses, so Casa activists made great display of the profanation, transformation, and destruction of religious icons.[3] The Constitutionalists likewise saw the Church as a redoubt of Spanish colonialism that submerged Mexico's masses in superstition and ignorance, and as a source of support for Huerta.

In a powerful gesture of this common hostility toward the Church, the Constitutionalists evicted the nuns and orphans from the Saint Brigit Convent and turned the building over to the Casa del Obrero Mundial, along with a printing press expropriated from a Catholic paper. Once in the convent, leaders smashed the religious icons and set up instead a "rationalist school" inspired by Spanish anarchism. In October 1915, when the Casa had outgrown the convent, Carranza expropriated the Palacio de los Azulejos (House of Tiles). This was another symbolic swipe at Mexico's old-regime privileges. The spectacular blue and white tile–covered colonial palace—the "seigniorial building of Mexico's bourgeoisie"—was home to the exclusive Jockey Club and the Centro Vasco, whose board of directors then included the Irigoyens, Albaitero's son, and Iriarte's nephews.[4] Only the horror that the bread barons must have felt as they removed their fine furniture could have matched the enthusiasm of the incoming workers. The Constitutionalists' material subsidies and rhetorical encouragement seemed to be an unequivocal sign that the revolution was opening new possibilities.[5] When had workers humiliated their employers with such high drama? When had the underdogs dreamed of such support from authorities?

Constitutionalists further took aim at the Spanish bakery owners in the semiofficial radical press that presented a Carranza bent on destroying the privileges that foreigners had enjoyed under Porfirio Díaz. The press sympathetically noted that his government was becoming "more socialist every day" as the president carried the revolution into the daily life of the city where humiliation and repression by Spaniards continued unabated.[6] Accusations of bakery malfeasance were regular features in *El Popular* and *Acción Mundial*, which were edited by the radical painter Dr. Atl. "On the corner of Ciprés and Rosa Streets," one article related, "there is a panadería, property of some . . . Spaniards where I observed the following":

A large group of poor people were on the sidewalk waiting for bread, when a servant boy began the "innocent" chore of hurling buckets of water onto the sidewalk, forcing the poor women to step aside. I asked him who had ordered such a stupid thing and he answered, his *"patroncito."* I headed to the door of the bakery and was met by one don Eusebio, a gachupín, with airs of "I've got the king by his ear," who told me that he was in his house and could do as he pleased.[7]

The piece concluded opaquely, "What a shame of brooms and ropes!" and then added, more forcefully, "Alas, what a shame of guillotines!"[8] Another article complained that "ninety-nine percent of the bakery owners in the capital are Spaniards—wolves of the same litter. They have agreed to divide the flour among themselves."[9] A writer for *El Pueblo* accused the Soto Street Panadería of "wickedly mocking the public." Women arrived around midnight, in anticipation of the five o'clock opening, but went "home without any bread for their little ones' breakfast," for the bakery secretly sold bread at high prices to peddlers who raised prices even further. Bakeries were even poisoning the public with "highly dangerous substances in order to satisfy their exaggerated speculations."[10]

La Acción Mundial accused the owner of the Ancha Street Panadería, "a *peninsular* named 'don Jesús,'" of hoarding flour instead of baking bread. "He inhumanely mistreats the women who buy bread." The sardonic use of the honorific *don* underscored the repudiation of persistent colonial deference. Like the original conquistadores, these Spaniards had been poor nobodies in their country but came to riches in Mexico through greed and guile. Don Jesús, the article continued, "surely hasn't known hunger lately, but it probably seemed interminable to him in his own land."[11] Once he had eaten, the article implied, don Jesús proceeded to profit from the hunger of Mexicans.

Conservatives looked on with profound dismay: armed workers, evicted nuns, and occupied colonial palaces all proved that Carranza was a social radical virulently opposed to "privilege." An American observer noted that in addition to turning the Palacio de los Azulejos, the "most exclusive and aristocratic club," over to Mexican and foreign anarchists, Carranza had also "plundered other well-furnished edifices."[12] Woodrow Wilson's interior minister likewise feared that intransigent, murderous radicals had taken over. "The Marats of Mexico," he wrote, in reference to the French Jacobin Jean Paul Marat, "onetime grocers and longshoremen, butchers and bakers," were now in control of the country.[13]

The Constitutionalists further confirmed conservatives' fear (and radicals' hope) of revolutionary transformation of everyday life when they set up socialist bakeries run by the bakers' union. In October 1915, only days after their employers vacated the Palacio de los Azulejos, the bakers joined the Casa del Obrero Mundial.[14] Two weeks later, in early November, they published a series of demands in *El Popular*. As part of a modern workers' movement, their demands were identical to those that the typographers' union had made the day before: eight-hour shifts, compensation for injuries, higher wages, and the exclusive authority to hire and "resolve any difficulties among workers." The list concluded with an ultimatum. If owners did not respond within ten days, the bakers threatened to close down their shops.[15]

After the catastrophe of the previous months, making sure that the city had food was a central political imperative for the Constitutionalists. Pablo des Georges was still overseeing the final threshing in San Andrés Chalchicomula. A strike would disrupt the food supply beyond bakeries: previous experience showed that residents compensated for bread with more tortillas, which led maize merchants and tortilla makers to raise prices. As a result, the poorest families who ate the least bread suffered the most. Shortages would jeopardize not only Carranza's authority in the city but, as the accusations from the American Red Cross indicated, his international standing as well. The Spanish government was already preparing legal demands for reparations for the damage caused by the riots of the previous summer. In October 1915, only days before the bakers' union published their demands, the U.S. president Woodrow Wilson had tentatively extended recognition of Carranza's authority.[16] Another wave of hunger and riots could only hurt Carranza's efforts to gain legitimacy within and beyond Mexico.

A bakers' strike would also highlight the political contradictions inherent in the Constitutionalists' accords. In addition to their pact with the Casa del Obrero Mundial, government officials had made agreements with the bakery and mill owners. When the Constitutionalists drew up contracts with Florencio Sánchez to mill Pablo des Georges's wheat and with Arrache & Córdoba to bake the bread that the government was to distribute among the poor, they considered labor as a passive component, a factor they could take for granted. But now the government had to contend with workers who were anything but passive. If a strike broke out, the Constitutionalists could no longer satisfy both owners and workers. The class antagonism in panaderías meant that the Constitutionalists had to walk an increasingly fine line. Erring on either side could jeopardize the food supply and, consequently, the government's claim to authority.

Mexico City governor César López de Lara attempted "several times" to negotiate a settlement.[17] López de Lara was another foreigner in the city (he was a general from the northern state of Tamaulipas) who was somewhat baffled by the complicated relationships around bread. When owners flatly rejected the bakery workers' demands, López de Lara sent them to the Bureau of Conciliation and Arbitration. The front page of *El Pueblo* showed the dark-skinned bakers arriving at the bureau, dressed in the overalls and cloth caps of the urban proletariat. The Navarrese bakery owners, including Antero Arrache, Manuel Erreguerena, Andrés Barberena, and Marcelino Zugarramundi, a whole head taller than the bakers, arrived in solemn business suits. Unable to come to an agreement, the two groups left the bureau and met again with the governor. The bakers reduced their demands to two: that owners raise their wages and recognize their union as the official representative of the workers.[18]

The owners refused any discussion of the union's legality. As for wages, they asserted that workers had recently received raises. Finally, they insisted that it was impossible to shorten shifts or fix any duration to them at all. "Bread production," they alleged, "is subject to many contingencies that do not depend on man, such as temperature changes that delay or accelerate labor."[19] Volume, which coincided with consumption, was the base of production, and this logic prevailed over the fixed "clock-time" demanded by workers. The owners claimed that shifts that ended after eight hours, regardless of the amount of bread produced, undermined this principle.[20] Furthermore, bakers should be content to have work at all. Mechanization, proclaimed the owners, was rendering "manual labor insignificant."

This mechanization bluff, which has misled modern historians, failed to dissuade the bakers.[21] Few bakeries had followed the example of Los Gallos and El Factor in mechanizing production so extensively, and even these shops relied heavily on the manual labor and artisan dexterity of bakers. Two decades later, a 1935 census of the 238 registered bakeries in Mexico City indicated that there were 265 manual dough-cutting machines and 155 dough mixers, but only thirty-five frosting mixers, two mechanical sifters, four refrigerators, and fifteen "other" machines.[22] As late as 1968, the bakery trade publication *Pan* noted that "bread baking will always be a handicraft" since bolillos, the most commonly consumed pieces, lost their freshness "shortly after being removed from the oven." It is unlikely, the article continued, "that the structure of bakeries will undergo any significant modification in the near future since the nature of the product makes the industrialization of production very difficult."[23] If bakery owners continued to rely on bakers' skill and strength in the late 1960s, in 1915 labor was nothing less than employers' highest concern. The owners offered to "allow workers back into the workrooms, without exceptions" if the bakers "renounced their pretensions." The bakers declined the offer and declared a strike.[24]

The impasse sent Constitutionalist officials scrambling for a solution that would appease workers and at the same time avoid a disruption of the bread supply. The government had neither the will nor the leverage to pressure either side to yield. On the one hand, the commercial circuits that supplied the city with wheat, flour, and bread remained in the power of the Basques and their associates, who had increasingly closed ranks in the face of government intervention and union pressures. Without their cooperation, there would be no steady supply of bread. On the other hand, the administration could not afford to upset its alliance with the Casa del Obrero Mundial by sending the gendarmes to break the strike. The Constitutionalists needed workers' support in order to govern the city, not least because the Red Battalions had recently returned but had yet to turn in their guns.[25] The strategic arsenal of the workers could involve more than just strikes.

The Constitutionalist city council agreed to a politically brilliant solution that at once allowed owners to disregard workers' demands, employ many of the unionist bakers, and provide the public with cheap bread. It also granted the government important political legitimacy. The council decided to rescind the contract it had established with Arrache & Córdoba to supply bread to municipal institutions and give it instead to the bakers' union.[26] These were the socialist bakeries. The city government provided the union with flour at cost as well as the rudimentary bakery facilities in the Belem Prison and the Castañeda Hospital.[27] In addition to supplying the public hospitals, orphanages, and asylums, the unionist bakers sold bread to the public at half the price of commercial bakeries from four municipal outlets: El Paraíso, El Asalto, El Centinela, and Las Delicias Taurinas.

According to municipal receipts, these four outlets received massive amounts of bread—between 8,400 and 13,900 pieces a day.[28] The city council turned over large amounts of money to the union in order to run the bakeries and the outlets. On November 13, 1915, the government accounting office recorded a payment of one thousand pesos. Another, four days later, was for three thousand pesos. On December 2, the sum that the union received jumped to 10,000, pesos but then it dropped to 8,000 pesos on the twenty-first and finally to 3,743 pesos at the end of the month.[29] The government also provided bakers with employment in the kitchen corps of the Constitutionalist Army.[30]

General Juan Mérigo even offered one thousand pesos "as spontaneous support" for the bakers' union.[31]

Owners were free to refuse workers' demands and, of course, the millers who supplied the socialist panaderías had no complaints. But private shops now had to contend with serious competition from the unionists who sold bread from baskets in front of their shops.[32] Governor César López de Lara declared that the arrangement encouraged "true competition between panadería owners and unionized workers that will yield benefits for the consuming public."[33] The competition was not between owners and union workers, though, but rather between the private sector and government subsidies that established socialist bakeries. The council's was a radical move that severely compromised the power of the Spanish owners. If extended, it threatened to put them out of business.

Yet this experiment in socialism lasted only two months. By the end of 1915, the food crisis had passed its worse point, and the union-run municipal bakeries were closed. What appeared to be a radical challenge to the Spanish capitalists had merely been a stopgap measure. The government had subsidized union workers in order to avoid a strike. In practice, the measure weakened workers' bargaining power by siphoning off the strikers while leaving the rest to labor as always inside the private bakeries. The solution did not address the growing antagonism between workers and employers, not to mention the tensions between the Casa del Obrero Mundial and the Constitutionalists.

"Blessed are the idealists"

Just under the surface of the pact between Constitutionalists and the Casa lay deep, irreconcilable differences. Carranza's goal was to centralize political authority under his guidance, fortify the power of the state, and defend private property. For him, the alliance with anarchists was a transitory, expedient means to gain support from the largest organization of workers in the capital. Better to deal with the workers, and gain revolutionary bona fides in the process than to leave the door open to the Zapatistas, who also courted workers. The Casa, by contrast, hoped that the alliance with the Constitutionalists would give workers leverage to make material demands, such as higher wages, that would attract more workers. Someday, perhaps, they would dismantle the bourgeois state and institute a more just system of production. For the moment both sides benefited from the pact, yet it soon became clear that each expected more than the other was willing to cede.

Both sides talked about "socialism," but they did not refer to the same concept. For labor radicals, socialism was a system in which workers took over or dissolved the state. For Constitutionalists, it was a vague, paternal, state-centered philosophy in which "the government looks after the interests of the wage workers and establishes fair relations between capital and labor."[34] That is, the state's role was to arbitrate between the two elements of production in order to foster social equilibrium. By definition, this ideological vision could not have satisfied the principles of anarchism or communism, for it did not contemplate the disappearance of either capitalism or the state. But this was the vision of socialism that prevailed and became central to the new government's role in reshaping class relations after the revolution.

The Casa del Obrero Mundial had internal disagreements as well. Most members sustained the anarchist belief that the state per se was the source of repression. Worker liberation, they argued, would spring from the formation of self-governing voluntary associations that remained autonomous from state tutelage. Production cooperatives and artisan workshops would eliminate the inequalities and injustices of capitalist factories. Meanwhile, workers were to engage in "direct action," that is, to protest directly against bosses with strikes and boycotts without mediation from the state and without allying with parties or involving themselves in other "political" activities, such as supporting candidates or even voting in elections.

This principle put the anarchists of the Casa at odds with the minority communists, who posited that liberation would come from the conquest of the state. In contrast to the anarchist vision of a stateless society, the communists aimed to build a noncapitalist state, a "dictatorship of the proletariat."[35] Although, as evidenced in the very "political" pact with the Constitutionalists, strategic pragmatism prevailed over ideological orthodoxy. If radicals of different stripes were flexible enough to ally with the emerging government, it would seem that they could have also found sufficient common ground among themselves. They all agreed that oppressed workers were to be the protagonists in a revolutionary future. Yet disagreements between communists and anarchists over what that future looked like and how to build it strained the unity of the labor movement. These internal tensions help explain why the Casa was unable to withstand attacks by the Carranza government when the pact with the Constitutionalists soured.

In March 1916, sixteen hundred Casa del Obrero Mundial–affiliated workers went on strike to demand payment in metal instead of the devalued bills issued by the Constitutionalists. Each enemy faction of the civil war had its own currency that it imposed upon the regions it occupied, and workers were wary of receiving wages in bills that were subject to unpredictable political fortunes and wild inflation. Merchants often refused to accept the factional bills and demanded payment in gold. Like the workers, they wanted money whose value was solid and universally accepted. The strike paralyzed the city and revealed the Casa's ability to mobilize mass workers; however, it did not withstand Carranza's reaction. The president evicted the Casa from the Palacio de los Azulejos and returned the building to its former tenants.[36] But the definitive clash came in the summer of 1916 when the Casa called a general strike, again demanding payment in hard currency. The strike left the city without transportation, electricity, or bread.

Carranza imposed martial law, deported foreign activists, threatened strikers with the death penalty, and declared the Casa seditious and illegal. He also closed down the radical paper *Acción Mundial* and sent its editor, the extravagant painter Dr. Atl, into exile in Los Angeles.[37] "Although the revolution had as one of its main objectives the destruction of capitalist tyranny," Carranza declared furiously, "it will not permit the creation of a tyranny of workers."[38] The new Labor Department chief stressed that "strikes were more or less justified in the time of Díaz and Huerta, but now are absolutely inappropriate and inconvenient given that the Constitutionalist authorities support the working class."[39] According to this circular logic, organized labor had exceeded its function by disrupting the balance between labor and capital, disturbing public order, and threatening the authority of the political leaders who had granted workers support.

The crackdown on the Casa gave Carranza the opportunity to reformulate the relationship between his government and organized labor. In September 1916, he called a convention, to take place in Querétaro in November, in order to draft a new constitution.[40] By then the war was winding down. Obregón had soundly defeated the Villistas in the battle of Celaya, and Constitutionalist forces were trouncing Zapatistas in a brutal scorched-earth policy in Morelos. With the convention, the Constitutionalists sought to legitimize their authority and codify crucial gains of the revolution. The resulting Constitution of 1917 gave the state wide-ranging powers with which to address Mexico's social inequality. Under Article 27, land became a public good that the government could expropriate from haciendas and distribute to the landless. Article 28 criminalized food speculation and monopolies.

Most significant for workers was Article 123, which spelled out the "right to dignified and socially useful employment" and codified a vision of state-supported equilibrium between labor and capital. It defined workers and employers as partners, but since workers had little leverage to redress grievances, the article mandated minimum conditions and affirmed workers' right to form unions and carry out strikes. Day shifts were to last eight hours; night shifts, seven. The minimum wage was to satisfy the "material, social, and cultural necessities of the families" of individual workers. Workers had the right to one day of rest a week and twenty days of paid vacation a year. Article 123 also established new mechanisms of state intervention in labor disputes. Officials from the newly created Bureau of Conciliation and Arbitration were to mediate cases of labor conflict. Only they could decide if strikes were "licit," which meant those strikes that "have as their objective to achieve a balance between the different factors of production, harmonizing the rights of labor with the rights of capital."[41] The Constitution reflected an understanding of the state's role as the arbiter of social order and mediator between forces. Without its oversight, the strongest collective group would create a "tyranny" over the weakest. Although Carranza opposed the benefits that the Constitution granted to workers, Article 123 articulated the Constitutionalists' vision of balance between two partners in a national community. This approach sought to temper the individualism of liberal capitalism while, at the same time, respecting private property and encouraging entrepreneurialism by treating labor and capital as inseparable constituents of national development.[42] Social equilibrium, rooted in a sense of the common good, would replace class warfare.

Consequently, the government threw its support behind a new union hub, the Confederación Regional de Obreros de México (CROM), formed in 1918, which complemented this vision of state-supported social equilibrium. Leaders of the CROM saw collaboration with the government as a viable means to improve the position of workers. A small group of anarchists formed an ephemeral organization, the Gran Cuerpo Central de Trabajadores, but most radicals—both anarchists and communists—joined the CROM.[43] After the trouncing that Carranza gave the Casa del Obrero Mundial, this is perhaps no surprise. As Luis Morones, the general secretary of the CROM, declared in 1918, "Blessed are the idealists, for they shall inherit all the disasters!"[44] The official sponsorship allowed the new hub to provide material benefits for workers in ways that the anarchist holdout never could. Furthermore, radicals found a place in the CROM because the affiliated unions maintained considerable independence from the central leadership in the early years.[45]

This autonomy among individual unions, as well as the ideological pragmatism and eclecticism, was evident in the bakers' union, which belonged to the CROM but closely associated with groups that loosely mixed communism and anarchism. Indeed, the bakers shifted between labor hubs, but the union leader remained, from roughly 1916 until 1930, Genaro Gómez, the "caudillo of the bakers." Gómez was uneducated, probably illiterate, but with his "thick and authoritarian voice" and "bitter character and appearance," he was a man who commanded respect.[46] He was a man of action, not of idle contemplation of utopias. When José Valadés, then a young middle-class radical new to activism, approached Gómez to request the bakers' union hall for "red" events, the union leader scoffed: "Such well-healed egalitarians [*catrines igualitarios*]? Would we take off our shoes to give them to some poor baker? If we really wanted to be equal, would we dare to leave our little books and make bolillos instead?" Gómez was among the founding members of the Mexican Communist Party in 1919. Antonio Ruiz, secretary general of the bakers' union in 1920, was also a member of the Mexican Communist Party as well as an organizer of the short-lived Latin American Bureau of the Third International.[47]

Their communist affiliation put Gómez and Ruiz at odds with anarchists, who criticized the "political" nature of the communists and unionism in general. Nonetheless, this did not stop Gómez from participating in an obscure "combative group" led by anarchists from Spain and Peru.[48] The time was ripe for such actions—or at least for plans. The bakers' union was one of the few radical groups with a downtown headquarters, and activists of several persuasions and nationalities flowed through its office on Netzahuacóyotl Street. A group of Spanish anarchists who fled to Mexico from Cuba, where they had tried to kill president Mario García Menocal, found refuge there. Among them was the Basque anarchist Sebastián San Vicente, who led Gómez's combative group.[49] Italian anarchists, Russian communists, and American "slackers" (draft dodgers) and anarchists from the International Workers of the World held meetings there and slept on the benches.[50] The Mexican Young Red Socialists taught gymnastics and language classes and held cultural events in which children recited "red poetry" and *señoritas obreras* sang the "red hymn."[51] The Red Brothers installed a printing press to produce *El Soviet* in the bakers' offices.[52]

The red ideas whirling through the bakers' headquarters clearly drew inspiration from the Russian Revolution, the triumph of which was unfolding as the Constitutionalists were drafting the new constitution in Querétaro.

However, the beacon of hope that the Bolsheviks represented was filtered through the protean understandings of worker vindication in Mexico. Mexican radicals borrowed concepts from the Russian Revolution but, as historian Barry Carr writes, gave them meanings that were "quite different from those understood by the Bolsheviks." *Rojo*, for instance, did not necessarily denote communism, but rather the broader rejection of state tutelage. Likewise, the pages of *El Soviet*, the newspaper published in the bakers' headquarters, did not contain a single reference to Marx or socialism.[53]

How actual bakery workers may have interpreted this mix of vague ideas is practically impossible to determine. Union leaders made few declarations to the press, and reporters did not take any from rank-and-file workers. However, the union clearly pursued pragmatic, reformist goals, not radical actions aimed at smashing the state. There is no indication of communism or anarchism in their declarations, demands, or actions. They did not act like anarchists when they accepted formal arbitration—much less when they worked as municipal bakers during the brief socialist bakery experiment. They rarely formed collectives as anarchist ideologues prescribed. The few collectives that did arise were outside of Mexico City—such as the one named after the Italian-American anarchists Sacco and Vanzetti in the port city of Progreso, Yucatán—and unions invariably accused them of being facades for owners who wanted to break strikes.[54] Nor did they challenge the right of Spaniards, or anyone else, to own bakeries. Unlike some of Carranza's officials, they never called for the expropriation of bakeries.[55] The demands they made in November 1915 remained, by and large, the same throughout the decade of the 1920s: higher wages, shorter shifts, and compensation for injuries.

Had the socialist bakery experiment persisted, the impetus of the movement would have moved toward a more radical transformation of production, and the red ideas would have congealed into a more solid, coherent ideological platform. But given the Constitutionalists' sudden closure of the union bakeries, their repression of the Casa del Obrero Mundial, and their continued alliance with the dominant bakery owners, organized bakery workers focused on more mundane goals. Without state support, they lacked the resources to set up and operate union-run shops that could have employed their substantial numbers and challenge the primacy of the bread barons. Since workers could not free themselves from their employers, they struggled instead to gain concessions from them.

Although these objectives remained within the confines of capitalism, Article 123 restricted the free market, emphasized social balance, and—

on paper, at least—granted Mexican workers rights that no others in the world enjoyed outside of communist Russia. When we consider the brutalizing conditions in the bakery workrooms until then, these rights were deep and sweeping. The dreams of anarchism and communism, in which workers would lead society, dissipated. The struggle now was to make real the promises of Article 123. And a struggle it was, for the new revolutionary government, as it turned out, had something of a butcher's thumb when it came to social balance.

Bread Strikes and the "New" Labor Policy

In February 1919, the bakers' union restated its demands for shorter shifts, compensation for injury, higher wages, and union authority to hire and fire workers and to "resolve any difficulties among workers." The members added a call for a labor contract that would homogenize working conditions in all Mexico City bakeries.[56] But workers now faced more overt and concerted opposition from owners and the government. Carranza (whom the press celebrated as "the arbiter of the workers") had just helped undermine a strike at several Mexico City flour mills by negotiating with workers at Arrache's La Florida.[57] When the workers accepted, the strikers' unity broke down, and the movement collapsed.[58] Carranza's intervention thus prevented the simultaneous closures of the mills and the bakeries, which would have given workers in both sectors tremendous leverage.

Bolstered by the government's support for employers, the bakery owners refused to discuss a labor contract with unionists, repeating the argument that bread production was incompatible with standardized shifts. Iriarte's nephew Segundo Minondo alleged that his workers could not knead the usual eighteen sacks of flour in eight hours. Owner Ramón Andión said he would comply with seven-hour night shifts; however, if workers were unable to "knead the appropriate number of sacks," he would dock their wages. Another owner said that eight-hour shifts would drive him out of business.[59] Underlying owners' refusal to accept shifts was the assumption that such a system would give full course to workers' natural laziness. A work day measured in sacks gave bakers incentive to work as fast as possible, for as soon as they baked a determined amount of bread, they were free to leave. As long as the shelves and bins were full of bread, it mattered little to owners if workers took ten or fourteen hours. According to the same logic, though, work days measured in time provided no such motivations and would only encourage bakers to do as little as possible. The Bureau of Conciliation and Arbitration agreed, albeit in somewhat different terms. An official said that the bureau would study the possibility of eight-hour shifts in bakeries, but that the nature of bread production made them impractical. "Although bakers remain in workrooms twelve hours or more a day, they do not work continuously, but with intervals of idle time."[60]

Owners warned workers not to embrace eight-hour shifts. If clock-time were the ultimate measurement of their labor, workers would soon lose ground to machines. "Almost all bakeries," they said, were ordering machinery from the United States. "Bakeries will only need three workers at most, instead of twenty or thirty." The massive firings were to begin in a month.[61] Arrache & Córdoba claimed they had imported American machines precisely in order to "avoid the recent difficulties created by the demands of some bakery workers." They announced the imminent dismissal of eighteen bakers.[62] This threat, however, was another turn at the same bluff: six years later, Arrache & Córdoba's Recabado Street Bakery employed at least thirty-five workers, far more than most.[63]

It was not machinery that weakened workers' leverage over their employers, but rather several groups that undermined the ability of the bakers' union to paralyze the bread supply so as to create a problem of governability that would force authorities to intercede on their behalf. A reserve of unemployed workers, rival unionists, and numerous Mexican-owned, family-run bakeries all made available varying amounts of bread, and they all counted on support from the police.

On the first day of the strike, the governor of Mexico City sent out "considerable detachments of gendarmes" to cordon off panaderías and protect the replacement workers who kneaded inside. The unionists called them *esquiroles* (scabs), but the government referred to them with a more flattering term, *obreros libres* (free workers). The chief of police argued that the gendarmes were not breaking the union's strike, but rather defending the obreros libres' "indisputable right to work."[64] Bakers, he added, could carry out "protest movements," but the police would "repress all scandals." He called on the bakers to form "commissions of individuals to enter into bakeries and invite the obreros libres to cease their labors, but leave them in peace if they do not accept the invitation."[65]

This distinction between respectful "protest" and disruptive "scandals" had little to do with the negotiation procedures spelled out in Article 123 and much more resembled the arbitrary, paternalist repression that Porfirio Díaz had wielded before the revolution. Despite the new laws and bureaucracies set up to channel and resolve labor strife, conflicts continued to arise over what bakers and employers each understood to be traditional prerogatives. In May 1919, for instance, when maestro Lamberto Miranda Marte was reproached by the owner for drinking, he walked out with his oficiales. When the owner found replacement workers, Miranda and his bakers threatened them with a pummeling. Following the script from the previous century, the clerks tried to "reduce the scandalous bakers to order" until the police arrived and arrested them. The description in the semiofficial press was also reminiscent of the Porfirian era: Miranda, according to *El Pueblo*, was "an individual who continually worships Bacchus and was therefore unable to fulfill his obligations."[66]

These traditional conflicts emerged less frequently as unionism became ever more tangled up in the political struggles of the 1920s. The most poignant instance of politicization occurred when Luis Morones and other CROM leaders formed the Partido Laborista in support of Álvaro Obregón's bid for the presidency in 1920.[67] Obregón's allies revolted and assassinated Carranza when the outgoing president chose a relatively unknown civilian technocrat as his successor. When Obregón won the presidential elections, CROM leaders found themselves with plum positions within the state apparatus. Anarchists and communists in the CROM found themselves marginalized within the hub. The telephone, textile, and streetcar workers and bakers left the CROM and formed the Confederación General de Trabajadores (CGT) in

Table 5. Union affiliation among bakery workers, 1921.

BAKERY LOCATION	TOTAL WORKERS	CGT	CROM	NONUNION ("LIBRES")
Abraham González 22	10	3	4	3
Hamburgo 113	14	2	8	4
Guillermo Prieto 114	23	23	0	0
Artes 58	26	17	8	1
Lisboa 50	26	13	2	11
Bucareli 121	33	20	13	0
Insurgentes 297	39	27	12	0
Guillermo Prieto 60	66	63	0	3
Total	237	168	47	22

Source: "Relación de sindicatos y panaderos," AHCM, 1921, Gobierno del Distrito Federal, Negocios Internos, caja 1.

February 1921.⁶⁸ A group of bizcocheros (sweet-bread bakers) remained with CROM, but the majority of bakers joined the CGT (table 5).

This division among the bakery workers intensified the violence of strikes and weakened the CGT, who now had to struggle against enemies in the CROM, in addition to the police and employers. In September 1921, the union reiterated its demand for a labor contract and added days off during national holidays and the prohibition of night labor.⁶⁹ Again, the Bureau of Conciliation and Arbitration summoned the parties, but owners refused to attend any negotiation that included night shifts, which were one of the keystones of the industry.⁷⁰ Since consumers demanded fresh bread for breakfast, bakeries did most of their business in the early morning. Without night shifts, customers would have to gnaw on rock-hard bolillos and dried up *conchas*. The union declared a strike and entered into five days of conflict with the police and esquiroles. Some of the scabs were not obreros libres, as the police insisted, but actually unionists from the CROM, sent in to break the force of the CGT. At the beginning of the 6:00 a.m. shift, squads of CGT "baker police" (*panaderos policías*) prevented esquiroles from entering the bakeries and dragged out those who had already entered. They were able to close down one-third of the bakeries on the first day. However, on the second and final day, the real police broke the strike by standing guard in front of bakeries, allowing most of them to remain open.⁷¹

The failure of this strike exacerbated tensions between communists and anarchists within the CGT. In October 1921, the anarchist leadership expelled the communists, who allegedly had attempted a coup to take over the hub. The expelled communists formed the Confederación Sindical Unitaria de Mexico (CSUM). Genaro Gómez briefly joined them but then returned to the CGT. Historians and autobiographic accounts are vague and brief in their explanations of these conflicts.⁷² Whatever the underlying motivations, these shifts highlight the recurrent and acerbic disagreements between rival groups within the labor movement.

The bakers' union managed to remain intact under the leadership of Genaro Gómez. As if to prove the continued strength of the union, in January 1922 Gómez sent owners a list of demands that included compensation in case of death or accidents and the establishment of a medical fund.⁷³ Negotiations mediated by Celestino Gasca, the CROM leader and Mexico City governor, ended in failure. After completing the day shift at 6:00 p.m., the bakers declared a strike. They marched through downtown, past the central bakeries. They stopped first at the corner of Regina and Bolívar streets where nonunion bakers were beginning the night shift. The strikers charged inside, and one of the frightened clerks turned off the lights, "producing a terrible confusion in which punches and blows with sticks were exchanged amid great screaming and yelling." The strikers smashed the counter, took the cash register, and marched a couple of blocks toward the Risco Bakery on Isabel la Católica Street. The owner there called the police, who found the strikers in front of the bakery yelling at the esquiroles to stop working. The police and the strikers exchanged gunfire, and three bakers and one gendarme left in an ambulance. Other wounded strikers slipped away. Police then rushed to La Cabaña to disperse bakers who were attempting to knock down the door and to La Alhóndiga Bakery where they were stoning the building.[74] The next day, the police arrested two strikers who flashed knives at the esquiroles at the San Antonio Tomatlán Street Bakery and barely saved the life of Braulio Iriarte's chauffeur whom strikers had beaten and stabbed.[75]

The CGT streetcar workers declared a partial solidarity strike and threatened to stop the *tranvías* altogether if owners did not concede to bakers' demands. The Eúskaro mill workers also went back on strike, in part because the machinery had killed a worker and the manager, Iriarte's nephew Andrés Barberena, had allegedly refused to compensate the widow. With these pressures, the union gained concessions from owners—a fund for medical expenses, eight-hour shifts, and the promise to consider a labor contract.[76] However, six months later, in June 1922, the bakers and the streetcar workers were back on strike because owners had not fulfilled the agreements. "It would take a person more than a month to take out the files in this office related to ... complaints regarding the lack of medical care and medicine," noted a Labor Department official. Furthermore, he added, "although the precepts of the law are clear and precise ... very few bakery industrialists have reduced the lengths of shifts and the few that have done so always reduce the salaries in proportion."[77]

Nonetheless, the Mexico City government redoubled its defense of bakeries, and the unionists grew more incendiary. The police set up "veritable military posts" at bakeries, and the "obreros libres enjoyed ample guarantees." The city "did not lack bread, which was bought at the usual prices." When the obreros libres at the shop on Soto Street refused to join the strike, strikers shattered the glass windows, yelling "*¡Viva Lenin!*" Yet the streetcar workers and the bakers renounced their demands by the fourth day and settled for individual contracts and the reinstatement of their jobs.[78]

Faced with new worker demands in September 1924, owners assembled at the elegant park and restaurant El Tívolo de Eliseo and formed their own organization, the Union of Bakery Owners of the Federal District (Unión de Propietarios de Panaderías del Distrito Federal). The union established a fund to help owners endure strikes and encourage discipline among members. Associates pledged to adhere to the collective decisions of the union: anyone who negotiated individually with the bakers' union would be expelled. Likewise, as soon as workers seized any single bakery, all owners would close their shops and refuse to negotiate until workers withdrew.[79] The union met with Álvaro Obregón, who then personally wrote to the leaders of the bakery workers' union and asked them to postpone their strike until after September, the month of independence festivities, so that the "celebrations can go on without any unfavorable incidents."[80] A city without bread and the spectacle of police breaking a strike against Spanish bosses during the most patriotic month of the national calendar would have been an embarrassment for Obregón. The union agreed to call off the strike altogether.

The formation of the owners' union, which later changed its name to the Association of Bakery Owners of Mexico City, at first suggested a rapprochement not only with the government but also among owners after years of friction between Spanish and Mexican owners. The small Mexican-owned shops did not experience the class and ethnic divide that prevailed in the Spanish-owned bakeries. For them, the strikes were a boon, a time when they could boost production and sales. Given the pledge to resist workers' demands with a common front, such unity among owners, regardless of nationality, was fundamental. The Mexicans, at least, hoped that relations had improved since the years of the revolution when the Basque mill owners refused to sell them flour and that finally everyone was "going to work together toward common agreement." This was the case for a few wealthy Mexican businessmen with important political links who formed partnerships with the Basques. Aristeo Pérez, for instance, owned some thirty retail outlets in 1921, more than any other single owner, and at least two bread production workshops in partnership with Baztanese immigrant José Olave.[81] Pedro Laguna, who had at least three bakeries and co-owned La Esperanza flour mill with immigrant Eugenio Jubién, was the most visible partner. Laguna was also a federal senator and a key representative of the millers' lobby.[82]

Most Mexican owners lacked the political power and wealth of men like Laguna, whom they excoriated as "Hispanicized," and felt marginalized by the Basques. Partners of Iriarte who had immigrated from Arizkun, a hamlet in the Baztán Valley, formed the core of the owners' association.[83] Their common idiosyncrasies, impenetrable language, family ties, and identity as foreigners gave cohesion to their businesses and to the bread trade in general. These ethnic resources had allowed them to dominate the trade. Under intense pressure from their workers, they tightened their already closed circle even further.

Excluded from governance of the owners' association and cut off from resources, the Mexican owners soon complained that "the TRUST formed around the Eúskaro flour mill, which controls everything from the wheat fields to the bakeries, refuses to consider our proposals and initiatives." The Mexican owners pleaded with the president for support: "You, Mr. President, must understand what a formidable enemy we have. [The Spaniards'] greed is so enormous that they want to ruin our small shops."[84] Yet the Mexican owners received no official support; the president did not bother to respond. What is more, they felt unfairly targeted by the government's recent scrutiny of bakeries.

In 1922 the Labor Department had carried out an extensive survey of Mexico City bakeries—asking, among other questions, how many workers they employed, how much they paid them, what machinery they used—and an examination of hygiene. These studies revealed an industry that paid little attention to cleanliness or technological innovations. Bakeries in general had much less machinery than Pedro Albaitero's Los Gallos had when it opened in 1888.[85] Likely in response to the findings of the hygiene study, the government drafted a health code for bakeries that, if applied, would have required shops to take a significant leap forward.

Bakery floors had to be made of cement or tiles, and not of wood or dirt, "in order to allow for the daily cleaning of the establishment" and to "prevent the propagation of rats." The ceiling and walls were to be painted with oil-based paint. The mixing troughs had to be always covered to prevent dust from mixing with the dough. Kneading tables, machinery, as well as planks, boxes, or baskets used to store or transport bread were to be "fastidiously and scrupulously cleaned." The flour pantry was to be "perfectly ventilated," its walls painted, and the ceiling and floor made of cement or tile. The retail section needed ample ventilation and sunlight. The countertop had to be made of granite. All merchandise was to be in showcases, protected from "dust, flies, and consumers' hands." Clerks and bakers were to take breaks in separate rooms with potable water and plumbing. There had to be at least two "English-style toilets" made of tile that measured two meters in the clerks' lounge and at least four or five in the bakers' rest area. The workroom had to have a sink with running water for workers to wash their hands.[86]

These provisions drew a picture of what ideal bakeries could look like, someday. Meanwhile, inspectors grappled with deficiencies that were much more urgent, widespread, and fundamental—such as cockroaches and filth. The missing granite countertops and English-style toilets were the least of their troubles. Of twenty-two bakeries visited in 1925, all but three were in "miserable sanitary conditions." Inspectors found adulterated flour, dark workrooms, piles of garbage, "a huge existence of flies," and a "multitude of holes in the walls [indicating] an abundance of rats." The report recommended the immediate closure of five panaderías.[87]

Both Mexicans and Spaniards owned these shops, but the Mexicans felt particularly vulnerable. Excluded by the Basques, ignored by the president, pressured by their workers, and now scrutinized by government inspectors, they struggled to direct attention away from themselves and toward their poorest of competitors, the small Mexican bakers who often operated without a license. Onofre Madrigal wrote to the Department of Public Health describing the "clandestine panaderías": "Dirty and sick workers make bread with dirty utensils; at night the bread stays in filthy stalls in the midst of lamentable promiscuity where many people sleep, lacking the most elemental hygienic practices, crowded in an atmosphere poisoned by the humors of their bodies and their very excrement." This alone, he insisted, "could explain the shocking mortality that dominates our poor classes."[88]

Madrigal's letter highlights the isolation that middle-class Mexican owners experienced. Barriers of ethnicity kept them from joining the Basques, their scant political clout kept them from the halls of power, and their ongoing conflicts with the bakers' union kept them from making common cause with the small Mexican producers. Indeed, the continual strikes drove an ever deeper wedge between the bakeries whose workers belonged to the union and those that relied on labor from family members. National identity—as Mexicans who had to struggle with Spaniards—brought together men like Onofre Madrigal and José Segura whose workers demanded shorter shifts and higher wages. But it could hardly extend to the lower-class Mexican producers who did not face such pressures.

From Crumbs to Victory

So far, the bakers had gained little in their struggle to achieve the promises of Article 123. Police batons and scab labor from the CROM had broken every strike. However, the political fortunes of the CROM began to wane. Its leader, Luis Morones, had first risen to prominence under the protection of Álvaro Obregón, but accusations that he had ordered the murder of a prominent congressman had turned Morones into a political liability for Obregón, who distanced himself from the union leader toward the end of his presidential term in 1924.[89] Morones, however, made sure to cultivate close ties with Obregón's successor, Plutarco Elías Calles, and the CROM remained a central political actor.

After a Catholic militant assassinated Obregón in 1928, on the eve of his second presidential term, many of Obregon's supporters suspected that Morones was behind the assassination. In order to prevent yet another splintering of the "revolutionary family," Calles reluctantly removed Morones and other CROM-istas from the administration and installed interior minister Emilio Portes Gil, a personal enemy of Morones, as interim president.[90] In order to further weaken the CROM, Portes Gil lent support to its rivals, particularly the CGT. Subsequently, without attacks from the CROM, the bakers' union was able to close bakeries and thus use bread as a lever to pressure both owners and the government.[91] Until then, the government had justified its strikebreaking with the argument that bread was essential to the city's functioning. Once the CROM lost its influence, keeping bread available required negotiating.

This government support would have been a boon for the CGT, but by then the anarchist union hub was in shambles. A decade of battles with police and the CROM had diminished its numbers and strength, and state sponsorship discredited what little remained of the CGT's former vigor.[92] The CGT leadership seems to have grown more rigid and dogmatic, which increased the already existing tensions among the leadership and followers.[93] Their most important contingent, the textile workers, had already abandoned the hub in 1924, after the CGT "submerged them in defeat, poverty, demoralization, dispersion, and helplessness."[94]

The bakers themselves, in contrast, benefited from the shift, largely because of the continued leadership of Genaro Gómez, who had remained at the head of the union for the previous fifteen years. His relations with the CGT anarchists had already been strained for years. The bakers' union acted largely independently of the hub, which the bakers left in mid-1928 in order to form an independent organization—the Sindicato de Trabajadores de la Industria del Pan del Distrito Federal—with a new headquarters on Bolívar Street.

Their new leverage was clear in the bakers' final strike of the decade, in May 1928. "We believe that we are acting within the law," they insisted, in reference to their constitutional right to strike. The "bread industry," they continued, "is in the hands of a foreign monopoly that exploits the sons of Mexico."[95] This allusion to the Spanish ownership of bakeries, the only one by the bakers' union, stressed the imbalance between labor and capital that Article 123 aimed to correct. For officials, however, workers disrupted balance when they damaged the public good. Since bread was essential to the daily subsistence of residents, the city government had the obligation to break the strikes. But the bakers questioned this premise by stating that "the strike will not cause suffering for society, for the food of Mexicans is the tortilla. Those who eat bread are the wealthy and people who ape the professional, mercantile civilization. The bread industry does not provide a public or community service."[96] Therefore, they asked, why is the government protecting a foreign monopoly? However, this appeal to tortilla nationalism was counter to what the unionist bakers—not to mention owners and officials—knew perfectly well.

By then Mexico City had more than two hundred formal bakeries, and the urban working class depended more than ever before on bread. With the city's reliance on bakers' labor, the strike was to reach unprecedented success. During the four days that it lasted, bread was so rare that the presence of it was a sign of treachery, as shown by a curious row during the strike. Four striking bakers were at La Imperial, a downtown cantina, when they saw a man walk by with a "sack of bread." When they tried to take it, the man stabbed one of the bakers, killing him, and ran off with the bread. Some hours later, according to the crime pages of *El Universal*, María Guadalupe Blanco Hernández went to the cantina where, according to neighborhood women, her husband, Ignacio Rodríguez, had been in a fight. By asking the police if he was the dead man, she unwittingly implicated her husband. "The police took her to see the body, but it was not her husband. Thus, she revealed who the murderer was."[97]

Given the union's ability to practically paralyze bread production in the city, owners agreed to negotiate. Clearly in a position of tremendous advantage, the union accepted nothing less than total victory. Owners agreed to sign a collective contract that standardized wages, set the workday at eight hours, and recognized the union as the legal representative of workers.[98] Previously, only owners had a cohesive sense of organization, linked by family and ethnic ties. Now, the formal institution that fought for improved conditions for the hundreds of bakery workers—a bigger chunk of the loaf, as it were—went a long way toward making real the ideal of social equilibrium between labor and capital. The workers did not bring down capitalism and the bourgeois state, but considering the deplorable working conditions of only a few years before, theirs was a remarkable achievement.

CHAPTER SEVEN

Unionists, *Tlalchicholes*, and *Canasteros*

⁂ THE SPANISH MONOPOLY HAD PROVEN ITSELF TO BE AN ESSENTIAL partner of the governments that emerged in the revolution and its aftermath. Hunger coincided with the brutal factional battles, and the government's ability to see that people were fed became a crucial sign of political legitimacy. Likewise, scarcity, inflation, and adulteration were signs of corruption, complicity, or ineptitude. In their efforts to ensure the food supply, authorities did not regard the bakery workers as allies. For the first decade after the revolution, they tried to keep labor strife from disrupting the bread supply by sending the police to guard panaderías while replacement workers baked inside. In 1928, though, bakery workers realized the deferred promise of improved working conditions and support by the revolutionary government. The collective contract did not make the heat, the filth, and the cramped quarters in panaderías disappear, but bakers began to work shorter shifts for better pay in accordance with the Constitution of 1917. They had finally approached the much-touted social equilibrium—the notion that labor and capital could confront each other, if not harmoniously collaborate, on somewhat equal terms.

For the new political leaders who saw themselves as the fulcrum that sustained this balance, keeping bread on shelves involved complications that no one had foreseen. The collective contract was an important step toward resolving the decades-long conflicts between bakery workers and owners, but it gave rise to new challenges that threatened to disrupt the precarious equilibrium. The state's challenge was to improve working conditions in order to prevent strikes without causing a rise in the price of bread that would erode the spending power of all of the other workers. Such an adjustment required that owners put more of their profits into the hands of the workers. Owners agreed, reluctantly, but not without conditions that drastically altered the relationship between markets and politics.

Basques, Mexicans, and *Tlalchicholes*

The union and owners agreed to a contract when the Spanish monopoly was at its peak. The movement of immigrants from the hamlets of Navarre into Mexico City continued to drive the expansion of bakeries and fortify the Basque leadership of the industry.[1] There were some 238 legally licensed bakeries in Mexico City, and Spaniards, more than half of whom came from Navarre, owned 175 of these shops.[2] As evidenced by the size and strength of their businesses, their dominance was more than numerical. Nationally, the average total value of (reported) investments for each Spanish-owned bakery was $22,242, while the Mexican-owned ones averaged only $6,195. Likewise, the reported annual value of production for Spanish bakeries averaged $56,600, whereas Mexican ones averaged only $28,447 (table 6).[3]

Undergirding the industry's formal leadership were the ethnic connections among the Baztanese. The owners' association president was Victoriano Loperena Illarregui, a native of Arizkun who arrived in Mexico in 1913 and became a board member of Braulio Iriarte's Modelo Beer. Anastasio Espinosa Suquilvide, also from Arizkun, arrived in 1909, and three of his brothers followed him to Mexico and into the bread business. Hipólito Arrechea Perurena arrived from the Baztán hamlet of Almandoz in 1926, months before his brother Gabriel. Feliciano Anaut left the village of Uztarroz in 1921 with his brother Teodoro. Together they ran a bakery in the Mexico City suburb Tacuba, where they also managed the San José flour mill founded by the Basque Laureano Arrubarrena.[4] These immigrants strengthened what Pedro Albaitero had accomplished under Porfirio Díaz—the integration of wheat, flour, and bread into a fairly cohesive commercial enterprise.

The bulk of Mexican owners resented the Basques' dominance but had little choice but to accept their leadership. After the collective contract went into effect, differences between the Mexican owners and the Spaniards

Table 6. Investments and capital of Spanish- and Mexican-owned bakeries in entire country, 1935.

NATIONALITY	NUMBER OF BUSINESSES	VALUE OF INVESTMENTS			
		SUM ($)	PROPERTY ($)	MACHINERY, TOOLS ($)	VEHICLES, FURNITURE ($)
Mexican	514	3,184,185	2,831,183	209,035	143,967
Spanish	172	3,825,640	3,530,580	180,085	114,975
Averages	Mexican	6,195		406	
	Spanish	22,242		1,047	

NATIONALITY		VALUE OF STOCK ($)		
	FUEL	RAW MATERIALS	FINISHED PRODUCT	VALUE OF PRODUCTION
Mexican	6,564	174,695	1,107	14,621,988
Spanish	9,802	291,212	595	9,735,166
Averages	Mexican			28,447
	Spanish			56,600

NATIONALITY	WAGES AND SALARIES PAID ($)			
	SUM	MANAGERS	EMPLOYEES	WORKERS
Mexican	2,592,609	175,316	143,256	2,274,037
Spanish	2,101,594	89,000	182,027	1,830,567

Source: Secretaría de Economía Nacional, *Segundo censo industrial*, 143, 348.

persisted but became less threatening than the conflicts with the small Mexican producers who did not hire union labor and had no obligation to comply with the union contract. In fact, after 1928 almost everyone—Mexican owners of medium-sized bakeries, the Spaniards, unionized workers, and the government—found in the small Mexican producers the main threat to the delicate balance.

The small producers were bakers who ran their own shops and employed mostly family labor. Some of their shops were legally licensed, but others were *tlalchiches*, informal bakeries with brick and adobe ovens hidden in tenements. Until the late 1920s, their operators—*tlalchicholes*—had not provoked much attention. Since their flour came from the same mills, they were clients of the Basques. They had not, so far, competed directly with the dominant bakeries. Most served neighborhoods on the periphery of the city that was rapidly expanding with the waves of rural migrants.[5]

These shops rarely show up in the archives until the mid-1920s, when a little information about them appears. Long-time residents in the city who had established modest workshops before the 1920s owned some, while others belonged to recent migrants to the city.[6] Many owners were former bakery workers who had served as replacement labor during the strikes of the previous years. Displaced by the union contracts, these self-described "simple workers emancipated from the tyranny of foreign capitalists" set up their own bakeries.[7]

The small producers peddled bread in plazas, at market stands, or among the clusters of *canasteros* (named for their baskets, or *canastas*) who sold fruit, tortillas, and herbs in the streets around the public market. They also sold through the small neighborhood grocery stores known as *tendejones*.[8] Located throughout the city, tendejones supplied residents with their basic needs of sugar, candles, and lard. But what brought customers in on a daily basis was bread. The tendejones were especially important in the poor neighborhoods where many rural migrants settled, away from commercial centers.[9] As an owner of a *tendejón* in Magdalena-Contreras on the western edge of the city, noted, "The very setting of this area makes it hard for people to purchase goods in established bakeries." Furthermore, he pointed out that "most people lack available cash" and therefore bought bread in local tendejones that sold on credit.[10] The small producers, together with these petty retailers, provided bread to the poorest working-class families.

Many of the small producers were informal, "clandestine" bakers who operated without a municipal license and in archaic conditions. In the tenements where some worked, "squalidness [was] taken to inconceivable limits," according to government investigators. Poor families piled together in "innumerable improvised bedrooms," and children with chronic diarrhea exhaled "*mal humor.*" The "state of the toilets" was "horrible."[11] Owners of unionized bakeries insisted that all small producers and the retailers who sold their bread languished in filth. Market vendors who bought from the small producers allegedly exposed bread to "bad air, lice and an infinity of parasites that later go on to the consuming public." The vendors "have syphilis, tuberculosis, and leprosy and never wash their hands, etc. etc."[12]

There was more to this hygiene discourse than a concern with cleanliness. Inspection reports show that no bakery was up to the stringent requirements of the health code. Rats and cockroaches plagued practically every shop. Nor did a business license from the municipality necessarily define the limit between formal and informal shops. Even major owners failed to obtain licenses for all of their shops. Fines from these transgressions were another business expense, though receipts of returned fines suggest that owners could make deals with inspectors.[13]

The defining characteristic of the small producers—what put them suddenly in the center of the bread battles—was their nonunion workforce. Since they hired mostly family members, not union bakers, they did not have to pay the higher wages, contribute to a medical fund, or fulfill the other requirements spelled out in the collective contract. The owners of the larger bakeries insisted that they could not honor their contract with the union as long as the small producers had such unfair advantages. The only problem was that many of the small producers were not violating any law. Since they were not bound by the same restrictions as the "monopoly," they could sell cheaper bread, undermine the dominance that the Basques had held for the last half century, and disrupt the balance between labor and capital.

Bakery Regulations

The federal government promulgated a series of bakery regulations for Mexico City in January 1929, six months after unionists and owners signed the contract. The regulations and the contract were separate and distinct documents. While the contract defined the wages, work day, benefits, hiring policies, and other issues that pertained to unionized bakeries, the new laws governed all bakeries in the capital regardless of unionization. Indeed, nothing in the regulations was explicitly linked to unionization or the working conditions defined in the labor contract. Their ostensive objectives were to ensure hygienic, inexpensive bread and, ironically, to prevent the formation of monopolies. Nonetheless, the practical function of the regulations was to create conditions that would allow the owners and union workers to comply with the contract. In other words, they restricted nonunion bakeries' access to the market.

The new laws reflected the state's more robust bureaucracy put into place under Plutarco Elías Calles (1924–1928). When a Catholic extremist assassinated Álvaro Obregón in 1928, on the eve of the general's second presidential term, Calles took advantage of the death of the charismatic hero of the revolution to expand his own power. He declared the end of the era in which politics revolved around "indispensable men." Instead, modern bureaucratic rule was to institutionalize the revolution's achievements, manifested in the newly formed National Revolutionary Party.[14]

At the center of this supposedly impersonal structure of government, though, was Calles himself. His presidential term ended in 1928, five months after Obregón's assassination, but he extended his authority through his handpicked successors—Emilio Portes Gil, Pascual Ortiz Rubio, and Abelardo L. Rodríguez.[15] As the new party machine jettisoned electoral democracy, it also gave the state unprecedented stability most apparent in the fact that, unlike Madero, Carranza, Obregón, and dozens of other political figures, Calles and his successors were not assassinated. The government was no longer focused on its mere survival and could turn to urban public works, the regulation of the economy, and control of public space.

The bakery regulations thus reaffirmed the state's role as arbiter of the formal sector of the economy. They mandated that bakeries fulfill several new requirements in order to obtain a license. Bakeries had to meet the health code and be easily visible to inspectors. Their production areas (*fábricas*) had to open directly onto the street and display a sign on the outside, no smaller than a square meter. In order to professionalize bread production and ensure hygienic conditions, fábricas could not be located "within tenements or apartments, but only in buildings that are not directly connected with residences." Retail outlets (*expendios*), as well as street vendors and small neighborhood grocery stores, could only sell bread from licensed fábricas.

Other provisions placed more explicit restrictions on the market and generated the greatest controversies. The first limited the physical distribution of bakeries by imposing a minimum of five hundred meters between fábricas and three hundred meters between expendios. The second introduced price fixing, a measure that had not been applied to bakeries since the disappearance of the Fiel Ejecutoría with independence. The initial price was set at five cents for two pieces of bread with a total weight of 160 grams. Finally, the laws established a "mixed commission" (*comisión mixta*) that included owners, unionists, and government officials who were to advise the city government on "prices, weight, quality, and other circumstances pertaining to bread."[16] Although the laws did not grant the commission any enforcement authority, the members delegated inspectors—unionist bakers—to collaborate with police and health inspectors in the persecution of violators.[17]

The new policies protected the dominant unionized bakeries tacitly, through language that appeared to defend the small producers. Authorities claimed that the distance requirements and the minimum prices kept predatory competitors from establishing shops next door to small bakeries and driving them out of business by dumping cheap bread. In practice, however, the distance requirements guaranteed—indeed, codified—the dominance of the bakeries already located in the central neighborhoods. Similarly, the prohibition of "persons or associations that effectuate any combination that could constitute improper competition" did not refer to the simultaneous ownership of wheat fields, mills, yeast factories, and bakeries, but rather to the small producers' strategy of selling cheaper bread. While officials claimed that price ceilings would ensure a minimum caloric intake for working-class families, enforcement focused almost exclusively on shops where bread cost less or weighed more. There is little evidence of punishment for underweight bread and none for other violations by dominant bakeries that, for instance, had upstairs dormitories for employees and workrooms located in basements where they could not open directly onto the street.[18]

Conflicts began soon after the promulgation of the regulations, when the Health Department declared that it would close all panaderías that did not comply with the health code in a week. If inspectors followed the letter of the law, they would have closed practically all of Mexico City's bakeries. But they clearly aimed the campaign at the small, nonunion shops. One small producer whose shop was closed turned to the courts, arguing that the Health Department was responding to "maneuvers by the large bakery owners who want to have control. The small establishments are closed without appeal even if they comply with the dispositions of the health department."[19] The court granted an injunction (*amparo*) against the closures and ruled that the distance requirements violated Article 28 of the Constitution of 1917, which prohibited "any act or measure that stifles or endeavors to stifle free competition of any production, industry, trade or public service."[20]

Consequently, President Abelardo L. Rodríguez eliminated the distance requirements, acknowledging that they had "exclusively favored a reduced number of people."[21] The Mexico City governor likewise conceded that the distances "protected the monopoly of basic food items." He stressed that the modification to the regulations proved that the government "had set out energetically to destroy the monopoly."[22] At the same time, federal congressmen accused mill owners of overcharging and overweighing flour despite falling wheat prices.[23] With this assault on the bread barons from the highest echelons of the three bodies of government, newspaper headlines boldly announced the "END OF THE MONOPOLY."[24]

The court also ruled that the minimum prices were "absurd." The judges declared that "beyond the interests of one group, it is in the true public interest that bread be sold as cheaply as possible." One magistrate asked rhetorically, "Are we really going to prosecute people for selling cheap bread?"[25] On this point, however, the president and the local government were firm. They argued that the minimum prices would remain since they protected small producers from "ruinous competition" masked by an "apparent benefit of the public."[26] In reality, however, the minimum prices were a crucial barrier against what the dominant owners called "*competencia desleal*"— the "disloyal" or "unfair" competition by the small producers that threatened to undermine the balance between labor and capital as framed in the collective contract.

Regulations were largely successful in their primary objective of ensuring the bread supply by containing labor strife. There were only four strikes in the 1930s, and actions in the following decades were scattered and short lived.[27] Nonetheless, these strikes and other disagreements over the labor contract drove the enforcement of the regulations and, consequently, the policing of the formal market. As the annual expiration date of the contract approached, union leaders invariably presented new demands and accused owners of neglecting their obligations. Each time, owners refused, arguing that they were barely breaking even. Negotiations then led to new adjustments in the regulations, followed by waves of persecution against the small producers and petty retailers. On the occasions that negotiations failed, strikes broke out, and then negotiations resumed. Owners and the union signed a new contract and drafted new regulations. While they never mentioned labor conditions or unionization, the stipulations regarding signage, hygiene, distance, and prices were inseparable from the government-sponsored arbitration between the mostly Spanish owners and the bakers' union. The regulations were, in sum, the crucial instrument behind the complex class negotiation, a mechanism to end the chronic strikes in bakeries that were so disruptive to everyday life in the city.

Policing the Formal Market

The first labor conflict under the new regulations occurred in September 1932. Since the collective contract limited shifts to eight hours, owners expected bakers to work more intensively. In response, the union demanded payment based on a percentage of the daily value of production rather than fixed wages. Owners and the union disagreed over what percentage, and the owners refused to submit to arbitration.[28] The city governor offered to forgive the owners' fines, "persecute clandestine bakeries, and exert influence over the health department to prohibit the sale of bread in plazas."[29] There was no agreement and the union declared a strike that shut down the major bakeries in the city. Strikers broke windows and took bread from at least two nonunion bakeries that remained open.[30]

Negotiations ended the strike five days later and brought a new contract. New regulations contained important advantages for both the union and the owners, as well as new pressures for the small producers.[31] The contract granted workers 15, 16, or 17 percent of the production profits, based on the degree of mechanization. The more rudimentary the shop, the more the workers earned, which further favored the more capitalized panaderías. It also established four paid holidays plus four yearly paid vacation days and a "workers' saving fund" into which 5 percent of workers' salaries was to be deposited and matched by 5 percent of daily profits. Owners were also to pay eight cents per worker per day for a medical fund.[32]

In exchange for these concessions, the government reinstated the distance limitations that President Rodríguez had repealed the year before.[33] This decision restored the key instrument of attack on the small producers, who immediately complained of the "unbearable situation" of inspectors from the mixed commission who confiscated bread, issued heavy fines, and even threw the small producers in jail.[34] In order to restrict the small producers' access to consumers, inspectors also pursued the small grocery stores. This was doubly bad for the small retailers. First, the dominant owners stopped selling bread to them; then, inspectors fined them for selling bread from the small producers.[35]

Small producers and retailers wrote directly to the president, protesting that "this law has only benefited the large business owners and damaged the small ones." They pleaded with him "to intervene on behalf of small commerce in order to end the effects of the decree."[36] Another accused the city government of supporting "the large bread industrialists who are ruining the tendejones by prohibiting the free sale of bread."[37] Some small producers, attempting to appeal to authorities' responsibility to ensure the nation's well-being, argued that the minimum official price would drive them out of business, to the grave detriment of future generations of Mexicans. Without wheaten bread, one small-bakery owner insisted, Mexicans would have to eat "tortillas, tamales, and squash," which were, "chemically speaking," inferior sources of starch. "Biologically speaking," wrote the owner, these foods would "produce an anatomical constitution with notable qualities of backwardness." What right, he asked, "does the current generation have to leave such a poor inheritance to the future generations? And, consequently, what role does the state play in the resolution of these problems?"[38] The president's office, unmoved, forwarded these letters to the municipal officials whom the small producers and retailers accused of corruption and abuse.

The next year, as the contract approached its expiration, owners and the union exchanged a series of threatening comments in the press. Owners argued that high wages were forcing them to close.[39] The union responded that owners amassed huge fortunes, "despite the primitive, colonial administration that constitutes the foundation of the city's bread industry."[40] If their profits allowed them to "vacation so often in old Europe," surely they could pay "fair wages."[41] A new contract and new regulations appeared in October 1933, before this volley grew into a strike. The government changed the official price, or more precisely the weight, of bread. Two pieces still cost five cents, but their total weight fell from 160 to 110 total grams.[42] This shift gave owners a greater profit margin that, in turn, allowed them to meet the workers' demands, without having to renounce their trips to old Europe.

The small producers formed their own association, the National Union of Small Bread Producers (Unión Nacional de Pequeños Industriales del Pan, URPI), and defiantly announced their offer to sell heavier bread cheaper—three pieces for five cents.[43] Rhetorically, they turned the regulations around in order to advance their interests. The government's clear favoritism toward the Basque and other Spanish owners, and the persecution of Mexican bakers who were willing and able to sell cheaper bread, allowed them to situate themselves as heroic defenders of the public good. They were—or at least strove to present themselves as—poor bakers, independent family businesses fighting against the monopoly of greedy Spaniards. URPI leader Sebastián Moreno wrote to the president, "It is inexplicable that small bakers are imprisoned and mistreated when they sell inexpensive bread in order to alleviate the hunger of the people."[44] Furthermore, the Constitution of 1917 clearly supported their grievances. Article 5, for instance, provided for the freedom of business, Article 28 specifically prohibited the monopolization of foodstuffs, and Article 33 granted the president the authority to expel "inconvenient foreigners."

The small producers urged the president to enforce Article 33, arguing that the "Spanish monopoly" violated Article 28. Instead, they suffered "brutal offensives," in which police "broke down bakery doors and arrested poor peddlers." The mixed commission confiscated so much bread from the small bakeries and market stalls that the small producers said they were "being destroyed."[45] Another complained, "The legal office of the city government harasses us with excessive fines because it is in connivance with the monopolists."[46]

While the mixed commission was pursuing small producers and petty retailers in favor of the dominant bakeries, officials insisted that the regulations served the general public's well-being. In a choice example of strained political language, the Mexico City governor declared that any detriment to consumers was entirely imaginary. The small producers' offer of three pieces of bread for five cents was simply a ploy to trick consumers, "particularly in the poor neighborhoods in the city," who were apparently unable to recognize how much bread they actually purchased. Customers "must realize that it is more advantageous to buy higher quality and weightier bread than a larger number of pieces."[47] He did admit that the official prices were making pieces of bread smaller but insisted this was a positive change since lighter pieces of bread meant less onerous drudgery for bakers. Prohibiting the sale of heavier bread was therefore "eminently revolutionary."[48] Gullible consumers "in poor neighborhoods" could feel satisfied knowing that their ever-smaller bolillos were in fact emblems of revolutionary justice, a triumph for workers. Yet they angrily protested that while inspectors diligently closed small shops that sold *overweight* bread, they did not punish those whose bread was *underweight*. On rare occasions when inspectors fined panaderías for bread that was too light, owners often docked the expense from workers' wages.[49]

Consumers remained outside of these negotiations altogether. Regulations mandated the inclusion of "consumer groups" in the commissions that set the official price and weight of bread and encouraged "popular action" to "denounce violations." However, the only consumer to serve on the commission was a union representative.[50] The tendentious opposition press, in contrast, was happy to air their grievances. The daily *El Nacional* reported that "a multitude of people, mostly women," went to the paper's office to complain of the size and weight of bread. It was "the greatest abuse they had ever seen."

Consumers, the paper concluded, "have to pay the consequences of the problems ... between workers and bosses in the bread industry."[51] Another observer mused, "Is this the justice that the revolutionaries have been bragging of?"[52]

The press seized upon the ironies of this top-down imposition upon consumers, whose well-being the laws supposedly defended. *El Fantoche* parodied the regulations, noting that according to the new laws bakers could only adulterate their flour with 40 percent plaster. Only 28 percent could be worm ridden. The weight of bread could be anywhere between 100 and 437 grams, "depending on the state of the scale." Day-old bread, known as pan frío (cold bread), could be up to three weeks old and would be sold for two-thirds the price of fresh bread, or *pan caliente* (warm bread). On hot days, bread baked any time in the previous year could be sold as *caliente*. Violators of the regulations would suffer "three days of ... bread and water."[53]

Cárdenas and the Confederación de Trabajadores de México

After Lázaro Cárdenas assumed the presidency in 1934, he broke with Calles and sent his former political mentor into exile. However, Cárdenas continued many of the policies and ideas of previous administrations, particularly the understanding of the state as the necessary arbiter of class balance. Cárdenas identified the revolution as a "movement that distances itself from the anachronistic norms of classic liberalism and from those of communism as practiced in Soviet Russia."[54] He envisioned a state with "greater, more frequent, and deeper" intervention in the market, though without imposing centralized control.[55] Like Calles, Cárdenas set out to develop a state that would offer political representation and material benefits to certain sectors of the population in return for their support of state authority.[56]

The bakery struggles revealed the degree to which Cárdenas had to constantly navigate between the conflicting demands of owners, workers, small producers, and consumers. The president sanctioned the regulations with his signature, but the owners and the union collaborated with authorities in their drafting and enforcement.

Crucial to Cárdenas's political project was the renewed effort to centralize workers into a single quasi-official labor hub, the Confederación de Trabajadores de México (CTM). Leaders from the CTM called on independent unions such as that of the bakers to join what Cárdenas called the "unification of the proletariat." Historians disagree about whether the CTM represented a state-led neutralization of the labor movement or a radical commitment to real proworker reform.⁵⁷ What is clear is that the CTM strengthened the state by incorporating organized workers as a crucial constituency. Unions that did not contribute to this end, regardless of how they may have benefited workers, became targets of state repression.

The leader of the bakers' union, Genaro Gómez, opposed joining the CTM, but divisions among bakers, and perhaps discontent over Gómez's long dominance, facilitated the bakers' incorporation. One hand-scrawled letter from a bakery worker pleaded with Cárdenas to "help the bakers' union liberate itself from the Leader Genaro Gómez Tapia who for fourteen years has divided the Union, keeping the bakery worker from claiming his rights because this man is in connivance with certain industrialists."⁵⁸ In November 1935, a faction of the union led by Amado Villegas expelled Gómez and his close ally Victoriano Muñoz and accused them of being "Trotskyite thieves" in the communist paper *El Machete*.⁵⁹ Police and armed CTM-istas seized the headquarters, and Gómez fled with fourteen thousand pesos of the union's funds, refused to give over the combination to the safe that held the rest, and set up another union a few blocks down the street.⁶⁰

For two years, both rival factions claimed leadership of the bakers. The Villegas faction had the headquarters and state support, but Gómez had the money and continued to administer the labor contract, which meant that he collected the eight cents a day per worker that owners gave to the medical fund. However, a new contract with Villegas's signature would marginalize Gómez and allow the union to join the CTM-affiliated Federation of Workers and Peasants (FROC). In April 1936, the union led by Villegas declared a strike. Gómez denounced it as a maneuver by the Spanish owners to muscle out his supposedly more combative union.⁶¹ Gómez claimed to still represent the majority of bakers, but when the strike broke out, only "a half dozen bakeries" where his people worked remained open.

The striking bakers now turned their violence against both Gómez and the small producers. Ironically, Gómez and the small producers came together and asked the president for protection.⁶² Their request was of little avail. Strikers approached the Flor de la Colonia Bakery, tore down the metal curtain, destroyed the furniture, and began to fight with the bakers inside. The police arrived and "prudently invited the workers to leave." The strikers then turned to a Chinese café that made bread, shattered its windows, and dragged the *"chinitos"* out to the street, where the police rescued them. They set another bakery on fire.⁶³

Consumers once again had to forgo their daily bread. Working-class families usually compensated for their lack of meat and vegetables with bread. The bread that sleepy workers dipped in black coffee, that children dipped in watery hot chocolate, was, in the words of one newspaper columnist, the "ally of tortillas." Bakery strikes, the columnist argued, were more threatening to the daily life of the city than the labor commotion in other sectors such as the bottle factories. "Mexico can live without leaders, without glass, without streets, and even without buses. But it cannot live without tortillas or baked flour."[64] Mexican consumers had become too accustomed to *chilindrinas*, *conchas*, *besos*, *ojos de pancha*, and "a thousand other" pieces that required intricate details and were "among the world's most luxurious." The function of bread, he insisted, was to "nurture, not to adorn tables," and Mexican bakers should make simple, large loaves.[65]

Bakery strikes shook the entire food supply. As usual, families bought more tortillas and crackers, which prompted grocers to raise their prices. "Mexico City Has No Bread!" exclaimed the headlines of *La Prensa*. "And the price of tortillas—higher than the clouds!" A kilogram of tortillas had gone from eighteen to thirty-five cents.[66] Dairy workers then said they would join the bakers in a solidarity strike.[67] Fortunately for consumers, they did not carry out the threat. No bread, expensive tortillas, and no milk: this would have been a painful sacrifice for consumers for the sake of an incomprehensible conflict between rival unions, Spanish owners, and Mexican producers.

Negotiations between Villegas's faction and owners yielded a new contract, which likely attracted the few followers that Gómez had managed to retain. New regulations came out two months later with provisions that further limited retail sales outside of bakeries. The Mexico City government declared that it would not issue any new licenses to retail outlets that were not part of established bakeries regardless of their location. In theory, peddlers and tendejón owners who had already received licenses could continue.[68] However, many complained that city officials refused to renew their permits.[69] A widow who ran a tendejón in Plaza Garibaldi wrote the city government to ask, "Is it possible that such a decision has been made, which will damage us poor people who lack fábricas and only subsist thanks to our bread sales?"[70] When the small producers wrote to the government requesting that the minimum prices be canceled, authorities responded that their request was impossible "because the objective of the restrictions on the free sale of bread is to prevent illicit competition and the formation of monopolies."[71]

Authorities continued to justify their defense of the Spanish monopoly by insisting that they were actually fighting monopolies.

The union headed by Villegas officially joined the CTM in July 1937 during a massive ceremony in the Palace of Fine Arts. The CTM national leader Vicente Lombardo Toledano declared that "the entire proletariat of Mexico should imitate the spirit of cohesion that is taking place among the bakers."[72] Yet anything but cohesion was apparent among the bakers. In December, the bakery owners met with Villegas at the city government office to sign an agreement in which they acknowledged Villegas's faction as the exclusive representative of the union bakers. Just before they signed the agreement, Gómez and his bakers burst in and began brawling. Gómez and his son were stabbed before police and firemen broke up the fight.[73] Days later, a defeated Gómez agreed to join the "unification" under the CTM.[74] In January 1938, José Siroub, mayor of Mexico City, together with the director of the Central Board of Conciliation and Arbitration, formalized the "fusion" of bakers by canceling the registries of all unions except for the one affiliated with the CTM.[75]

The new Sindicato Único (the "Only Union") demanded higher wages in January 1938. When owners refused, the bakers launched a strike with new levels of violence. At La Purisima on Héroe de Nacozari Street, strikers broke the counters, threw dough onto the floor, damaged machines, and beat the workers inside. When these workers tried to flee out a window and onto the roof, strikers in the street bombarded them with rocks, causing one to fall to his death. The police arrived at another bakery, not to protect the workers inside, but rather to convince them to stop working.[76] Strikers threw rocks at La Jalisciense on Pino Suárez Street and drenched the owner in cold water. At El Bosque on Chapultepec Avenue, they scattered the long line of customers, rushed inside, broke the counters, and took the bread. Strikers closed the highways that entered the city from the outlying towns of Azcapotzalco and Naucalpan in order to keep bread from entering. When they found a man walking down the street with a basket of bread, they gave him a pummeling and took the bread.[77] The strike went on for five days and ended when owners agreed to a new contract with increased wages.[78]

A week later, new regulations lowered the weight of bread from 110 to 75 grams. Violations were punishable by fine of two hundred pesos for the first offense, four hundred for the second, and closure for the third.[79] Another wave of closures and confiscation crashed upon the small producers, who complained to the president of "hostile treatment" by the mixed commission inspectors.[80] The inspectors also patrolled the markets looking for canasteros.

They took "nearly forty" to jail.[81] At one small bakery, the mixed commission dragged a clerk to jail where she remained for five days.[82] The small producers claimed that the mixed commission closed twelve bakeries one day and ten a week later. The next week it protested the closure of ten more.[83] A large crowd of neighbors gathered in front of one small bakery to protest the closure." Customers were also indignant about the decreasing size of the bread on the shelves. The pieces were of "such miniscule proportions that they could only throw them back at the vendors."[84]

The head of the Board of Conciliation and Arbitration applauded the cooperation between government officials, unionists, and owners "to combat the nefarious clandestine bakeries," including the "so-called small producers who have adopted a posture of open rebellion."[85] Whereas authorities previously had maintained a rhetorical stance that contradicted the real effects and purpose of the regulations, they now emphasized the alliance of the state, the union, and owners against the threat that the small producers represented toward the achievements of the revolution.

Although unionist bakers acted together with their employers to attack the small producers and retailers, and even came to act as de facto shock troops for the Spanish monopoly, relations between the union and the major bakery owners remained extremely contentious even without strikes. The union continually accused owners of mistreating workers and cheating customers; owners countered that outside agitators with selfish hidden motives within the union were causing consumers to suffer. Conflicts climaxed in August 1938. Leandro González Uzcanga, the CTM leader of the bakers' union, was in negotiations at the Board of Conciliation and Arbitration with Spanish owner Argimiro López Fernández, when the two began to exchange heated words. After López yelled "vulgar and harsh expressions" such as "I am going to teach you to be a man," both men began to fight. González Uzcanga pulled out his pistol and shot the owner, who "fell to the floor and expired minutes later." Two of his Basque clerks picked up the body.[86]

The reactions to the murder went from sympathy to dismay. *El Nacional* observed that the Spanish owner was a large man, a "Herculean individual" known for his "harsh language." He allegedly had an "African hate" for the union leader. The paper published the union's extensive list of grievances—murders, injuries, exploitation—that the Spanish owners had committed against unionists and had led to the growing antagonism.[87] In contrast, the more probusiness *Excélsior* echoed the owners' association's denunciation of the "cowardly and treacherous assassination . . . by a delinquent who for a long time had been provoking bosses." The paper noted that López had only recently opened up his own shop after working for several years as a clerk in another Spaniard's bakery.[88] The CTM representatives declared that González Uzcanga was a victim "forced to defend his life" and said they would defend his innocence.[89]

The trial began twelve days after the murder and lasted through November. González Uzcanga insisted that he acted in self-defense and rolled up his pants to show wounds on his legs. When a detective pointed out that the injuries were clearly older than the incident, González Uzcanga admitted that they came from an earlier accident but insisted that López had ripped off the scabs when he kicked him. The court sentenced him to the federal penitentiary, from where he continued to harangue owners and incite workers to strike.[90]

The deep rift between owners and the union brought no consolation to the small bakeries. Their persecution continued and was intensified by the continued antagonism, which the government struggled to resolve at the cost of the small producers. The most naked violence against small producers occurred during the strikes when unionists beat them up and stole their bread. The duller but more destructive violence against the small producers came with union-owner resolutions, when the regulations further restricted the small producers' ability to freely engage in the bread market.

The government's assault on small producers and petty vendors was "revolutionary," much like its insistence that consumers should eat smaller, lighter pieces of bread. The cynicism of this justification was not lost on those whose livelihood was threatened—certainly not on the canasteros who worked a few blocks from the central plaza in the Abelardo L. Rodríguez Market. The market opened in 1937 and was named for the president who insisted that the regulations aimed to protect small producers and vendors. The irony does not end there. Soon after the market opened, the government commissioned a team of artists led by Diego Rivera to paint murals depicting revolutionary accomplishments and pending grievances. One mural had three panels, the first of which showed porcine capitalists sitting around a table counting gold coins. In their top hats and black suits, the capitalists resembled caricatures of Wall Street fat cats more than Spanish shopkeepers, but the recent history of hunger profiteering and labor strife made clear who the Mexican worker's local nemesis was. In the second panel, skeletal workers drudged along in tattered overalls; behind them smoke billowed from sacks of burning grain. In the final panel, indigenous peons loaded trucks with the same sacks—Mexico's agricultural bounty, soon to become ashes for the peons and gold for the capitalists. The caption reads, "The capitalists destroy grains to raise prices while workers and peasants die of hunger. Let us destroy the capitalist system and eliminate the exploiters."

The mural's unmistakable message—the wealthy become fat by impoverishing the poor—sought to highlight the government's commitment to continue the struggle against lingering injustices. This insistence could not have convinced vendors who sold bread inside the same market. Inspectors raided the market and confiscated all the bread in the market, forcing the working-class families who frequented it to buy their bread from the same foreign capitalists the mural denounced.[91]

The Counterrevolutionary Reaction

By the late 1930s, this incongruence exposed the government to increasing criticism. As Cárdenas reached the end of his term, conservative opposition arose from his support for organized labor, implementation of "socialist education," extensive land reform, and anticlericalism.[92] His local concerns were compounded by events in Europe, where fascists had toppled liberal republican governments in Spain, Italy, and Germany. Nazi sympathizers in Mexico formed the Golden Shirts (Camisas Doradas) to fight communism and the "Jewish threat," both of which were, in their view, one and the same.[93] The right-wing *sinarquista* movement, which claimed to have thirty thousand members in 1938 and was growing quickly, took up the cause of Catholics, business owners, small producers, veterans, and other groups who opposed Cárdenas.[94]

As the persecution of small producers increased—and as the weight of bread diminished—it became ever more difficult for the government to justify its bread policy. Bluster about "revolution" rang hollow, as officials argued that the assaults on the small producers benefited organized workers. The small producers insisted that they benefited the "Spanish monopoly." "It is not true that the Revolution protects the proletariat," the small producers exclaimed. "The authorities are supporting the capitalists who victimize the proletarians. The city government has used the regulations to favor the tyranny of foreign capitalists, covering up the existence of monopolies."[95] This argument must have been compelling to customers, who saw the weight of bread decrease even further. The weight of bolillos now oscillated between forty and eighty grams.[96] Why, commentators asked, was the revolutionary government going to such lengths to support the Spanish monopoly? "Since colonial times, the bread industry has been the exclusive economic activity of the dominant caste. The Mexican people eat scraps of stale bread because they are still a humiliated and vanquished race that pays a bitter tribute of hunger and deprivation."[97] In the rhetoric of the small producers, the bread battles were not between labor and capital but rather between Spaniards and Mexicans.

Advisers to Lázaro Cárdenas warned that the bakery struggle made the government vulnerable to criticism from the right. "The Reaction," wrote Cárdenas's friend and collaborator Dr. Jesús Díaz Barriga, "takes any disruption caused by the revolutionary efforts and uses it against the government." The bread conflicts were especially damaging because "a large number of people of limited economic possibilities, canasteros and small producers, have had to be eliminated." This was particularly embarrassing since the "large producers" whom the regulations protected were making bread whose "weight and quality have diminished in an alarming fashion ... for the simple reason that [bakery owners] are not willing to lower their profits, accustomed as they are to an anachronistic system that has yielded them enormous riches." The report urged the president to find employment for the small producers in state-sponsored cooperatives, where they would "make toys or any other objects for which there is a market." Otherwise, they might join the forces of "Reaction." Díaz Barriga reminded Cárdenas that "in other countries, it is among groups such as small producers that Fascism has recruited its infantry."[98]

This political pressure, added to the street violence against small producers and the growing discontent among consumers, strained the government's ability to present its actions regarding bakeries as a coherent policy. The government's bind was to satisfy bakery workers' demands without causing a rise in the price of bread or pushing owners toward the political opposition. The most expeditious way to resolve the pressures was to shave ounces from consumers' bread and restrict the rights of the small producers. But Cárdenas was becoming aware of the political costs of persecuting Mexican businesses that sold cheap bread.

One of Cárdenas's problems was that he professed to support all sides of the conflict, a position that did not result in social equilibrium between contending interests but rather in ongoing violence and less bread for the city. On the one hand, in January the president met with a group of small producers and canasteros and assured them that the government would defend their right to produce and sell bread.[99] On the other, he did nothing to act on this pledge, and government functionaries continued to harass and publically criticize the small producers. The day after the president's meeting,

Figure 5. "Canastero," Mexico City, ca. 1930. Fondo Casasola, Inventory No. 205. Courtesy of the Fototeca Nacional of the Instituto Nacional de Antropología e Historia.

representatives from the CTM and the FROC accused the small producers and vendors of trying to erode the power of organized labor. Unionists redoubled their vigilance against the canasteros selling in markets and plazas. They closed several bakeries and marched through downtown in public protest against nonunion shops.[100]

A few days later, announcers on President Cárdenas's weekly radio broadcast, *The National Hour*, denounced the "illegal competition" and the "reactionary agitation" of the small bakery owners.[101] A group of unionists, together with an official inspector, then raided market vendors and poured gasoline on their bread. When one canastero tried to defend his mother's basket of bread, a unionist inspector took out a pistol and shot into the air. Other canasteros grabbed the inspector, disarmed him, and hit him with his own pistol. The police intervened and arrested not the inspector but the first canastero.[102] The brigades closed more shops, destroyed their tools and counters, and beat up operators.[103] While the unionist bakers celebrated the "Day of the Baker" at the Hidalgo Theater, the small producers and canasteros protested that by allowing the persecution, the government was disregarding the promises Cárdenas had made to them.[104] When the small producers' representatives met with city officials in February, unionists charged into the offices and ran them out. The small producers declared they would no longer meet with authorities.[105]

The focus of the bread struggles had shifted toward the small producers, but conflicts continued between the large owners and the union. Leandro González Uzcanga was released from prison in late February—six months after the murder—and the union declared a strike in late March.[106] Strikers attempted to burn down a bakery cooperative and kidnapped two workers. Vicente Lombardo Toledano, leader of the CTM, blamed the violence on the "bosses' constant provocations."[107] After nine days, owners and the union arrived at an agreement. The owners were to deposit ten thousand pesos as insurance against future violations of the collective contract.[108]

Cárdenas called on the unionist bakers to consider the families who suffered the consequences of their strikes. In a tacit recognition that the bread struggles had swirled out of control, certainly out of the control of officials, he "exhorted" the union leaders to "collaborate with the government."[109] Social equilibrium, the middle path between state communism and liberal capitalism, was supposed to rest on the regulating force of the state. A more secure well-being for working-class families was supposed to be the payoff. Instead, two antagonistic forces—the union and large owners—had come to wield enormous and practically autonomous authority over the bread trade.

The president took measures to reassert the state's authority by cancelling the mixed commission. The governor of Mexico City, Raúl Castellano, declared that the commission had "damaged the collective interest and strengthened, through new forms, the old monopolistic tendency." In his declaration, he expressed what had been obvious for the last ten years. "The large bread producers are willing to improve the conditions of their workers if, in exchange, the government gives a legal form to their monopoly and, furthermore, delegates to them sufficient authority to persecute and exterminate their competitors."[110] In canceling the commission, while at the same time asserting the government's commitment to defending workers' rights, Cárdenas managed to reframe the bread conflicts as a struggle between workers and employers. The persecution suffered by the small producers and vendors, in this view, was tangential to the heart of this class struggle.

This approach drastically reduced the conflicts and kept bread on shelves. Strikes after 1939 were short and isolated. The brutal persecution of small producers ended. There were no more bread sales in groceries or markets, but the small bakeries continued to operate quietly on the margins of the large shops, with or without licenses. The large shops continued to dominate, spreading across the expanding city. Like the political maneuvers, this relative social peace concealed complex negotiations. Owners expressed their indignation in an open letter to Cárdenas. "Our blood has been offered in futile defense; it is unjust that now we are made to appear like exploiters of a people we respect and love."[111] They need not have been quite so concerned, for the distance requirements and price fixing remained in effect. The regulations and the union continued to bolster their monopoly.

The government added another element that encouraged owners to collaborate with unions. In 1942 Manuel Ávila Camacho, Cárdenas's successor to the presidency, instituted a program in which the government sold subsidized flour to bakeries for the production of bolillos. The program, which continued through the mid-1980s, helped keep the price of bread stable, but bakeries frequently sold underweight bread and thus increased their profits. More important still, many bakeries used the flour to make expensive sweet breads, whose price was not subject to government regulation.[112]

In one sense, this corruption funneled government assistance away from its intended beneficiaries, working-class citizens. Yet more importantly, the history of the bakery regulations shows that the ostensible goals of policy can conceal the unwritten objectives. The misuse of subsidized flour allowed bakeries to reap greater profits and comply with the contractual obligations with workers. The aim of price fixing, likewise, was not primarily to guarantee consumers access to bread, but rather to deny nonunionized bakeries access to the market. By no means does this sort of game of mirrors render policy irrelevant or directionless. That rules are not enforced according to their explicitly stated functions does not mean that they are not fulfilling a purpose. Like the bank of a billiard table that directs a ball in the opposite direction from that in which it is hit, regulations that ostensibly opposed monopolies actually codified them. And the small producers, petty vendors, and consumers—not the Spanish monopoly, the supposed class enemies of the proletariat—footed the bill.

Conclusion

❦ IN THE MURAL IN THE ABELARDO L. RODRÍGUEZ MARKET, CHUBBY capitalists count money they have extracted from workers whom artificial scarcities have reduced to walking skeletons. Placed anywhere else, the mural would be a simple denunciation of inequality, an accusation that the rich profited from the hunger of the poor. What could be greedier, more inhumane, than the intentional destruction of food so that the poor would go hungry and pay more of their wages to the food barons? Surrounded as it was by fruits, vegetables, herbs, chicken, pigs' feet, enchiladas, and baskets of bread in a public market built by a government that emerged from a revolution that pledged to end such glaring inequalities, the mural took on additional meanings. It implied that the market, named after the political ally of Plutarco Elías Calles, who occupied the presidency between 1932 and 1934, operated according to more just principles—that government intervention could be a counterweight to the exploitation of capitalism. With government support and regulation, this physical market—and markets more abstractly—could be an idealized site of social equilibrium.

The raids by officials and unionists on the canasteros drastically complicated the dichotomy presented in the mural between rich and poor, between exploitative and just markets. Panadería owners did grow wealthy from the labor and wages of workers, but the scrappy actors fighting on the floor of the market formed a tangled array whose conflicts and interests went beyond the black-and-white struggle between greed and sustenance.

If the capitalists in the mural wore wool berets instead of top hats, they would be more clearly identifiable as Basques and other Spaniards who consolidated the "Spanish monopoly" in Mexico City during the reign of Porfirio Díaz. Díaz fortified the Basques' enterprises by, among other actions, encouraging immigration, strengthening the police force, and keeping in check protests by Mexican workers. The rise of the Basques was not entirely concomitant with Díaz's, for their roots lay in the fragmented, relatively open market that resulted from the postindependence collapse of the colonial gremio, the quasi-official owners' guild that dominated the market with tacit support of local authorities. By the time that Díaz had secured a firm grip on political power in the mid-1880s and foreign capital began to flow into the Mexican economy, Pedro Albaitero had already extended a business network that rested on the familial and ethnic identity of immigrants from the hamlets of the Baztán Valley. Still, Díaz's regime allowed this network to flourish.

The Basques' success in the bread trade was symbolic of how Díaz had transformed the nation. For supporters of the dictator, Mexico had become stable and prosperous after internal instability and foreign invasions had ripped apart the country during its first half century of independence. Under Díaz, foreigners disembarked in Mexico from steamships not gunboats. They were armed not with cannons but with capital and ingenuity. The French established textile mills, Americans opened mines, Britons set up banks. The Basques rebuilt the fractured conduits of victual provisioning, reopened the decaying flour mills, and spread panaderías throughout the growing city. As a result, Mexico City residents had access to bread like never before. If bread was a sign of well-being and urban civility, then rarely had Mexico City enjoyed so much comfort and sophistication than during Porfirio Díaz's belle epoque.

Detractors countered that Díaz built his vision of progress on the backs of ordinary Mexicans. He extended privileges to foreigners yet undermined the ability of citizens to shape their own political and economic fates. To illustrate their argument, critics pointed to the underside of the panaderías. The lives of bakers had always been onerous and poverty stricken. But when owners locked them up in 1895, bakers experienced a degree of coercion and humiliation usually reserved for prisoners and slaves. Some of the new panaderías and flour mills had dazzling steam-powered machinery from Europe and the

United States. Most shops, though, remained archaic, dangerous, and filthy. As the collapsed roof at La Florida showed, progress did not necessarily heighten the value of workers' lives. The immigrants rebuilt the bread trade, but they also established a monopoly reminiscent of the colonial gremio, which led some to question whether the Basque panadería owners were really modernizing entrepreneurs or exploitative gachupines like their colonial predecessors.

The caption to the Abelardo L. Rodríguez Market mural—"Let us destroy the capitalist system and eliminate the exploiters"—suggested that the revolution (and the government that contracted the muralists) aimed to redress these grievances and defend ordinary Mexicans from merciless hunger profiteers. In this retribution, Spaniards played a key role. Many revolutionaries saw the war as a continuation of independence and the violence as a way for Mexicans to assert their sovereignty over foreigners who had, in their view, usurped crucial aspects of the economy and subjugated local workers. Revolutionary caudillos routed Spaniards from regional flashpoints such as Morelos and Chihuahua. In Mexico City, Obregón humiliated the foreign shopkeepers by forcing them to sweep the city streets. Venustiano Carranza's aide urged the first chief to "smash the head[s]" of the Spanish grocers and bakery owners whom he called "the apocalyptic monster of our history." Spaniards and their businesses came to symbolize the vestiges of colonialism bolstered by Porfirian xenophilia.

Instead of becoming targets of retributive violence during the revolution, however, bakery owners continued to run their shops. Some made handsome profits. At the height of the war, hungry residents, particularly women desperate to feed their families, sacked bakeries and grocery stores while newspapers aired rumors that Spaniards were hoarding wheat and selling adulterated bread. This whirlwind of hunger and desperation in the capital did not crescendo into direct physical attacks on the Spanish owners or into forced deportation orders like those Pancho Villa issued in Chihuahua. Perhaps not enough people believed the rumors of hoarding or equated their own suffering with the prosperity of the bakery owners. Or perhaps the panadería owners were not as widely resented as the Hispanophobes suggested. After all, despite a legacy of distrust of Spaniards in general and of bakery owners in particular, panaderías were neighborhood institutions. The mostly female clientele had dealings every day with Spanish clerks and owners. Maybe these housewives and daughters did not share the intense anti-gachupinismo of the entirely male newspaper editorialists who excoriated the panadería owner as a latter-day conquistador.

City residents in 1915 may have understood that the "Spanish monopoly" controlled the flow of wheat, flour, and bread and believed that violence against local shops would have disrupted the already precarious food supply. The politicians and the caudillos from northern states who gradually formed the revolutionary government centered in Mexico City certainly took this view. They understood that food was an intimate link between governors and governed, that bread was an indispensable condition of political legitimacy, and that in order to gain traction in a city where they were outsiders, they needed to rely on the Basque bread barons. The bakery owners became crucial intermediaries between the new state and the populace.

The early alliance with these bakery owners allowed the new revolutionary leaders to distribute food and thus claim political victories. It also put them in an awkward position when the Mexican bakery workers, strengthened by their association with the broader labor movement, resumed the strikes they had been carrying out since 1895. The government that had pledged to defend the rights of Mexicans against the exploitation of foreign capitalists was in fact doing the opposite, supporting the latter while undermining bakery workers' attempts to improve their deplorable working conditions.

The strikebreaking was part of the political imperative to see that residents, especially workers in other lines besides bakeries, had access to bread, but it meant denying the legitimacy of the panadería workers' demands. The police who guarded bakeries while replacement workers kneaded inside were, therefore, fulfilling a social duty by ensuring the food supply. Though hardly revolutionary—this was, after all, similar to the policy the Díaz regime pursued—the approach was consistent with governmental concerns for the welfare of the populace. The new authorities, like their predecessors, were much more concerned with bread consumers than with bread workers. Before 1928, when panadería workers won the collective contract, the notion of regulation emphasized the balance between the right of consumers to have bread at accessible prices, on the one hand, and the right of producers and retailers to earn reasonable profits, on the other. The rights of panadería workers were incidental. This neglect was clear when the government made agreements with Basque-owned panaderías to produce bread for the municipality during the months of hunger in 1915. Officials did not consider the workforce as anything but part of the bakery. They soon discovered, with surprise, that workers had pending demands against their employers and were preparing to launch a major strike that same year. The "socialist" panadería experiment was not a sign of deep social change but of government officials scrambling to tread lightly among the volatile mix of adversaries in the bread trade and to find resolutions to problems they were only beginning to understand.

By the late 1920s, when authorities had to take the demands of the panadería workers seriously, when ensuring the food supply required hammering out a deal between labor and capital, their approach shifted into a distinct, but no less awkward, position. After the union and the major owners signed the collective contract, the challenge was to prevent the smaller producers and vendors from undermining the tenuous balance forged between the contending parties. Arguably, the important achievements of improving the well-being of the vast majority of panadería workers and, by extension, preventing labor strife from disrupting the food supply justified the persecution of small producers and canasteros. Perhaps these smaller actors were aberrations incompatible with the "social equilibrium" between organized labor and capital.

Yet there were other losers. The attack on the small producers and retailers was also an attack on the public's access to markets and on the transparency of law. Secretive negotiations drove the enforcement of the bakery regulations to the detriment of groups redefined as outsiders. This yielded an especially wide gap between law and practice and between rhetoric and practice. The health code became an instrument not of cleanliness but of politics. Smaller, more expensive bolillos became, according to officials, a revolutionary achievement. The definition of the formal market was subordinated to political concerns related to class negotiation and helped create the informal sector.

Monopolies, or similar forms of dominance, were hardly new to the bread trade. But the postrevolutionary phase of the "Spanish monopoly" was qualitatively different and sheds some light on the corruption, politicization, and rigidity of many markets in Mexico during the twentieth century after the revolution. During the colonial period, regulations supported the bread gremio, but their primary aim was to protect the interests of consumers from merchants' greed. Regardless of the policy's internal contradictions and the discrepancies between levels of government, the regulations were congruent with the overall objective of fomenting a stable market that would reliably provide the populace with bread. The following period, which emerged from the free-trade reforms of the 1810s and the subsequent economic and political turbulence, offered new opportunities for small producers and vendors who had previously operated on the margins of the formal market that had been limited, in practice, to the gremio. This period ended with the arrival of wealthier, mostly foreign, entrepreneurs who, after around 1850, progressively displaced these smaller actors and set the stage for the dominance of the Basque immigrants. This displacement occurred in a context of increasingly robust capitalism in Mexico in which these small actors were unable to compete with larger panaderías who could sell more bread for less. The dominance of the postrevolutionary Spanish monopoly, by contrast, did not rest on competition but rather on the manipulation of regulations that repressed competition. Such arrangements may suggest why monopolistic groups still dominate key sectors of the Mexican economy.

As the misuse of subsidized flour shows, the political formation of the formal bread market generated unexpected costs, which increased after 1945, as the ruling Party of the Institutional Revolution (PRI) built its power, in part, on its intimate association with unions that became corrupt and complacent. Panaderías continued to grow apace with the ballooning population of Mexico City—between 1945 and 1955 their numbers in Mexico City jumped from 520 to 938—but panadería workers found they had little leverage to negotiate with their employers. Today, the once mighty bakers' union occupies a small room in the very back of the large building that bakers under Genaro Gómez purchased in 1928. Bakers today complain that the union does little to defend their rights or bring them out of the precarious economic circumstances under which most Mexican wage laborers suffer.

Perhaps this is why most bakers I met preferred to discuss topics that had more meaning to them than the union. They expressed a deep love of their craft. They celebrated the aesthetic value and taste of quality bread and lamented the mediocrity of many panaderías. Though unrecognized by the bakery owners' chamber of commerce that periodically organizes bread festivals and exhibits, these maestros were proud that their creativity, dexterity, and labor continue to produce the remarkable plethora of bread on display at the Mexico City panaderías today, many of which were the sites of the actions and conflicts depicted here. If bread continues to serve the public's well-being, it is thanks to the worn, flour-covered hands of the bakery workers.

Notes

Introduction

1. In usage during the periods studied here, *monopoly* described not so much an exclusive hold on a particular trade, but rather a group of businessmen who collectively dominated a market and marginalized weaker competitors through what the latter perceived as unfair and illicit competition. This was more of an oligopoly than a monopoly: a core of dominant actors with small competing interests on the fringes. The "monopolists" ran independent businesses and competed among themselves but coalesced when other groups—retailers, workers, or small producers—challenged or hindered their collective interests.
2. For information on the Mexican bread tradition, see Barros and Villar, *El santo olor de la panadería*; Iglesias and Salinas Alvarez, *El pan nuestro de cada día*; and Barros and Buenrostro, *Panaderías de Tlaxcala, ayer y hoy*.
3. Works that have inspired this approach include, among others, Bauer, *Goods, Power, and History*; Mintz, *Sweetness and Power*; Auslander, *Taste and Power*; Reid, *Paris Sewers and Sewermen*; and Hobsbawn and Scott, "Political Shoemakers."
4. Bulmer-Thomas, *The Economic History of Latin America Since Independence*; Middlebrook, *The Paradox of Revolution*; Collier and Collier, *Shaping the Political Arena*; and Brachet-Marquez, *The Dynamics of Domination*.
5. Helstosky, *Garlic and Oil*, 66.
6. Humboldt, *Political Essay on the Kingdom of New Spain*, 423–24.

7. Molina Enríquez, *Los grandes problemas nacionales*, 279. Criollos are of Spanish descent but born in Mexico. Unless otherwise noted, all translations are the author's.
8. Génin, *Notes sur le Mexique*, 148.
9. Fernández y Fernández, *El Trigo en Mexico*, 2:206.
10. Ibid., 2:152.
11. Humboldt stressed that his judgments derived from "mere approximations . . . calculations never before ventured" (*Political Essay on the Kingdom of New Spain*, 71, 425).
12. García Acosta, *Las panaderías, sus dueños y trabajadores*, 186.
13. One of the foundational myths regarding the myriad types of bizcochos in Mexico is related to the construction of the cathedral in Mexico City. Since the stucco walls needed hundreds of egg whites, the nuns took the yolks and created new sweet breads.
14. Prieto, *Memorias de mis tiempos*, 30.
15. Cuéllar, *Chucho el ninfo*, 41–42.
16. Octaviano Herrero to Srio de Fomento, Tehuacan, Puebla, Sept. 30, 1885, AGN Fomento-Agricultura, caja 6, exp. 6; "Se perseguirá y castigará a panaderos adulteradores," *El Radical*, May 3, 1915.
17. "Las panaderías y bizcocherías. El veneno actual," *El Mundo*, Oct. 14, 1890.
18. "El monopolio del pan," *El Popular*, Dec. 4, 1897.
19. Etados Unidos Mexicanos, *Sexto censo de población*, 46, 82.
20. Rudé, *The Crowd in History*, 47–65, 108–22; Thompson, "The Moral Economy of the English Crowd in the Eighteenth Century"; Tilly, "Food Supply and Public Order in Modern Europe"; Kaplan, *Provisioning Paris*; Wright, "The Politics of Urban Provisioning in Latin American History"; Hufton, *Women and the Limits of Citizenship in the French Revolution*, 39–42; Taylor, "Food Riots Revisited." For more recent work, see Ochoa, *Feeding Mexico*; Elena, "Peronist Consumer Politics and the Problem of Domesticating Markets in Argentina"; Horowitz, Pilcher, and Watts, "Meat for the Multitudes"; and Helstosky, *Garlic and Oil*.
21. The literature on Basque migration is vast. Key general works include Douglass and Bilbao, *Amerikanuak*, and, more recently, Moya, *Cousins and Strangers*, and Azcona Pastor, *Possible Paradises*. For debates on socialization, see Kasdan, "Family Structure, Migration and the Entrepreneur"; Brandes, "On Basque Migration"; Douglass, "Reply to Brandes"; Kasdan and Brandes, "Basque Migration Again"; Douglass, "Reply to Kasdan and Brandes"; and Twinam, "Jew to Basque." For studies of specific contributions of Basque immigrants in Mexico, see, among many others, Garritz, ed., *Aportaciones e integración de los vascos a la sociedad mexicana en los siglos XIX–XX*; Garritz, ed., *Los vascos en las regiones de México siglos XVI a XX*; Herrero, *Los empresarios mexicanos de origen vasco y el desarrollo del capitalismo en México*; Arcelus Iroz, *Presencia de Navarra en México*, 197; Idoate Ezquieta, *Emigración navarra del valle de Baztán a América durante el siglo XIX*.
22. For discussion of who constituted a "citizen," see Chambers, *From Subjects to Citizens*; Guerra, "El soberano y su reino"; and essays in Guerra and Lempérière, eds., *Los espacios públicos en Iberoamérica*.

23. Anderson, *Outcasts in Their Own Land*.
24. Elena, "Peronist Consumer Politics and the Problem of Domesticating Markets in Argentina," 113.
25. Ochoa, *Feeding Mexico*.

Chapter One

1. López de Gómara. *Historia de las Indias y conquista de México*, 1:352.
2. Quoted in Pilcher, *¡Que Vivan los Tamales!*, 35.
3. Bauer, "La cultura material," 434–62; Humboldt, *Political Essay on the Kingdom of New Spain*, 72; García Acosta, *Las panaderías, sus dueños y trabajadores*, 186; Camelo, "La importancia de la comida como identificación de un pueblo."
4. The Crown compiled existing laws and added more in 1724. See "Ordenanzas de la Fiel Executoria, de la mui noble y mui leal ciudad de México," May 24, 1724, in *Colecscion de ordenanzas de la mui noble ynsigne y mui leal e ymperial ciudad de Mexico*, ed. Francisco del Barrio Lorenzot, AHCM, Ayuntamiento, Ordenanzas, tomo 3, vol. 433a.
5. Lee, "Grain Legislation in Colonial Mexico."
6. "Ordenanzas de la Fiel Executoria."
7. For prices from the eighteenth century to 1812, see AHCM, Real Audiencia, Fiel Ejecutoría–Panadería, vols. 3824–30.
8. Guemez Pacheco de Padilla Horcasitas y Aguayo, Conde de Revillagigedo, *Instrucción reservada que el conde de Revilla Gigedo dio á su succesor en el mando, Marqués de Branciforte, sobre el gobierno en este continente en el tiempo que fué su virey*, 79; García Acosta, *Las panaderías, sus dueños y trabajadores*, 41. See sample of these brands in Barros and Buenrostro, *Panaderías de Tlaxcala, ayer y hoy*; Barrio Lorenzot, *El trabajo en México durante la época colonial*, 236; AHCM, Ayuntamiento, Real Audiencia, Fiel Ejecutoría, Condenaciones, vol. 3791, exp. 4.
9. The modern Spanish spelling of *zeal* is *celo*, but during in the colonial era the word was most commonly written with a *z*.
10. For a recent interpretation of how liberalism influenced ideas of political economy in nineteenth-century Mexico, see Gómez Galvarriato and Kourí, "La reforma económica."
11. For Jovellanos's views on political economy, see Sociedad Económica de Madrid, "Informe sobre la ley agraria," and Polt, *Gaspar Melchor de Jovellanos*, 92–105.
12. Fisher, "Imperial 'Free Trade' and the Hispanic Economy"; Brading, *Miners and Merchants*, 114–28; Stein and Stein, *Apogee of Empire*, esp. chaps. 8–9; and Costeloe, *Response to Revolution*, 117–59.
13. Rudé, *The Crowd in History*, 47–65, 108–22; Thompson, "The Moral Economy of the English Crowd in the Eighteenth Century"; Tilly, "Food Supply and Public Order in Modern Europe"; Kaplan, *Provisioning Paris*; Wright, "The Politics of Urban Provisioning in Latin American History"; Hufton, *Women and the Limits of Citizenship in the French Revolution*, 39–42; Taylor, "Food Riots Revisited."

14. "Pedimento del procurador en la solicitud del apoderado del trato de panaderías," Mexico City, 1779, AHCM, Ayuntamiento, Panaderías, vol. 3453, exp. 93.
15. "Real cédula sobre que no se mezclen varios negocios en una sola representación," Aug. 21, 1748, in Dublán and Lozano, eds., *Legislación mexicano ó colección completa de las disposiciones legislativas*, 1:10.
16. "Ordenanzas de la Fiel Executoria."
17. The city council (*cabildo* or ayuntamiento) was composed entirely of men born in New Spain until 1772 reforms required that three of the six members be Spanish born. Yet even the latter "identified with creole political objectives" (Anna, *The Fall of the Royal Government in Mexico City*, 26–28).
18. Kizca, "The Great Families of Mexico."
19. Sánchez de Tagle, "El inicio de la reforma borbónica en la ciudad de México"; Sánchez de Tagle, "Las reformas del siglo xviii al gobierno."
20. AHCM, Real Audiencia, Fiel Ejecutoría–Panadería, vol. 3842, exp. 14.
21. García Acosta, *Las panaderías, sus dueños y trabajadores*, 219; Castilleja, "Asignación del espacio urbano."
22. *Empeñar*, in fact, means "to pawn."
23. "Cuenta y relacion jurada que yo don Joseph Manuel de Lara doi a la junta municipal del Colegio de San Pedro y San Pablo del año de 1775," Feb. 1, 1776, AGN, Indiferente Virreinal, caja 0053, exp. 016.
24. Cope, *The Limits of Racial Domination*, 90.
25. Quoted in Romano, *Mecanismo y elementos del sistema colonial americano*, 198.
26. AGN, Sept. 3, 1794, Instituciones Coloniales, Tribunal Superior de la Justicia de la Ciudad de Mexico, Corregidores (México), Procesos Civiles, caja 13 A, exp. 110; Cope, *The Limits of Racial Domination*, 90.
27. Brading, *Miners and Merchants in Bourbon Mexico*, 26–30.
28. Barrio Lorenzot, "Autos de panaderos de 1761," 13.
29. García Acosta, *Las panaderías, sus dueños y trabajadores*, 91–95.
30. Charles IV to Viceroy Antonio María Bucareli y Ursúa, Aranjuez, May 8, 1773, AGN, Instituciones Coloniales, Reales Cedulas Originales y Duplicados, Reales Cedulas Originales, vol. 102, exp. 122.
31. Sánchez de Tagle, "Las reformas del siglo xviii al gobierno," 178.
32. For fines in the eighteenth century, see AHCM, Ayuntamiento, Real Audiencia, Fiel Ejecutoría, Condenaciones, vol. 3791, exp. 4; AHCM, Ayuntamiento, Real Audiencia, Fiel Ejecutoría, Causas, vol. 3785, exps. 8, 9, 9 bis, 13–15, 18.
33. "Testimonio del expediente sobre facultades de la Fiel Ejecutoría," Mexico City, May 26, 1801, AHCM, Real Audiencia, Fiel Ejecutoría–Panadería, vols. 3829 and 141.
34. D. Juan Vicente de Guemez Pacheco de Padilla Horcasitas y Aguayo Conde de Revillagigedo, "Bando en que se manda cumplir exactamente el art. 43 de las ordenanzas de la Fiel Executoria acerca de que los molineros no tengan panaderias, ni compren trigos para revender a los panaderos," Mexico City, Nov. 20, 1789, AHCM, Ayuntamiento, Bandos, caja 92, exp. 22; García Acosta, *Las panaderías, sus*

dueños y trabajadores, 199; Suárez, *La política cerealera en la economía novohispana*, 153–54; Artís E., "La organización del trabajo en los molinos de trigo," 195–97; Artís E., *Regatones y maquileros*, 23.

35. D. Juan Vicente de Guemez Pacheco de Padilla Horcasitas y Aguayo Conde de Revillagigedo, "Bando sobre prohibicion a compras de trigo a molineros," Feb. 3, 1790, AGN, Gobierno Virreinal, Impresos Oficiales, vol. 51, exp. 68; Revillagigedo, *Instrucción reservada que el conde de Revilla Gigedo dio á su succesor*, 79–80.
36. Revillagigedo, *Instrucción reservada que el conde de Revilla Gigedo dio á su succesor*, 79–80.
37. Francisco Xavier Venegas, "Circular sobre exitar a los labradores para que conduzcan trigo de los graneros a los molinos de esta capital," Mexico City, Sept. 17, 1811, AGN, Indiferente Virreinal, caja 5291, exp. 023; Juan García de la Cuesta to Francisco Xavier Venegas, Toluca, Sept. 26, 1811, AGN, Indiferente Virreinal, caja 5291, exp. 023; Miguel Domínguez to Francisco Xavier Venegas, Querétaro, Nov. 30, 1811, AGN, Indiferente Virreinal, caja 5291, exp. 023.
38. "Postura del pan para el quadrimestre que comiensa el primero de enero del siguiente año de 1812," AHCM, Real Audiencia, Fiel Ejecutoría–Panadería, vol. 3830, exp. 193.
39. Ibid.
40. Francisco Xavier Venegas, "Providencias para evitar la escasez de carne," Feb. 5, 1812, AHCM, Fondo Ayuntamiento, Bandos, caja 91, exp. 264; Venegas, "Se concede la libertad de fabricación y venta de pan," Jan. 7, 1813, AHCM, Fondo Ayuntamiento, Bandos, caja 92, exp. 279; Venegas, "Decreto del libre comercio de tocinería," Feb. 6, 1813, AHCM, Bandos, caja 92, exp. 281; Venegas, "Se declara extinto el gremio de veleros; Libertad en la fabricacion y comercio de velas de cebo," Feb. 9, 1813, AHCM, Bandos, caja 92, exp. 28; Félix María Calleja, "Decreto de la libre venta de maiz," Apr. 15, 1814, AGN, Instituciones Coloniales, Ayuntamiento, Mercados, vol. 6, exp. 8.
41. Fiscal de Hacienda to Félix María Calleja, Mexico City, Mar. 20, 1814, AGN, Instituciones Coloniales, Ayuntamiento, Mercados, vol. 6, exp. 8.
42. Secretaría del Exmo Ayuntamiento, "Varias reflexiones," 1813, AHCM, Fondo Ayuntamiento de México, Sección Panaderías, vol. 3453, exp. 92.
43. Costeloe, *Responses to Revolution*, 122.
44. See discussion of these and other reforms in Anna, *The Fall of the Royal Government in Mexico City*, chap. 5.
45. Viceroy Francisco Xavier Venegas to Fiscal de lo Civil, Mexico City, Jan. 31, 1813, AGN, Instituciones Coloniales, Ayuntamiento, Mercados, vol. 6, exp. 9; Venegas, "Providencias para evitar desordenes en la venta de carnes," Mexico City, Mar. 1, 1813, AGN, Instituciones Coloniales, Ayuntamiento, Mercados, vol. 6, exp. 12.
46. Manuel de Amaya to Ayuntamiento, Mexico City, Nov. 3, 1814, AGN, Instituciones Coloniales, Ayuntamiento, Mercados, vol. 6, exp. 12.
47. See debates around this proposal in AGN, Instituciones Coloniales, Ayuntamiento, Mercados, vol. 6, exp. 12.

Chapter Two

1. Citing similar instances of economic participation by previously marginalized actors, Voss calls this trend "*gente baja* initiative." Such lower-class producers and vendors, he argues, "were very much active players in the post-independence economy—mostly out of necessity but with some vision of improvement and even mobility" (Voss, *Latin America in the Middle Period*, 137).
2. Noting that a drop in the price of flour had not caused a similar decrease in the price of bread, one resident angrily wrote the municipal president of Mexico City that "the commissioners in charge of overseeing panaderías, which are so vital to the public, are not fulfilling their duty" (Lorenzo Justiniano Araujo to Presidente del Ayuntamiento, Mexico City, Nov. 23, 1823, AHCM, Fondo Ayuntamiento de México, Sección Panaderías, vol. 3453, exp. 86).
3. "Prevenciones de policía respecto de las panaderías y multas a los conventores," in Arrillaga, ed., *Recopilación de leyes*, 261.
4. José Valeriano to President of Ayuntamiento, Nov. 27, 1834, AHCM, Fondo Ayuntamiento de México, Sección Panaderías, vol. 3453, exp. 88.
5. "Medidas para evitar abusos en el comercio de panaderias," in Arrillaga, ed., *Recopilación de leyes*, 608–9.
6. "Providencia sobre precios de pan," in Arrillaga, ed., *Recopilación de leyes*, 192–93.
7. "Prevenciones sobre panaderías, y que no se encarezcan el pan, maiz y harina," in Arrillaga, ed., *Recopilación de leyes*, 278–79.
8. González Navarro, *Los extranjeros en México y los mexicanos en el extranjero*, 1:187–93.
9. Costeloe, *The Central Republic in Mexico*, 149–83.
10. "Necesidad de una buena policia," *Siglo Diez y Nueve*, Oct. 11, 1841.
11. Luis Gonzaga Vieyra, "Decreto sobre precios de pan," Mexico City, Dec. 1, 1841, AHCM, Ayuntamiento, Monedas de Cobre, vol. 3284, exp. 15; Manuel Marañón, Bartolomé Guardarramos, Luis Prieto, José María Moreno, Luis Reyes, José Rosas, Fernando Zúnigas, José María Picazo to Ayuntamiento, Mexico City, Nov. 16, 1841, AHCM, Ayuntamiento, Monedas de Cobre, vol. 3284, exp. 15. "Decreto de Luis Gonzaga Vieyra, comestibles libres de derechos," *Siglo Diez y Nueve*, Oct. 11, 1841; "Decreto de Juan Orbegozo, gobernador del departamento," *Siglo Diez y Nueve*, Oct. 11, 1841.
12. "Cobre," *Siglo Diez y Nueve*, Dec. 13, 1841.
13. "Moneda de Cobre," *Siglo Diez y Nueve*, Nov. 30, 1841; Shaw, "Poverty and Politics in Mexico City," 26–28; Costeloe, *The Central Republic in Mexico*, 81.
14. "Decreto de Juan Orbegozo, gobernador del departamento," *Siglo Diez y Nueve*, Oct. 11, 1841; Administración Principal de Rentas to Presidente del Ayuntamiento, Mexico City, Nov. 30, 1841, AHCM, Ayuntamiento, Monedas de Cobre, vol. 3284, exp. 15.
15. Bustamante, *Apuntes para la historia*, 33.
16. Cabildo del Ayuntamiento to Presidente de la República, Mexico City, Nov. 30, 1841, AHCM, Ayuntamiento, Monedas de Cobre, vol. 3284, exp. 15.
17. Miño Gijalva, "Población y abasto de alimentos en la ciudad de México," 60.
18. Aguas en General, July 1843, AHCM num. 35, exp. 11.

19. Aguas, Desierto de los Leones, Feb.–Dec. 1843, AHCM, num. 51, exp. 8.
20. Zamacois, *Historia de Méjico*, 263.
21. Fowler, *Santa Anna of Mexico*, 222; Bustamante, *Apuntes para la historia*, 33.
22. Miño Gijalva, "Población y abasto de alimentos en la ciudad de México," 60; Thomson, *Puebla de los Angeles*, 140; López Mora, *El Molino de Santa Mónica*, 188; Peralta Flores, *La hacienda de Santa Mónica*, 29; Artís E., *Regatones y maquileros*, 191.
23. AHCM, Fondo Ayuntamiento, Sección Aguas Molinos, Dec. 1826, vol. 170, exp. 11; Ibid., Oct. 1826, vol. 170, exp. 10.
24. Jonathan Loesse to Presidente del Ayuntamiento, Mexico City, Feb. 26, 1840, AHCM Fondo Ayuntamiento de México, Sección Panaderías, vol. 3453, exp. 88.
25. Bakery Owners to Presidente del Ayuntamiento, Mexico City, Nov. 27, 1834, AHCM, Fondo Ayuntamiento de México, Sección Panaderías, vol. 3453, exp. 87.
26. Quoted in González Navarro, *Historia moderna de México*, 156. See also Walker, *Kinship, Business, and Politics*, 22–23; Haber, *Industry and Underdevelopment*.
27. "Sobre que [estrangeros] pueden tener carnicerías, panaderías y otros comercios de esta clase," AHCM, Ayuntamiento, Comercio e Industria, May 21, 1830, and Aug. 7, 1830, vol. 522, exp. 3.
28. AGN, Pasaportes y Cartas de Seguridad, several exp. in vols. 1–55.
29. Pani, "De coyotes y gallinas."
30. Flores Caballero, *Counterrevolution*; Pi-Suñer Llorens, "Negocios y política a mediados del siglo xix," 88–89; González Navarro, *Los extranjeros en México y los mexicanos en el extranjero*, 1:69–77.
31. Sims, *The Expulsion of Mexico's Spaniards*, 6; Bernecker, *De agiotistas y empresarios*, 181; Meyer Cosio, "Empresarios españoles después de la independencia."
32. Falcón, *Las rasgaduras de la desconolización*, 120; González Navarro, *Los extranjeros en México y los mexicanos en el extranjero*, 1:363.
33. Coatsworth, "Obstacles to Economic Growth in Nineteenth-Century Mexico"; Marichal, "Avances recientes en la historia de las grandes empresas," 22; Gómez Galvarriato and Kourí, "La reforma económica."
34. Chowning, "The Contours of the Post-1810 Depression in Mexico"; Hernández Franyuti, ed., *La ciudad de México en la primera mitad del siglo xix*; Cardoso, "Características fundamentales del período 1821–1880"; Pérez Toledo, *Los hijos del trabajo*.
35. Bakery Owners to Presidente del Ayuntamiento, Mexico City, Nov. 27, 1834, AHCM, Fondo Ayuntamiento de México, Sección Panaderías, vol. 3453, exp. 87. Eight of the names are illegible, making it impossible to know if they were newcomers or not. The legible names are José Valeriano, Manuel Marañón, Manuel Ortiz de Montellano, Francisco Báez, Marín de Zúniga, Manuel Echave, Joaquín Barrios, José María Liccozo, Luis Meyer, A. Caso, Plácido María de V., as well as José María Nava and Manuel Rodríguez, who appear in earlier lists printed in García Acosta, *Las panaderías, sus dueños y trabajadores*, app. 3. In 1831 the new owner Miguel Marañón, for instance, requested access to water for his bakery so that he would not have to deal with roving water vendors with whom bakery workers traded alcohol for stolen ingredients (Manuel Marañón to Ayuntamiento, Mexico City, June 30,

1831, AHCM, Ayuntamiento Gobierno del Distrito Federal, Aguas: Mercedes en Arrendamiento, vol. 65, exp. 44).
36. Walker, *Kinship, Business, and Politics*, 44.
37. "Prevenciones de policía respecto de las panaderías y multas a los conventores," in Arrillaga, ed., *Recopilación de leyes*, 261.
38. Gayón Córdova, *Condiciones de vida y de trabajo en la ciudad de México en el siglo XIX*, 11, 34.
39. Opposing this "simplistic" belief held by bakers with a more "scientific" view that abrupt temperature changes damaged their lungs, the article's author argued that bakers brought diseases on themselves when, hot from the oven and the labor, they drank cold water—not to mention "*licores fuertes*." When they slept, they did not cover themselves with proper clothes and thus exposed themselves to "the strong impressions of atmospheric air" ("Los panaderos," *El Semanario Artístico*, Aug. 2, 1844, 3–4). I am grateful to Claudio Robles for this reference.
40. "Decreto sobre dotación del fondo municipal de la capital de México, sancionado en 6 de octubre de 1848," AHCM, Ayuntamiento, Ordeñas de Vacas, vol. 3392, exp. 32.
41. Ramo Panaderías, AHCM, vol. 3453, exp. 94; Archivo General de Notarías, not. 426, vol. 2881, pp. 74–76; Archivo Histórico del Tribunal Superior de Justicia del Distrito Federal (AHTSJDF), Ramo Molinos, vol. 78, Molino Blanco y Prieto, 1857, cited in Gómez Gerardo, "Tradicionalismo e innovaciones tecnológicas en la producción de harina en el valle de México en el siglo xix"; Torres, "Una empresa agroindustrial."
42. Calderón, *La república restaurada*, 104–7, 416.
43. "Representación que la municipalidad de Veracruz eleva al escm. sr. presidente de la república," *El Siglo Diez y Nueve*, May 6, 1852; *El Siglo Diez y Nueve*, May 16, 1852.
44. Gamboa Ramírez, "Las finanzas municipales de la ciudad de México," 40; Coello Salazar, "El comercio interior," 766–67.
45. Fowler, *Santa Anna of Mexico*, 297.
46. Manuel Ortiz de Montellano, Leandro Cuevas, Francisco Javier Y., Rodrigo Marañón, and Julián Garcia to Presidente del Ayuntamiento, Mexico City, Oct. 4, 1853, AHCM, Fondo Ayuntamiento de México, Sección Panaderías, vol. 3453, exp. 94.
47. Governor Azcárate to President of Mexico, Mexico City, Oct. 25, 1853, AHCM, Fondo Ayuntamiento de México, Sección Panaderías, vol. 3453, exp. 94.
48. Maillefert, *Directorio del comercio del imperio mexicano para el año de 1867*.
49. "Panadería francesa," *Le Trait d'Union*, July 31, 1869.
50. "Multas panaderías," Aug. 5–23, 1869, AHCM, Fondo Ayuntamiento de México, Sección Panaderías, vol. 3453, exp. 96–103.
51. AHCM, Ayuntamiento, Real Audiencia, Fiel Ejecutoría, Causas, vol. 3785, exp. 9; "Panaderías," *Boletín Oficial*, no. 4, Sept. 3, 1841, AHCM, Ayuntamiento, Historia Revoluciones, vol. 2279, exp. 12; Moreno Toscano, "Los trabajadores y el proyecto de industrialización."
52. AHTSJDF, Ramo Molinos, Molino de Valdés, 1873.

53. Apolonio Atempaneca and ninety other retailers to Gobernador de la Ciudad de México Juan Baz, Mexico City, July 26, 1869, AHCM Jurados, vol. 2740, emphasis added.
54. Morales, "Espacio, propiedad y órganos de poder en la ciudad de México en el siglo XIX."
55. Apolonio Atempaneca and others to Juan Baz, Mexico City, July 26, 1869, AHCM Jurados, vol. 2740.
56. Angel de la Lama, who had five downtown bakeries, conceded to a discount of half a real, one-sixteenth of a peso (that is, around six cents on pieces that could cost between twenty and thirty cents). Teodoro Weis agreed to give the same discount at his bakery on San Lorenzo Street but none at the one on San Juan. Francisco Prieto allowed a half real for some pieces at his bakery on Aldana Street and a whole real for others at his shop on Tacuba ("El negocio del pan," *La Iberia*, Aug. 4, 1869).
57. Thompson, "The Moral Economy of the English Crowd in the Eighteenth Century"; Tilly, "Food Supply and Public Order in Modern Europe"; Hufton, *Women and the Limits of Citizenship in the French Revolution*, 39–42; Taylor, "Food Riots Revisited."
58. "Oficio del gobierno del distrito sobre que se cite a cabildo extraordinario, con el fin de tratar sobre las providencias que deben de tomarse para evitar el monopolio que pretenden establecer los dueños de molinos y panaderías," June 13, 1870, AHCM, Ayuntamiento, Policía en General, vol. 3634, exp. 608.
59. AHCM, June 15, 1870, Ayuntamiento, Policía en General, vol. 3634, exp. 608.
60. "Cabildo secreto sobre que se practique una visita en las panaderías," Nov. 15, 1874, AHCM, Ayuntamiento, Policía en General, vol. 3635, exp. 640.
61. AHCM, Feb. 2, 1853, tomo 2889, cited in Shaw, *Poverty and Politics in Mexico City*, 84–85.
62. "Abusos de operarios en las panaderías," *El Siglo Diez y Nueve*, Nov. 4, 1854.
63. "El Lincoln de los oficiales de panaderías," *El Monitor Republicano*, Feb. 19, 1861.
64. Pimentel, *Memoria sobre las causas*, 202–3.
65. Zarco, *Crónica del congreso extraordinario constituyente*, 289.
66. Ibid., 605–6.
67. *Código penal para el Distrito Federal*, 178.
68. Baz, "Decreto sobre condiciones de trabajo," *Boletín Republicano*, Nov. 30, 1867; Baz, "Panaderías y tocinerías," 24–27.
69. Aguirre, *The Criminals of Lima and Their Worlds*, chaps. 1–2; Rivera-Garza, "Dangerous Minds."
70. "Abusos de operarios en las panaderías," *El Siglo Diez y Nueve*, Nov. 4, 1854.
71. Baz, "Decreto sobre condiciones de trabajo," *Boletín Republicano*, Nov. 30, 1867.
72. Ayuntamiento, Cárceles: Panaderías, AHCM, Dec. 30, 1868, vol. 507, legajo 1.
73. Governor Azcárate to President of Mexico, Mexico City, Oct. 25, 1853, AHCM, Fondo Ayuntamiento de México, Sección Panaderías, vol. 3453, exp. 94.

Chapter Three

1. Falcón, *Las rasgaduras de la desconolización*, passim; González Navarro, *Las ideas políticas de Lucas Alamán*; Marti, "Lucas Alamán, Pioneer of Mexican Historiography"; González Navarro, *Los extranjeros en México y los mexicanos en el* extranjero, 1:223.
2. Pani, "Cultural nacional, cánon español"; Falcón, *Las rasgaduras de la desconolización*, 15–27; Pérez Montfort, *Hispanism y falange*, 15–19.
3. Alcázar, *El gachupín*, 30–31.
4. Azcona Pastor, *Possible Paradises*, 321.
5. Ruiz de Gordejuela Urquijo, "Cincuenta años de presencia vasca en México"; González Navarro, *Los extranjeros en México y los mexicanos en el extranjero*, 217.
6. Douglass and Bilbao, *Amerikanuak*, chaps. 3 and 5.
7. Thomas, *The Spanish Civil War*, 61.
8. Moya, *Cousins and Strangers*, 93.
9. Azcona Pastor, *Possible Paradises*, 312.
10. Lhandé, *L'emigration basque*, quoted in Iriani, "Los vascos y las cadenas migratorias."
11. Alday Garay, "Presencia baztanesa en las regiones de México."
12. Kasdan, "Family Structure, Migration and the Entrepreneur." For debates on whether or not non-heirs were socialized for emigration and entrepreneurship, see Brandes, "On Basque Migration"; Douglass, "Reply to Brandes"; Kasdan and Brandes, "Basque Migration Again"; Douglass, "Reply to Kasdan and Brandes"; Twinam, "Jew to Basque."
13. Azcona Pastor, *Possible Paradises*, 349–53.
14. Moya, *Cousins and Strangers*, 24; Azcona Pastor, *Possible Paradises*, 296–303.
15. Azona Pastor, *Possible Paradises*, 359–60; Arcelus Iroz, *Presencia de Navarra en México*, 197; Idoate Ezquieta, *Emigración navarra del valle de Baztán a América durante el siglo XIX*, 12–15.
16. Azona Pastor, *Possible Paradises*, 363.
17. Booker, *Veracruz Merchants*; Calderón de la Barca, *Life in Mexico*, 40.
18. Lida, "El perfil de una inmigración," 29.
19. "Albaitero certifica al cirujano callista," *La Sociedad*, Feb. 12, 1864.
20. "Testamento público abierto otorgado por la Señora Mercedes Albaitero de Yrigoyen, el 25 de febrero de 1910," AGN, TSJDF, caja 0066, fol. 013103; Baptismal record of Cipriana Cornelia Merced del Rosario Albaitero García in Family History Library Catalog of the Church of Jesus Christ of Latter-day Saints, www.familysearch.org; "Rejón Viuda de Albaitero. Información ad perpétuam," May 19, 1910, AGN, TSJDF, caja 0002, fol. 000157.
21. Luisa's brother Andrés was christened in Tacubaya in 1850. See the García Rejón genealogy in the christening record of Andrés García Rejón y Piñón, Jan. 24, 1850, Asunción, in Vital Records Index of the Family History Library Catalog of the Church of Jesus Christ of Latter-day Saints, www.familysearch.org, batch no. C619624, fiche no. 35207. On Joaquín García Rejón, see Benson, *The Provincial Deputation in the Harbinger of Political Autonomy, Independence, and Federalism*, 153; Zanolli Fabila, "Inversiones mercantiles en el agro yucateco a finales de la época colonial."

22. Walker, *Kinship, Business, and Politics*, 70.
23. Maurer, *The Power and the Money*, 13–26; Rosenzweig, "Moneda y bancos"; Potash, *Mexican Government and Industrial Development in the Early Republic*.
24. Mestre Ghigliazza, *Efemérides biográficas*, 286; Schell, *Integral Outsiders*, xii–xiii.
25. Marriage record of José Arrache and María García Rejón y Piñón, Nov. 28, 1874, La Candelaria, Tacubaya, DF, Family History Library Catalog of the Church of Jesus Christ of Latter-day Saints, www.familysearch.org, batch no. M643217, source call no. 0652544.
26. AHCM, July 24, 1874, Ayuntamiento Gobierno del Distrito Federal, Sección Contratas, vol. 561, exp. 23.
27. Quoted in MacGregor, *México y España*, 41–42; Schell, *Integral Outsiders*, xii.
28. Lida, "El perfil de una inmigración," 30.
29. Busto, *Estadística de la República Mexicana*.
30. "Población según la ocupación principal," in Ministerio de Fomento, *Censo general de la República Mexicana, 1895*, 45–65.
31. "Subscripción en favor del ejército de Cuba. Ramo de panaderías," *El Correo Español*, Oct. 24, 1895.
32. "Impuestos municipales. Panaderías," *El Municipio Libre*, July 17, 1896; Gamboa Ramírez, "Las finanzas municipales de la ciudad de México," 42.
33. Arcelus Iroz, *Presencia de Navarra en México*.
34. Family History Library Catalog of the Church of Jesus Christ of Latter-day Saints, www.familysearch.org, batch no. M643217, source call no. 0652544; "Testamento público abierto otorgado por la Señora Mercedes Albaitero de Yrigoyen, el 25 de febrero de 1910," AGN, TSJDF, caja 0066, fol. 013103; AHCM, 1888, Ayuntamiento Gobierno del Distrito Federal, Sección Agua Molinos, vol. 170, exp. 32.
35. On chain migration via uncles and nephews, see notary records collected in Idoate Ezquieta, *Emigración navarra del valle de Baztán a América durante el siglo XIX*; Bazant, "The Basques in the History of Mexico"; Mörner, "Inserción del fenómeno vasco en la emigración europea a América"; Iriani, "Los vascos y las cadenas migratorias"; Brading, *Miners and Merchants in Bourbon Mexico*.
36. Baptismal record of Pedro María Eustaquio Albaitero García, Family History Library Catalog of the Church of Jesus Christ of Latter-day Saints, www.familysearch.org, batch no. C619755, source call no. 0285896.
37. "Los bizcochos para los pobres, y el arancel," *El Siglo Diez y Nueve*, Sept. 23, 1892.
38. "Una gran construcción," *El Tiempo*, June 21, 1887.
39. Steen, *Flour Milling in America*, 33–34, 122; Storck and Teague, *Flour for Man's Bread*.
40. "Los bizcochos para los pobres, y el arancel."
41. López Rosado, *Historia del abasto de productos alimenticios en la ciudad de México*, 245–46.
42. "Visita a la panadería de los Sres. Albaitero y Arrache," *Diario del Hogar*, Jan. 11, 1890.
43. Estados Unidos Mexicanos. *Estadística gráfica: Progreso de los Estados Unidos Mexicanos: Presidencia del Sr. General Don Porfirio Díaz*, 215.

44. "La fabricación de pan con maquinaria," *Diario del Hogar*, Dec. 10, 1889.
45. Ibid.; "La fabricación de pan en 'Los Gallos,'" *Diario del Hogar*, Feb. 7, 1890.
46. "Asalto escandaloso," *El Demócrata*, July 3, 1895.
47. Tenorio-Trillo, "1910 Mexico City," 103.
48. Lear, "Mexico City," 78; Johns, *The City of Mexico in the Age of Díaz*, 7–42; Tenenbaum, "Streetwise History"; Tenorio-Trillo, "1910 Mexico City."
49. "El Sr. D. Pedro Albaitero," *El Correo Español*, Apr. 19, 1900; "D. Pedro Albaitero," *El Correo Español*, Apr. 20, 1900.
50. "Juan Irigoyan pide 15 pajas en arrendamiento," 1887, AHCM, vol. 170, exp. 24; Arriola Ortiz, *Recordando otros tiempos*, 47; Alday Garay, "Presencia baztanesa en las regiones de México."
51. Alday Garay, "Presencia baztanesa en las regiones de México."
52. Gaarder, "The Basques of Mexico," 55.
53. Alday Garay, "Presencia baztanesa en las regiones de México."
54. According to Mercedes's will, their children were Pedro, Manuela, Mercedes, Alfonso, Manuel, María Antonia, and Joaquín, who in 1901 were fifteen, ten, six, five, three, and eleven days, respectively, when Mercedes passed away in February 1901 ("Testamento público abierto otorgado por la Señora Mercedes Albaitero de Yrigoyen, el 25 de febrero de 1910," AGN, TSJDF, caja 0066, fol. 013103).
55. Alday Garay, "Presencia baztanesa en las regiones de México."
56. Herrero, *Braulio Iriarte*; Arriola Ortiz, *Recordando otros tiempos*, 47.
57. Figueroa Doménech, *Guía general descriptiva de la República Mexicana*, 1:310; Iglesias and Salinas Alvarez, *El pan nuestro de cada día*, 166–69.
58. "Impuestos municipales. Panaderías," *El Municipio Libre*, July 17, 1896.
59. Salazar, *El empresario industrial*, 66.
60. Fernández y Fernández, *El trigo en Mexico*, 1:62.
61. Acta constitutiva de Molino El Eúskaro, libro 3, vol. 76, fs. 283, num. 584, del Registro Público de la propiedad y el Comercio del D.F., quoted in Salazar, *El empresario industrial*, 77–78.
62. Arcelus Iroz, *Presencia de Navarra en México*, 205.
63. "Fábricas de pan y bizcochos," *Boletín Mensual del Departamento del Trabajo*, Feb. 1922; Arcelus Iroz, *Presencia de Navarra en México*, 237; "Junta española de auxilio," *El Correo Español*, Mar. 12, 1914; Alday Garay, "Presencia baztanesa en las regiones de México."
64. "En la 5º Comisaría se distribuyeron 20,000 panes," *Mexican Herald*, June 30, 1915, 1, 2.
65. Alday Garay, "Presencia baztanesa en las regiones de México."
66. Fernández y Fernández, *El trigo en Mexico*, 2–4.
67. Ibid.
68. Arcelus Iroz, *Presencia de Navarra en México*, 196–225.
69. "Fábricas de pan y bizcochos," *Boletín Mensual del Departamento del Trabajo*, Feb. 1922.
70. See the brilliant analysis of immigrant entrepreneurship in Waldinger, *Through the Eye of the Needle*.

71. Cardona, *México y sus capitales*, 224, quoted in Salazar, "Extraños en la ciudad," 225–50.
72. Marcos, *México y los españoles*, 14–15.
73. This figure was based on the estimated cost per diem of the following necessities: food, $1.42; clothes, $0.40; room, $0.50; other expenses, $0.43; savings, $0.25. Dorantes, "El trabajo en México."
74. "Robo en una panadería. Operarios que se fugan robando," *El Imparcial*, June 6, 1899; Moreno Sánchez, "Vida de trabajo en la panificadora 'El Antiguo Fénix.'"
75. Herrero B., *Los empresarios mexicanos de origen vasca y el desarrollo del capitalismo en México*.
76. Figueroa Doménech, *Guía general descriptiva de la República Mexicana*, 651; Schell, *Integral Outsiders*, 22. On "ethnic enclaves," see Portes, "The Social Origins of the Cuban Enclave Economy of Miami"; Kaplan, "The Creation of an Ethnic Economy"; Cobas, "Ethnic Enclaves and Middleman Minorities"; Aldrich and Waldinger, "Ethnicity and Entrepreneurship." On the limits of ethnic niche markets, see Auster and Aldrich, "Small Business Vulnerability, Ethnic Enclaves and Ethnic Enterprise."
77. Lida, "El perfil de una inmigración"; Secretaría de la Economía Nacional, *Estadísticas sociales del Porfiriato*; Ministerio de Fomento, *Censo General de la República Mexicana, 1895*, 8–9, 32–33; Secretaría de Fomento, *Censo general de la República Mexicana, 1900*, 12–13, and *Censo General de la República Mexicana, verificado el 28 de octubre de 1900*, 38–39, 142–43.
78. Morales, "La expansión de la ciudad de México en el siglo XIX"; Haber, *Industry and Underdevelopment*, 27.
79. My description of these transactions comes from the lengthy dispute between owners and peddlers found in the correspondence of Jesús L. Lara to Director del Departamento del Trabajo José Colado, Mexico City, Dec. 12, 1914, AGN, Departamento del Trabajo, caja 71, exp. 4, fol. 1.
80. Of a sample of one hundred shops, twenty-nine hired between one and five persons; forty-six hired between six and ten; ten hired between sixteen and twenty; and seven hired between twenty-one and twenty-five. Only six hired more than twenty-six persons ("Fábricas de pan y bizcochos," *Boletín Mensual del Departamento del Trabajo*, Feb. 1922).
81. Lear, *Workers, Neighbors, and Citizens*, 64–66.
82. "Fábricas de pan y bizcochos," *Boletín Mensual del Departamento del Trabajo*, Feb. 1922.
83. Quoted in Pérez Herrero, "Algunas hipótesis de trabajo sobre la inmigración Española a México," 131.
84. "Panaderías," *La Voz de México*, Aug. 30, 1877.
85. "Editorial. Necesidades públicas," *El Siglo Diez y Nueve*, Aug. 8, 1881.
86. "El monopolio del pan," *El Popular*, Dec. 4, 1897.
87. "Españoles monopolizadores," *El Hijo del Ahuizote*, Oct. 23, 1898.
88. Carson, *Mexico*, 60.
89. Morgan, "Proletarians, Politicos, and Patriarchs," 154–55.

90. Haber, *Industry and Underdevelopment*, 48–51, 91–95; Haber, "Political Institutions and Financial Development."
91. Bunker, "Transatlantic Retailing."
92. The workers' paper *La Convención Radical Obrera* published a critique directed as much at the allegedly apathetic Mexican bourgeoisie as at foreigner capitalists. "If we want to be free and sovereign," the piece argued, "let us start by opposing our neighbors' avalanche of ambition with the efforts of our own industriousness" ("Aún es tiempo," *La Convención Radical Obrera*, Oct. 12, 1902, quoted in Villalobos Calderón, "*La Convención Radical Obrera*," 200).
93. "El monopolio del pan," *El Popular*, Dec. 4, 1897.

Chapter Four

1. "El derrumbe en la calle de jurado," *La Voz de México*, Sept. 1, 1889.
2. Marx, *Capital*, 1:358. For similar working conditions in Peruvian panaderías, see Aguirre, "Violencia y control social"; Hünefeldt, *Paying the Price of Freedom*, 187–94. For conditions in contemporary U.S. bakeries, which were only somewhat better, see Kaufman, *A Vision of Unity*, 23–33.
3. AHCM, June 1, 1875, Ayuntamiento, Policía en General, vol. 3635, exp. 743.
4. AHCM, Sept. 1880, Policía en General, vol. 3636, exp. 832.
5. Lear, *Workers, Neighbors, and Citizens*, 109.
6. Reyna, "Las condiciones del trabajo en las panaderías de la ciudad de México durante la segunda mitad del siglo XIX."
7. AHCM, July 24, 1874, Ayuntamiento, Gobierno del Distrito Federal, Sección Contratas, vol. 561, exp. 23.
8. Salvucci, *Textiles and Capitalism in Mexico*; Camarena Ocampo, *Jornaleros, tejedores y obreros*; Gayón Córdova, *Condiciones de vida y de trabajo en la ciudad de México en el siglo XIX*; Bortz, *Revolution Within the Revolution*, 88.
9. Centro de Estudios Históricos del Movimiento Obrero Mexicano, *La mujer y el movimiento obrero mexicano en el siglo XIX*, 169–70.
10. *El Desheredado*, Jan. 1875, quoted in Gayón Córdova, *Condiciones de vida y de trabajo en la ciudad de México en el siglo XIX*, 73–84; Villalobos Calderón, "*La convención radical obrera*," 73; Bortz, *Revolution Within the Revolution*, 86–88.
11. "Incendio de una fábrica de bizcochos," *El Siglo Diez y Nueve*, May 22, 1895; "Día de incendios," *El Demócrata*, Nov. 3, 1895; "Incendio en la panadería de Lerdo," *El Chisme*, June 7, 1900; "Quemado vivo," *La Voz de México*, Jan. 16, 1894.
12. Dorantes, "El trabajo en México."
13. "Decreto prohibe amasar con los pies," *La Patria*, Apr. 18, 1893.
14. Raat, "Agustin Aragon and Mexico's Religion of Humanity"; Villegas, *Positivismo y porfirismo*; Guerra, *México*, 1:185 and passim; Hale, *The Transformation of Liberalism in Late Nineteenth-Century Mexico*, 6–7; Knight, "El liberalismo mexicano desde la reforma hasta la revolución"; Weiner, *Race, Nation, and Market*, 26–31.

15. Weiner, *Race, Nation, and Market*, 33–42; Blum, "Conspicuous Benevolence"; Agostoni, "Discurso médico, cultura higiénica y la mujer en la ciudad de México al cambio de siglo"; Rivera-Garza, "Dangerous Minds"; Piccato, "'El Paso de Venus por el disco del sol.'"
16. *El Monitor Republicano*, Aug. 29, 1877, quoted in Anderson, *Outcasts in Their Own Land*, 69.
17. Lear, *Workers, Neighbors, and Citizens*, 40.
18. Ibid., 42; Piccato, *City of Suspects*, 42.
19. Lear, *Workers, Neighbors, and Citizens*, 41–42, 53.
20. "Traviesos mandaderos en las bizcocherías," *El Nacional*, Sept. 6, 1890.
21. "Riña," *El Tiempo*, Mar. 28, 1890.
22. "Maldad estúpida. Obrero que quema á otro," *El Popular*, Mar. 19, 1902.
23. "Veredictos populares," *El Imparcial*, Jan. 22, 1899.
24. "Riña en una panadería," *El Popular*, Aug. 30, 1902.
25. "Pan amasado con sangre," *El Tiempo*, Aug. 12, 1910.
26. Busto, *Estadística de la República Mexicana*; "Población según la ocupación principal," in Ministerio de Fomento, *Censo general de la República Mexicana, 1895*, 45–65.
27. "Los panaderos. Huelga inminente," *El Siglo Diez y Nueve*, July 20, 1895.
28. García Acosta, *Las panaderías, sus dueños y trabajadores*, 56–58.
29. Shaw, "Poverty and Politics in Mexico City," 83.
30. Agente de Agricultura Octaviano Herrero to Secretario de Fomento, Tehuacán, Puebla, Sept. 30, 1885, AGN, Fomento-Agricultura, caja 6, exp. 6.
31. Castro Gutiérrez, *La extinción de la artesanía gremial*; Pérez Toledo, *Los hijos del trabajo*.
32. "Contrato para pan en cárcel de Belem," Mexico City, Dec. 30, 1868, AHCM, Ayuntamiento, Cárceles: Panaderías, vol. 507, legajo 1.
33. Roumagnac, *Los criminales en México*, 44–46, 130, 157, 166–67, 282.
34. "Un muerto y un herido," *La Voz de México*, Jan. 4, 1894.
35. Piccato, "Politics and the Technology of Honor."
36. "La higiene en las panaderias," *La Patria*, June 21, 1901.
37. Ibid.
38. Secretaría del Exmo Ayuntamiento, "Varias reflexiones," 1813, AHCM, Fondo Ayuntamiento de México, Sección Panaderías, vol. 3453, exp. 92.
39. Díaz, "The Satiric Penny Press for Workers in Mexico."
40. Gamboa Ojeda, *La urdimbre y la trama*.
41. "Hoy no habrá pan," *El Universal*, Aug. 1, 1895.
42. "Escándalo promovido por unos panaderos," *El Monitor Republicano*, July 21, 1895; "La cuestión del día. La ciudad sin pan," *El Siglo Diez y Nueve*, Aug. 1, 1895; "La huelga de los panaderos," *El Tiempo*, Aug. 2, 1895.
43. "Los panaderos. Huelga inminente," *El Siglo Diez y Nueve*, July 20, 1895; "Escándalo promovido por unos panaderos," *El Monitor Republicano*, July 21, 1895.
44. "El asunto del día. La huelga de panaderos," *El Siglo Diez y Nueve*, July 31, 1895; "Hoy no habrá pan," *El Universal*, Aug. 1, 1895; "Huelga de panaderos," *El Tiempo*,

Aug. 1, 1895; "La cuestión del día. La ciudad sin pan," *El Siglo Diez y Nueve*, Aug. 1, 1895.
45. "La cuestión del día. La ciudad sin pan," *El Siglo Diez y Nueve*, Aug. 1, 1895. "Continúa la huelga de los panaderos," *El Siglo Diez y Nueve*, Aug. 2, 1895.
46. "Hoy no habrá pan," *El Universal*, Aug. 1, 1895.
47. "El asunto del día. La huelga de panaderos," *El Siglo Diez y Nueve*, July 31, 1895.
48. "Hoy no habrá pan," *El Universal*, Aug. 1, 1895; "Seguimos con los panaderos. Opiniones de la prensa," *El Siglo Diez y Nueve*, Aug. 3, 1895.
49. "Hoy no habrá pan," *El Universal*, Aug. 1, 1895.
50. "La huelga de los panaderos," *El Tiempo*, Aug. 2, 1895.
51. Ibid.
52. Hart, "Nineteenth Century Urban Labor Precursors of the Mexican Revolution"; Anderson, *Outcasts in Their Own Land*; Knight, "The Working Class and the Mexican Revolution"; Díaz, "The Satiric Penny Press for Workers in Mexico"; Thomson, "Popular Aspects of Liberalism in Mexico."
53. Taibo, ed., *La huelga de los sombrereros*, 119.
54. Díaz, "Planes de la Noria y Tuxtepec," 321.
55. Walker, "Porfirian Labor Politics."
56. "La huelga de los panaderos," *El Tiempo*, Aug. 2, 1895.
57. "El asunto del día. La huelga de panaderos," *El Siglo Diez y Nueve*, July 31, 1895.
58. "Continúa la huelga de los panaderos," *El Siglo Diez y Nueve*, Aug. 2, 1895.
59. "La huelga de los panaderos," *El Tiempo*, Aug. 2, 1895.
60. "El pan en la ciudad. Concluyó el escándalo," *El Siglo Diez y Nueve*, Aug. 5, 1895.
61. "Huelga de panaderos," *Gil Blas*, Oct. 26, 1895; "Huelga de panaderos," *El Demócrata*, Oct. 26, 1895.
62. "Escándalo en una panadería," *La Voz de México*, Apr. 4, 1897.
63. "Agresión a la policía y escándalo. 34 panaderos presos," *El Tiempo*, May 27, 1898.
64. "Huelga de panaderos," *El Imparcial*, Jan. 6, 1902.
65. Lear, *Workers, Neighbors, and Citizens*, 104.
66. Camarena Ocampo, *Jornaleros, tejedores y obreros*, 67–68.
67. Thompson, "Time, Work-Discipline, and Industrial Capitalism"; Whipp, "'A Time for Every Purpose.'"
68. *El Nacional*, Aug. 14, 1890, cited in Gutiérrez, "De panaderos y panaderías."
69. González, "El liberalismo triunfante," 986.
70. "Los panaderos se declaran en huelga," *El Imparcial*, July 4, 1907; "Los dueños de panaderías no dan trabajo á los hueguistas," *El Imparcial*, July 7, 1907; "Aumenta el número de panaderos huelguistas," *El Imparcial*, July 6, 1907.
71. "Los huelguistas vuelven á sus trabajos," *El Imparcial*, July 10, 1907.
72. "No regresan los panaderos a su trabajo," *El Imparcial*, July 22, 1911.
73. "La huelga de los panaderos," *El Tiempo*, July 22, 1911.
74. Quoted in Lear, *Workers, Neighbors, and Citizens*, 129.

Chapter Five

1. Coronel Ignacio C. Enriquez to Pablo des Georges, Sept. 21, 1915, AHCM, Ayuntamiento, Reguladora de Comercio, vol. 3853, exp. 15.
2. Lewis, *Pedro Martínez*, 92–93, 101–2; Riedlander, *Being Indian in Hueyapán*, 58.
3. Knight, *The Mexican Revolution*, 1:387; Katz, *The Life and Times of Pancho Villa*, 244.
4. "En el Centro Vasco," *El Correo Español*, Jan. 7, 1914.
5. Owners of flour mills and bakeries who donated money to the cause were Gaspar Rivera, Braulio Iriarte, Juan Irigoyen, Arrache & Córdoba, Andrés Barberena, Pedro Irigoyen, Manuel Erreguerena, Melitón Miguelena, Martín Saragardia, Joaquín Irigoyen, Segundo Minondo, Agustín Jáuregui, Eugenio Alonso, Eusebio Barberena, Esteban Lecumberri, Fermín Barberena, Fermín Boades, Juan Elizondo, Luis Albaitero, Marcelino Zugaramurdi, Melitón Echenique, Pablo Diez, Pedro Laguna, Ramón Zavala, Sebastián Morillo, Manuel Blanco y Blanco, and Gustavo Bueno. "Junta española de auxilio," *El Correo Español*, Mar. 12, 1914. See Gil Lázaro, "Hispanofobia en el norte de México durante la revolución mexicana"; Reed, *Insurgent Mexico*, 128–29.
6. "Banquete en el casino español," *El Correo Español*, Mar. 25, 1914, 2; Illades, "Propietarios españoles y la revolución mexicana."
7. "Estudio sobre el encarecimiento de la vida en México, hecho por el señor Licenciado Eduardo Fuentes," Sept. 27, 1915, CONDUMEX, Fondo XXI, carpeta 53, legajo 5861, doc. 1–2.
8. "¿Está a punto de estallar la crisis del pan?," *Diario del Hogar*, Nov. 8, 1914; "¿Para el día 22 no tendremos pan?," *El Monitor*, Dec. 15, 1914; "Diez mil sacos de harina serán traídos en breve de Jalisco," *El Radical*, Dec. 17, 1914.
9. Buchenau, *The Last Caudillo*, 70–72.
10. "¿Está a punto de estallar la crisis del pan?," *Diario del Hogar*, Nov. 8, 1914.
11. Rodríguez Kuri, "Desabasto, hambre y respuesta política, 1915."
12. Jesús L. Lara to Director del Departamento del Trabajo José Colado, Mexico City, Dec. 12, 1914, AGN, Departamento del Trabajo, caja 71, exp. 4, fol. 1.
13. José Colado to Marcelino Zugarramundi; P. Albaitero y Cía.; F. Aguerrebere; Albaitiero y Cía; Marin Alzuarte; Benito Andión; Ramón Andión; Arrache y Córdoba; Andrés Barberena; E. Barberena; J. Barberena; Berea y Cía; Baudes y Minondo; Panificadora Mecánica; Cofinio y Saracho; A. Arriola; R. Hernández; J. Galarza; J. Elizondo; Echenique y Cía; M. Echenique; J. E. Freyre; S. Hernández Rosas; F. Echandi; P. Diez; G. Echande; Jaimerena y López; J. Oteiza; J. Ortiz; Irigoyen y Cía; J. Meoqui ("La Moderna"); B. Iriarte; P. Laguna, Reza y Damía; E. Reynosa; J. Romero; M. Perochena ("La Baztanesa"); L. Senosian; F. Velasco; J. Viera., Mexico City, Dec. 17, 1914, AGN, Departamento del Trabajo, caja 71, exp. 4, fol. 1.
14. Quoted in Yankelevich, "Hispanofobia y revolución."
15. José Colado to Propietarios, Mexico City, Dec. 17, 1914, AGN, Departamento del Trabajo, caja 71, exp. 4, fol. 1.

16. José Colado to Director del Departamento del Trabajo Atenedoro Monrroy, Mexico City, Dec. 19, 1914, AGN, Departamento del Trabajo, caja 75, exp. 3, fols. 15–18.
17. "Una multa de quinientos pesos por vender el pan bastante pequeño," *El Monitor*, Dec. 30, 1914.
18. Salazar and Escobedo, *Las pugnas de la gleba*, 1:55; MacGregor, *México y España*, 62–63; Lear, *Workers, Neighbors, and Citizens*, 266–67.
19. Agrupación de Fabricantes Mexicanos de Pan y Bizcochos del Distrito Federal to Eulalio Gutiérrez, Mexico City, Dec. 21, 1914, AGN, Departamento del Trabajo, caja 71, exp. 3, fols. 15–22.
20. "Los acapadores de harina tratan de arruinar a los panaderos pobres de dejar sin pan a la clase media," *El Radical*, Dec. 18, 1914; Agrupación de Fabricantes Mexicanos de Pan y Bizcochos del Distrito Federal to Eulalio Gutiérrez, Mexico City, Dec. 21, 1914, AGN, Departamento del Trabajo, caja 71, exp. 3, fols. 15–22; "Los panaderos en pequeño quieren llegar a un arreglo con los acaparadores," *El Monitor*, Dec. 23, 1914; "Los panaderos ante el presidente de la república," *El Radical*, Dec. 22, 1914.
21. "Los acapadores de harina tratan de arruinar a los panaderos pobres de dejar sin pan a la clase media," *El Radical*, Dec. 18, 1914; Agrupación de Fabricantes Mexicanos de Pan y Bizcochos del Distrito Federal to Eulalio Gutiérrez, Mexico City, Dec. 21, 1914, AGN, Departamento del Trabajo, caja 71, exp. 3, fols. 15–22; "Los panaderos en pequeño quieren llegar a un arreglo con los acaparadores," *El Monitor*, Dec. 23, 1914; "Los panaderos ante el presidente de la república," *El Radical*, Dec. 22, 1914.
22. Eulalio Gutiérrez to Ayuntamiento, Mexico City, Dec. 25, 1914, AHCM, Comercio e Industria, vol. 522, exp. 61.
23. Braulio Iriarte to Gobernador del Distrito Federal, Mexico City, Dec. 24, 1914, AHCM, Comercio e Industria, vol. 522, exp. 33.
24. José Segura to Presidente del Ayuntamiento, Mexico City, Jan. 5, 1915, AHCM, Ayuntamiento, Comercio e Industria, vol. 522, exp. 61; Jesús J. Gutiérrez to José Segura, Mexico City, Jan. 1, 1915, AHCM, Ayuntamiento, Comercio e Industria, vol. 522, exp. 61; "Los panaderos se congregarán hoy por la tarde," *El Radical*, Dec. 28, 1914.
25. "Exasemos de arina por que lla seme acabo y tendremos que dejar de trabar llo y los que trabajan en mi casa si ud no nos facilita el modo de seguir trabajando," Aniseto Martínez to José Segura, Mexico City, Jan. 1, 1915, AHCM Ayuntamiento, Comercio e Industria, vol. 522, exp. 61.
26. Román Hernández to José Segura, Mexico City, Dec. 29, 1914, AHCM, Comercio e Industria, vol. 522, exp. 61.
27. "Convenio entre molineros y fabricantes mexicanos de bizcochos," Jan. 13, 1915, AHCM, Ayuntamiento, Comercio e Industria, vol. 522, exp. 22.
28. Enrique Díaz Conti to Gobernador del DF, Mexico City, Jan. 15, 1915, AHCM, Ayuntamiento, Comercio e Industria, vol. 522, exp. 33.
29. "Vienen 16 furgones de trigo a la capital," *El Monitor*, Jan. 26, 1915.
30. "Mucha harina está descargándose en Buenavista," *El Radical*, Jan. 25, 1915.
31. MacGregor, *Revolución y diplomacia*, 303.

32. "Investigaciones hechas por uno de los comités americanos," Mar. 1915, AHCM, Ayuntamiento, Reguladora de Comercio, vol. 3853, exp. 11.
33. Rodríguez Kuri, *Historia del desasosiego*, 132–33.
34. Knight, *The Mexican Revolution*, 2:315; Lear, *Workers, Neighbors, and Citizens*, 274.
35. Rodríguez Kuri, *Historia del desasosiego*, 131; Buchenau, *The Last Caudillo*, 76–77.
36. Lear, *Workers, Neighbors, and Citizens*, 273; MacGregor, *Revolución y diplomacia*, 301–2.
37. *Le Courrier du Mexique*, Mar. 9, 1915, cited in MacGregor, *Revolución y diplomacia*, 304.
38. Rodríguez Kuri, "Desabasto, hambre y respuesta política, 1915," 146.
39. Moats, *Thunder in their Veins*, 170–71.
40. "Prices of Corn and Charcoal on Increase in City," *Mexican Herald*, Mar. 10, 1915.
41. "Se perseguirá y castigará a panaderos adulteradores," *El Radical*, May 3, 1915.
42. Böker, "Keeping House in Revolutionary Mexico City," 165–70.
43. "Prices of Corn and Charcoal on Increase in City," *Mexican Herald*, Mar. 10, 1915.
44. "El problema de la comida es pavoroso," *Mexican Herald*, May 19, 1915.
45. "Perdió a su hijo al querer comprar maíz," *Mexican Herald*, May 20, 1915.
46. "266 mujeres se desmayan en la venta del maíz," *Mexican Herald*, May 22, 1915.
47. "El pueblo hambriento ha empezado a castigar a sus infames verdugos," *El Combate*, June 25, 1915.
48. "Los grupos no hacen frente a los bomberos," *Mexican Herald*, June 27, 1915.
49. Francisco Angulo to H. Ayuntamiento, Mexico City, Jan. 6, 1915, AHCM, Ayuntamiento, Comercio e Industria, vol. 522, exp. 61.
50. "Ayer se repartió pan a los pobres," *El Combate*, July 1, 1915; "En la 5° comisaría se distribuyeron 20,000 panes," *Mexican Herald*, June 30, 1915.
51. "Despedida de soltero," *Mexican Herald*, July 16, 1915.
52. Ramírez Plancarte, *La ciudad de México durante la revolución constitucionalista*, 538–40.
53. Herrero B., *Braulio Iriarte*, 21–35.
54. Alday Garay, "Presencia baztanesa en las regiones de México."
55. "Oyamburu, Martín. Compraventa de casas en Guadalupe Hidalgo, D.F." Nov. 20, 1915, AGNDF, notary 1, vol. 83, num. 465, pp. 105–12; "Oyamburu, Martín. Compraventa de seis casas en Guadalupe Hidalgo, DF," Dec. 13, 1915, AGNDF, notary 1, vol. 81, num. 473, pp. 109–15; "Oyamburu, Martin. Se constituye la 'Compañía Petrolera,'" Dec. 29, 1915, AGNDF, notary 1, vol. 82, num. 489, pp. 131–53; "Oyamburu, Martín. Disolución de la sociedad 'Juan Ybarrola, sociedad en comandita,'" Apr. 16, 1918, AGNDF, notary 1, vol. 81, num. 728, pp. 278–82.
56. Ramírez Plancarte, *La ciudad de México durante la revolución constitucionalista*, 427–28.
57. "Comisión reguladora de precios," 1916, AHCM, Comisión Reguladora de Precios, caja 1.
58. Rodríguez Kuri, "Desabasto, hambre y respuesta política."

59. "El pan, los militares y los que hacen 'cola,'" *Acción Mundial*, June 20, 1916.
60. Quoted in Negri, *Official Statement Regarding the Food Situation in Mexico City after the Constitutionalista Occupation*, 4.
61. Ibid., 21.
62. Ibid., 27.
63. "Liga anti-española," Sept. 16, 1915, CONDUMEX, Fondo XXI, carpeta 53, legajo 5844; "León Girón to Venustiano Carranza, Tacubaya, D.F." Sept. 25, 1915, CONDUMEX, Fondo XXI, carpeta 53, legajo 5844.
64. CONDUMEX, Sept. 16, 1915, Fondo XXI, carpeta 53, legajo 5844.
65. León Girón to Venustiano Carranza, Tacubaya, D.F., Sept. 25, 1915, CONDUMEX, Fondo XXI, carpeta 53, legajo 5844.
66. Ibid.
67. "Estudio sobre el encarecimiento de la vida en México, hecho por el señor Licenciado Eduardo Fuentes," Sept. 27, 1915, CONDUMEX, Fondo XXI, carpeta 53, legajo 5861, doc. 1–2.
68. Lear, *Workers, Neighbors, and Citizens*, 270–71.
69. Salazar and Escobedo, *Las pugnas de la gleba*, 1:94–95.
70. "La inmigración ibera que viene a México no se compone de ladrones ni degenerados, sino de elementos sanos, laboriosos y dignos," *El Correo Español*, Sept. 26, 1915; CONDUMEX, Sept. 16, 1915, Fondo XXI, carpeta 53, legajo 5844.
71. "Arrache & Córdoba, guided by the noble goals expressed above, make their establishment available to the municipal president. All the material necessary for the production of bread will be paid for by the municipal president, and all the products of these materials will made available to him. The municipal presidency will pay the wages, salaries, and fixed costs of Cofiño and Saracho's mentioned bakery" ("Contrato entre ayuntamiento y panadería 'Los Gallos,'" Sept. 14, 1915, AHCM, Ayuntamiento, Reguladora de Comercio, vol. 3853, exp. 14).
72. "Acaparadores españoles," Sept. 27, 1915, CONDUMEX, Fondo XXI, carpeta 53, legajo 5867.
73. "Han llegado a un arreglo acerca de la venta del pan," *Mexican Herald*, Aug. 12, 1915.
74. Pablo des Georges, "Diario de mi viaje a San Andrés Chalchicomula," AHCM, Ayuntamiento, Reguladora de Comercio, vol. 3853, exp. 15.
75. Gamboa Ojeda, "La constancia mexicana"; Morales-Moreno, "Los molinos de la Asunción y San Miguel en Tecamacalco y Acatzingo, Estado de Puebla."
76. "Contrato entre ayuntamiento y panadería 'La Unión,'" Oct. 2, 1915, AHCM, Ayuntamiento, Reguladora de Comercio, vol. 3853, exp. 14.
77. Pedro Irigoyen to Álvaro Obregón, Mexico City, July 18, 1918, Fideicomiso Archivos Plutarco Elías Calles y Fernando Torreblanca Fondo FAO, serie 020500, exp. "223"/206, inv. 494, legajo 1, fol. 5.
78. AGN, Mar. 15, 1921, Presidentes, Obregón-Calles (henceforth cited as O-C), caja 185, exp. 602-B-1.
79. G. Elías to Plutarco Elías Calles, Ciudad Juárez, Chihuahua, Feb. 16, 1925, AGN, Presidentes, O-C, caja 319, exp. 814-I-1; Álvaro Obregón to Fernando Torreblanca, Cajeme, Sonora, Feb. 13, 1925, AGN, Presidentes, O-C, caja 319, exp. 814-I-1.

80. "El sindicato de panaderos presenta peticiones a los dueños de obradores," *El Pueblo*, Nov. 4, 1915; Huitrón, *Orígenes e historia del movimiento obrero en México*, 290.
81. Quoted in Rodríguez Kuri, "El año cero."
82. Rodríguez Kuri argues that "one of the main causes of the hunger in Mexico City [was] the dismantling—if not disappearance—of the state" (*Historia del desasosiego*, 143).

Chapter Six

1. Huitrón, *Orígenes e historia del movimiento obrero en México*, 290; Salazar and Escobedo, *Las pugnas de la gleba*; Hart, "The Urban Working Class and the Mexican Revolution"; Hart, *Revolutionary Mexico*; Knight, *The Mexican Revolution*, 2:316–21.
2. "Transcripción de reunión entre dueños, expendedores, Departamento del Trabajo," Dec. 19, 1914, AGN, Departamento del Trabajo, caja 71, exp. 3, fols. 27–51, 51v.
3. Carr, "The Casa del Obrero Mundial."
4. Alday Garay, "La comunidad baztanesa en la ciudad de México en los siglos XIX y XX."
5. Salazar and Escobedo, *Las pugnas de la gleba*, 121.
6. *El Pueblo*, May 24, 1915, quoted in Carr, "The Casa del Obrero Mundial."
7. The owner of this bakery was in fact Braulio Iriarte. "Eusebio" perhaps referred to Eusebio Goyeneche, Iriarte's nephew.
8. "Por las panaderías," *Acción Mundial*, June 16, 1916.
9. "¿Por qué no hay pan para el pueblo en las panaderías?," *Acción Mundial*, June 16, 1916.
10. "Una panadería como hay muchas," *El Pueblo*, May 7, 1916; "Están envenenando al público los panaderos," *El Pueblo*, Mar. 5, 1919.
11. "En la panadería," *Acción Mundial*, June 12, 1916.
12. Moats, *Thunder in Their Veins*, 187.
13. Quoted in Knight, *The Mexican Revolution*, 2:216.
14. "Sindicato de obreros y obreras del ramo de panadería," Oct. 21, 1915, AHCM, Ayuntamiento, Reguladora de Comercio: Diversos, vol. 3853, exp. 14.
15. "El sindicato de panaderos presenta peticiones a los dueños de obradores," *El Pueblo*, Nov. 4, 1915; Huitrón, *Orígenes e historia del movimiento obrero en México*, 290.
16. Ulloa, "La lucha armada," 1151; Illades, "Propietarios españoles y la revolución mexicana"; Illades, *Presencia española en la revolución mexicana*.
17. "Más sobre la huelga de panaderos," *El Pueblo*, Nov. 5, 1915.
18. "Los patrones y los panaderos huelguistas ante el señor gobernador del distrito," *El Pueblo*, Nov. 7, 1915.
19. "Más sobre la huelga de panaderos," *El Pueblo*, Nov. 5, 1915.
20. "Los patrones y los panaderos huelguistas ante el señor gobernador del distrito," *El Pueblo*, Nov. 7, 1915.
21. Lear, as well as Buffington and French, point to bakery mechanization as a sign of "de-skilling" (Lear, *Workers, Neighbors, and Citizens*, 65; Buffington and French, "The Culture of Modernity").

22. Secretaría de la Economía Nacional, *Segundo censo industrial, 1935*, 3:18:85–88.
23. "La panadería será siempre un artesanado," *Pan*, June 15, 1968.
24. "Aunque sigue la huelga de panaderos no faltará pan en la metrópoli," *El Pueblo*, Nov. 6, 1915.
25. The Red Battalions were disarmed in January 1916 (Hart, "The Urban Working Class and the Mexican Revolution").
26. Coronel Ing. Ignacio Enríquez to Cofiño y Zaracho, Mexico City, Nov. 1, 1915, AHCM, Ayuntamiento, Reguladora de Comercio, vol. 3853, exp. 14.
27. General César López de Lara to Coronel Ing. Ignacio Enríquez, Mexico City, Nov. 8, 1915, AHCM, Ayuntamiento, Reguladora de Comercio, vol. 3853, exp. 14; Coronel Ing. Ignacio Enríquez to "Casa del Obrero Mundial" Sindicato de Panaderos, Mexico City, Nov. 10, 1915, AHCM, Ayuntamiento, Reguladora de Comercio, vol. 3853, exp. 14; Coronel Ignacio C. Enríquez to "Casa del Obrero Mundial" Sindicato de Panaderos, Mexico City, Nov. 11, 1915, AHCM, Ayuntamiento, Reguladora de Comercio, vol. 3853, exp. 14; Luis Díaz to Ignacio Rodríguez, Presidente del Ayuntamiento, Mexico City, Nov. 12, 1915, AHCM, Ayuntamiento, Reguladora de Comercio, vol. 3853, exp. 14; Oficina de Contabilidad del Ayuntamiento to Ignacio Rodríguez, Presidente del Ayuntamiento, Mexico City, Nov. 13, 1915, AHCM, Ayuntamiento, Reguladora de Comercio: Diversos, vol. 3855, exp. 30.
28. "Relación de las cantidades de pan que recibieron los expendios números uno, dos, tres y cuatro correspondientes al Cuartel II," Oct. 3–22, 1915, Ayuntamiento Gobierno D.F., Reguladora de Comercio, Comisión Inspectores, vol. 3857, exp. 1.
29. Oficina de Contabilidad del Ayuntamiento to Ignacio Rodríguez, Presidente del Ayuntamiento, "Recibos por dinero entregado al sindicato," AHCM, Ayuntamiento, Reguladora de Comercio: Diversos, vol. 3855, exp. 30.
30. "De interés para los panaderos," *El Pueblo*, Nov. 8, 1915.
31. "Los patrones y los panaderos huelguistas ante el señor gobernador del distrito," *El Pueblo*, Nov. 7, 1915.
32. Huitrón, *Orígenes e historia del movimiento obrero en México*, 291.
33. "Los patrones y los panaderos huelguistas ante el señor gobernador del distrito," *El Pueblo*, Nov. 7, 1915; "Pronto tendremos pan barato en abundancia," *El Pueblo*, Nov. 8, 1915.
34. Silva Herzog, *El mexicano y su morada*, 48.
35. Carr, "Marxism and Anarchism in the Formation of the Mexican Communist Party"; Carr, *Marxism & Communism in Twentieth-Century Mexico*; Hart, "Nineteenth Century Urban Labor Precursors of the Mexican Revolution"; Hart, "The Urban Working Class and the Mexican Revolution"; Hernández, "Tiempos libertarios."
36. Lear, *Workers, Neighbors, and Citizens*, 326.
37. Casado Navarro, *Geraldo Murillo*, 34.
38. Quoted in Salazar and Escobedo, *Las pugnas de la gleba*, 205.
39. *Boletín del Archivo General de la Nación*, 3rd ser., 5, no. 1 (Jan.–Mar. 1981): 39–42, quoted in Lear, *Workers, Neighbors, and Citizens*, 290.

40. Niemeyer, *Revolution at Querétaro*; Blidstein, "Política y caudillismo en el congreso constituyente mexicano de 1917."
41. Estados Unidos Mexicanos, *Constitución política de los Estados Unidos Mexicanos*, "Artículo 123—Derecho al trabajo digno y socialmente útil."
42. Klarén, "Lost Promise"; Newton, "Natural Corporatism and the Passing of Populism in Spanish America."
43. Carr notes that bakers joined the Gran Cuerpo, but I have not found evidence of this (Carr, "Marxism and Anarchism in the Formation of the Mexican Communist Party"; Leal, *Agrupaciones y burocracias sindicales en México*, 85).
44. Quoted in Meyer, "Los obreros en la revolución mexicana."
45. This coincides with Gamboa Ojeda's findings: "Although at its highest levels of leadership, the CROM was a reformist organization, in its lower levels it was an organization that, due to a real internal autonomy and the need to confront employers, widely applied the tactics of revolutionary syndicalism, almost always at the urging of minor leaders at the state and local levels" (*La urdimbre y la trama*, 296–97).
46. Valadés, *Memorias de un joven rebelde*, 2:78; interviews with Alfonso Ortega Ríos, May 27, 2005, Mexico City, and Mario Anguiano Trejo, June 3, 2005, Mexico City.
47. Taibo, *Bolshevikis*, 63.
48. "San Vicente... was an anarchist from Guernica but he fraternized with the communists. He just didn't allow the communists to assume positions of leadership in the unions. To achieve his objectives he organized a very combative group with Speziale, Urmachea, Gómez, Pachoe, Rodolo Aguierre, and leaders from the streetcar and telephone workers" (Valadés, *Memorias de un joven rebelde*, 77).
49. "A group of ten or twelve Spanish anarchosyndicalists came from Cuba, fleeing from persecution by the government in Havana. Two or three were implicated in a terrorist attack against the authorities, and the president of Cuba. Of that group, José Rubio and Sebastián San Vicente stood out. The former was an enemy of compromise [*transaccionismo*] and he opened a deep abyss between unionism and the state, between communism and freedom. He always carried a Bakunninist catechism. He was an ascetic. He slept on the benches of the bakers' union" (Valadés, *Memorias de un joven rebelde*, 97–98; Taibo, *Bolshevikis*, 63).
50. Valadés, *Memorias de un joven rebelde*, 98; La Botz, "American 'Slackers' in the Mexican Revolution"; Carr, *Marxism & Communism in Twentieth-Century Mexico*, 25.
51. Taibo, *Bolshevikis*, 63; Valadés, *Memorias de un joven rebelde*, 78.
52. "Festival obrero," *El Pueblo*, Jan. 25, 1919; "Por la cultura obrera," *El Pueblo*, Jan. 31, 1919; "La semana obrera," *El Pueblo*, Feb. 15, 1919; "Sociabilidad obrera," *El Pueblo*, Mar. 7, 1919; "La primera escuela racionalista," *El Pueblo*, Mar. 15, 1919.
53. Carr, "Marxism and Anarchism in the Formation of the Mexican Communist Party"; Carr, "The Casa del Obrero Mundial."
54. Manuel Molas to President Manuel Avila Camacho, Progreso, Yucatán, Aug. 4, 1941, AGN, Presidentes, Manuel Ávila Camacho (henceforth cited as MAC), caja 596, exp. 523.1/51. Dozens of accusations of "false collectives" (*falsas cooperativas*) appear

between 1926 and 1939, mostly in Veracruz and Puebla. See AGN, Departamento del Trabajo, caja 974, exp. 4, fols. 35–36, and AGN, Presidentes, Lázaro Cárdenas del Río (henceforth cited as LCR), caja 383, exp. 432/476.

55. "Estudio sobre el encarecimiento de la vida en México, hecho por el señor Licenciado Eduardo Fuentes," Sept. 27, 1915, CONDUMEX, Fondo XXI, carpeta 53, legajo 5861, doc. 1–2.

56. "Los panaderos son ahora, los que quieren la huelga," *El Pueblo*, Feb. 18, 1919; Bortz, "The Revolution, the Labour Regime and Conditions of Work."

57. "El sr. presidente, árbitro de los obreros, resolverá sobre las peticiones de los molineros," *El Pueblo*, Mar. 2, 1919; "Hoy se reanudarán las labores en los molinos," *El Pueblo*, Mar. 3, 1919; "La industria harinera es en México un gran negocio," *El Pueblo*, Mar. 14, 1919; "Puede decirse que los conflictos obreros han quedado solucionados," *El Pueblo*, Mar. 16, 1919.

58. "Dentro de la más estricta justica y la más pura equidad, el gobierno resolverá el conflicto obrero," *El Pueblo*, Feb. 27, 1919; "¿Se declarará una huelga general?," *El Pueblo*, Feb. 25, 1919; "Los molineros insisten en sus deseos," *El Pueblo*, Feb. 19, 1919.

59. A sack equals forty-five kilograms of flour. "Encuéntranse exitados los tahoneros," *El Pueblo*, Mar. 17, 1919.

60. "Los panaderos son ahora, los que quieren la huelga," *El Pueblo*, Feb. 18, 1919.

61. "Sólo tres obreros emplearán los panaderos," *El Pueblo*, Apr. 1, 1919.

62. "Dificultades entre propietarios y trabajadores de amasijos," *El Pueblo*, Apr. 28, 1919.

63. *Boletín Mensual del Departamento del Trabajo*, "Fábricas de pan y bizcochos."

64. "Tumulto promovido por los obreros de una panadería," *El Pueblo*, Mar. 17, 1919.

65. "Los panaderos no han vuelto a las tahonas," *El Universal*, Jan. 19, 1922.

66. "El asunto de la panadería 'La Fama,'" *El Pueblo*, May 5, 1919.

67. Hall, *Álvaro Obregón*; Brachet-Marquez, *The Dynamics of Domination*; Clark, *La organización obrera en México*; Valadés, *Memorias de un joven rebelde*, 78.

68. Baeza Paz, "La Confederación General de Trabajo"; Hall, *Álvaro Obregón*; Meyer, *El conflicto social y los gobiernos del Maximato*, 126.

69. Manuel Ponce de León to Álvaro Obregón, Mexico City, Sept. 12, 1921, AGN Presidentes, O-C, caja 135, exp. 407-P-18.

70. "Los panaderos votaron la huelga general," *El Universal*, Sept. 13, 1921.

71. "Mayúsculo escándalo entre los panaderos y los esquiroles," *El Universal*, Sept. 16, 1921; "Fracasó la huelga de panaderos," *El Universal*, Sept. 17, 1921.

72. "Hay un escisión entre los líderes obreros," *El Universal*, June 2, 1922; Taibo, "Inquilinos del DF a colgar la rojinegra"; Carr, *Marxism & Communism in Twentieth-Century Mexico*, 29–30.

73. "Hoy estalla huelga de panaderos," *El Universal*, Jan. 17, 1922.

74. "La huelga de panaderos dio origen a sangrientos escándalos, ayer tarde," *El Universal*, Jan. 18, 1922.

75. "Los panaderos no han vuelto a las tahonas," *El Universal*, Jan. 19, 1922.

76. "Al fin pudieron tener un arreglo los panaderos huelguistas y los industriales," *El Universal*, Jan. 21, 1922.

77. "La huelga de tranviarios continúa pues no se logró llegar a un acuerdo," *El Universal*, June 18, 1922; José Rodríguez to Gobernador del Distrito Federal, Mexico City, Dec. 17, 1924, AGN, Presidentes, O-C, caja 135, exp. 407-P-18.
78. "La huelga de tranviarios continúa pues no se logró llegar a un acuerdo," *El Universal*, June 18, 1922; "El gobierno está resuelto a no permitir manifestaciones públicas de huelguistas," *El Universal*, June 19, 1922; "Terminó la huelga de tranviarios," *El Universal*, June 22, 1922.
79. Segundo Minondo, Angel Rosales, Arturo Leopoldo Romero, Agustín Orozco, Ruperto Luna, Antonio Armesto, Porfirio Barajas, Marcelino Yglesia, J. Hernández Rosas, Gabino Gutierrez, H. Ordóñez, Adolfo Fernández, Manuel Díaz, Michelena Hernández, Fernández y Calvin, Alfonso Ruiz, Juan Elizondo, Valentín Elizondo, Aurelio López, J. Romano, José Larrondo, Emilio Pérez, Manuel R. Martínez, Tiburcio Castillo, Simón Servión, Camilo Sánchez, Fermín Barberena, José Barberena y Hno., José Martínez, and José Rodríguez to Junta Central de Conciliación y Arbitraje Gobierno del Distrito, Mexico City, Sept. 12, 1924, AHCM, Ayuntamiento, Departamento Consultivo, Huelgas, exp. 2077.
80. Víctor Díaz, Manuel de la Torre, Miguel Segura, and Pablo Rivera to Álvaro Obregón, Mexico City, Sept. 13, 1924, AGN, Presidentes, O-C, caja 135, exp. 407-P-18; Martín Enriquez, Pablo Rivera, and Víctor Díaz to Dueños o Encargados de Bizcocherías del D.F. en General, Mexico City, Aug. 7, 1924, AGN, Presidentes, O-C, caja 135, exp. 407-P-18; Martín Enríquez, Pablo Rivera, Víctor Díaz, and Manuel de la Torre to Propietarios o Administradores de Bizcocherías del D.F., Mexico City, Aug. 26, 1924, AGN, Presidentes, O-C, caja 135, exp. 407-P-18.
81. "Licencias expendios pan bizcocho," 1922, AHCM, Ayuntamiento, Licencias, Panaderías, vol. 3210.
82. *Boletín Mensual del Departamento del Trabajo*, "Fábricas de pan y bizcochos"; Pedro Laguna to Alvaro Obregón, Mexico City, Jan. 23, 1923, AGN, Presidentes, O-C, caja 166, exp. 424-T-2.
83. "Una sociedad de los productores del pan," *Excélsior*, July 17, 1931. See Arcelus Iroz, *Presencia de navarra en México*.
84. Onofre Madrigal, D. Mondragón, J. Martínez, Norberto Castillo, Salvador E. Rosas, José E. Segura, and Agustín Orozco to Plutarco Elías Calles, Mexico City, May 8, 1926, AGN, Presidentes, O-C, caja 135, exp. 407-P-18.
85. Dorantes, "El trabajo en México."
86. AHSS, June 16, 1925, Fondo Salubridad Pública, Sección Servicios Jurídicos, caja 4, exp. 8.
87. The bakeries they recommended for closure were La Encantada at 108 Chapultepec Avenue; La Quemada, República del Salvador 75; La Vencedora Santísima; La Jalisciense, on the corner of Argentina and Ecuador streets; and La Flor de México, on the corner of Bolívar and Capuchinas streets (E. Alvarez and B. Parra to Secretaria General del Departamento de Salubridad Pública, Mexico City, Oct. 17, 1925, AHSS, Fondo Salubridad Pública, Sección Servicio Jurídico, caja 4, exp. 8).

88. Onofre Madrigal to Departamento de Salubridad Pública, Mexico City, Aug. 9, 1927, AHSS, Fondo Salubridad Pública, Sección Servicios Jurídicos, caja 4, exp. 8.
89. Clark, *La organización obrera en México*; Hall, *Álvaro Obregón*; Leal, *Agrupaciones y burocracias sindicales en México*.
90. Medin, *El minimato presidencial*, 26–30.
91. My gratitude to Ingrid Bleynart for insisting on this point.
92. Baeza Paz, "La confederación general de trabajo."
93. Salazar and Escobedo, *Las pugnas de la gleba*, 2:224.
94. Gamboa Ojeda, *La urdimbre y la trama*, 397.
95. "Lo que pasará si se reanuda la huelga de panaderos," *El Universal*, May 22, 1928.
96. "La escasez de pan fue ayer más grande," *El Universal*, May 17, 1928.
97. "Hombre muerto por un costal de pan," *El Universal*, May 19, 1928.
98. "Se suspendió la elaboración del pan en todo el Distrito Federal; Ayer fue votada la huelga," *El Universal*, May 14, 1928; "Tampoco hoy habrá pan; sigue la huelga," *El Universal*, May 15, 1928; "Entramos al tercer día de ayuno," *El Universal*, May 16, 1928; "La mitad de los panaderos de ciudad de Méjico se han declarado en huelga," *La Prensa*, May 17, 1928; "La escasez de pan fue ayer más grande," *El Universal*, May 17, 1928; "Armisticio en la huelga de pan," *El Universal*, May 18, 1928.

Chapter Seven

1. Arcelus Iroz, *Presencia de navarra en México*, 196–225.
2. Secretaría de la Economía Nacional, *Segundo censo industrial, 1935*, vol. 3, tomo 18. For a list of particular owners, see *Directorio de la Colonia Española 1937*. Arcelus Iroz, *Presencia de navarra en México*, 196–225.
3. These figures should be taken with reserve. In addition to faulty reporting and recording, they reflect the fact that practically all the Spanish-owned bakeries were located in cities, especially Mexico City, while the Mexican-owned ones were found in cities, towns, and villages. "Establecimientos, inversiones, existencias, valor de la producción, sueldos y salarios pagados al personal ocupado, número de directores, empleados y obreros y capacidad de equipo de fuerza motriz, por nacionalidad dominante según el monto del capital," in Secretaría de la Economía Nacional, *Segundo censo industrial, 1935*, 143, 345.
4. "Una sociedad de los productores del pan," *Excélsior*, July 17, 1931. See Arcelus Iroz, *Presencia de navarra en México*.
5. Sánchez Ruiz, "Planificación y urbanismo en la ciudad de México del siglo xx."
6. Interviews with Pascual Cortés Cruz, July 14, 2005, Mexico City, and Agustín Moreno, Aug. 3, 2005, Mexico City.
7. "Los vendedores de pan barato, perseguidos," *La Prensa*, Jan. 19, 1935.
8. Also spelled *tendajones* and known as *misceláneas* and *abarroterías*.

9. Kinsbruner, *The Colonial Spanish-American City*, 72–79; Kinsbruner, *Petty Capitalism in Spanish America*; Silva Riquer, "La organización de las tiendas pulperas en la ciudad de México."
10. José Espinosa de los Monteros to Lázaro Cárdenas, Mexico City, Sept. 23, 1937, AGN, Presidentes, LCR, caja 637, exp. 521/8.
11. "Hay repartidas innumerables habitaciones formadas de manera provisional y en pésimas condiciones de higiene [que] se caracterizan por el desaseo llevado a límites inconcebibles. El estado en que se encuentran los excusados es horrible" (Puga, "Higiene de la habitación").
12. Crecencio Pérez to Abelardo L. Rodríguez, Mexico City, May 12, 1933, AGN, Presidentes, Abelardo L. Rodríguez (henceforth cited as ALR), caja 202, exp. 561.8/5.
13. "Infracciones," 1919–1920, AHCM, Ayuntamiento, Infracciones, Sección Panaderías, vol. 2390. "Cantidad íntegramente devuelta a los Sres. Boades y Zugarramudi [sic] de una multa de $20.00 que depositó el día 30 de mayo de 1927." "Relación de multas," Mar. 10, 1929, AHSS, Fondo Salubridad Pública, Sección Servicios Jurídicos, caja 16, exp. 7–8.
14. Buchenau, *Plutarco Elías Calles and the Mexican Revolution*.
15. Córdova, *La revolución en crisis*; Medin, *El minimato presidencial*; Meyer, *El conflicto social y los gobiernos del Maximato*.
16. "Reglamento de la industrial del pan en el distrito federal," *Diario Oficial*, Jan. 15, 1929, 7–8.
17. "Decreto que modifica el reglamento de la industria del pan, en el distrito federal," *Diario Oficial*, May 27, 1931, 9–10.
18. *Boletín Mensual del Departamento del Trabajo*, "Fábricas de pan y bizcochos," Feb. 1922, 20–23. See description of living quarters above the Flor de México in Sendra de Servitje, *Vivir es luchar*, 51.
19. "Quieren el monopolio del pan los ricos extranjeros," *El Nacional*, May 3, 1930.
20. Branch and Row, "The Mexican Constitution of 1917."
21. "Ya se dio fin al monopolio de pan," *El Universal*, May 28, 1931.
22. "El precio del pan en México," *El Universal*, July 11, 1931.
23. "Para que el pueblo tenga pan barato, se pide la intervención del ejecutivo," *El Universal*, Aug. 1, 1931.
24. "Ya se dio fin al monopolio de pan," *El Universal*, May 28, 1931; "Decreto que modifica el reglamento de la industria del pan, en el distrito federal," *Diario Oficial*, May 27, 1931, 9–10.
25. "La suprema corte de justicia se declaró abierta y públicamente en favor del pan barato para el pueblo," *El Universal*, July 9, 1931; "Un reglamento absurdo que impedía al pueblo comprar el pan barato," *Excélsior*, July 9, 1931.
26. "El precio del pan en México," *El Universal*, July 11, 1931.
27. Flores Garza, "El desarrollo de la clase trabajadora en la industria de pan y pasteles en México en el periodo 1960–1975."

28. Owners proposed paying workers $1.00 for every $1.44 of bread; workers asked for $1.00 for every $1.20 of bread ("Pronta solución del conflicto del pan," *La Prensa*, Sept. 6, 1932).
29. "300 panaderías clausuradas el día de ayer," *La Prensa*, Sept. 3, 1932, 11.
30. "Buena parte de la ciudad se encuentra sin pan," *El Universal*, Sept. 3, 1932; "300 panaderías clausuradas el día de ayer," *La Prensa*, Sept. 3, 1932, 11; "Los panaderos están desde hoy en huelga," *El Universal*, Sept. 2, 1932; "Fracasaron las juntas realizadas," *El Gráfico*, Sept. 2, 1932; "Incidentes desagradables en la huelga de panaderos," *La Prensa*, Sept. 4, 1932; "La huelga en las tahonas," *El Universal*, Sept. 6, 1932, 9.
31. "Se solucionó ayer la huelga de panaderos," *El Gráfico*, Sept. 7, 1932, 3, 12; "La huelga de panaderos," *El Universal*, Sept. 7, 1932.
32. "La decisión sobre el pan," *El Universal*, Sept. 23, 1932; "Se ahonda el conflicto de los panaderos por el laudo que se dictó," *Excélsior*, Sept. 23, 1932; "Texto del laudo pronunciado en el conflicto de la industria del pan entre obreros y patronos," *El Nacional*, Sept. 22, 24, 25, 1932; "Intentan desconocer la sentencia. Los dueños de tahonas tratan de violar el laudo que dictó el general Cabral," *El Nacional*, Sept. 22, 1932.
33. "El pan y su reglamento," *El Nacional*, Sept. 21, 1932.
34. Gabriel Pacheco, José Baltazar, and Víctor Díaz to Abelardo L. Rodríguez, Mexico City, Sept. 22, 1932, AGN, Presidentes, ALR, caja 202, exp. 561.8/5; Marcelino Feria to Abelardo L. Rodríguez, Mexico City, Nov. 21, 1932, AGN, Presidentes, ALR, caja 202, exp. 561.8/5; Sebastián Moreno to Abelardo L. Rodríguez, Mexico City, Nov. 21, 1932, AGN, Presidentes, ALR, caja 202, exp. 561.8/5.
35. The Spanish bakery owner Mariano Redorta wrote on behalf of his colleagues, "We sell our bread exclusively in our own retail outlets [expendios]. Naturally, then, if we don't sell bread through stores and other sites where bread is sold, this bread must come from the Clandestine Bakeries" (Mariano Redorta to Secretaría de Salubridad, Mexico City, Nov. 5, 1937, AHSS, Fondo Salubridad Pública, Sección Servicios Jurídicos, caja 4, exp. 8).
36. José T. Orrico to Abelardo L. Rodríguez, Mexico City, Jan. 30, 1933, AGN, Presidentes, ALR, caja 202, exp. 561.8/5.
37. José T. Orrico and Ramón L. Sánchez to Abelardo L. Rodríguez, Mexico City, June 2, 1933, AGN, Presidentes, ALR, caja 202, exp. 561.8/5.
38. Ruperto Luna and Víctor Díaz to Abelardo L. Rodríguez, Mexico City, Sept. 27, 1932, AGN, Presidentes, ALR, caja 202, exp. 561.8/5.
39. "Siguen cerrando las panaderías," *Excélsior*, June 19, 1933; "Hay menos pan para la venta en la capital. Los tahoneros no han podido resistir los altos salarios y están cerrando," *Excélsior*, June 17, 1933.
40. "No existe problema en la industria del pan," *El Nacional*, June 20, 1933.
41. "El problema de la industria del pan," *El Nacional*, Sept. 18, 1933.
42. "Acuerdo por el cual se fija el precio y el peso del pan en el distrito federal," *Diario Oficial*, Oct. 13, 1933, 444–45; "Dos piezas por 5 ctvs.," *El Universal*, Oct. 14, 1933.
43. Aarón Sáenz to Sebastián Moreno, Mexico City, Oct. 30, 1933, AGN, Presidentes, ALG, caja 202, exp. 561.8/5.

44. Sebastián Moreno and Alfredo Torices to Abelardo L. Rodríguez, Mexico City, Oct. 20, 1933, AGN, Presidentes, ALR, caja 202, exp. 561.8/5.
45. "La pequeña industria está siendo destrozada por las cantidades de pan que diariamente se les decomisa no sólo a ellos sino también a los expendedores, con el pretexto de fabricar pan de tres por cinco centavos" (Sebastián Moreno to Lázaro Cárdenas, Mexico City, Jan. 14, 1935, AGN, Presidentes, LCR, caja 637, exp. 521/8). "Los locatarios en el ramo del pan, del mercado Alvaro Obregon están siendo perjudicados por la decomización que lleva a cabo la Comisión Reguladora del Ramo de Panaderías" (Isabel Bustamante to Lázaro Cárdenas, Mexico City, Jan. 21, 1935, AGN, Presidentes, LCR, caja 637, exp. 521/8).
46. Salvador Bejerano to Lázaro Cárdenas, Mexico City, Jan. 14, 1935, AGN, Presidentes, LCR, caja 637, exp. 521/8.
47. "Acuerdo por el cual se fija el precio y el peso del pan en el distrito federal," *Diario Oficial*, Oct. 13, 1933, 444–45.
48. Octavio B. Barona to Florentina García, Mexico City, Nov. 23, 1933, AGN, Presidentes, ALR, caja 202, exp. 561.8/5, emphasis added.
49. "Se está defraudando al pueblo con el pan," *El Nacional*, Oct. 12, 1932; "Inexactitudes sobre la cuestión del pan," *Excélsior*, Oct. 14, 1932; Salvador Pérez to Lázaro Cárdenas, Mexico City, Feb. 11, 1939, AGN, Presidentes, LCR, caja 637, exp. 521/8.
50. The Comité de Acción de Consumidores contra la Vida Cara, formed by several unions, designated Arturo Aramburu, who had served on the executive committee of the Sindicato de Obreros, Panaderos Bizcocheros y Reposteros del D.F., to represent consumers (Santiago Calzadilla to Jefe del Departamento Central, Mexico City, Apr. 13, 1936, AGN, Presidentes, LCR, caja 637, exp. 521/8).
51. "Se defrauda al público con el pan," *El Nacional*, Oct. 11, 1932.
52. "Poliedro: Pan y monopolios," *La Prensa*, Oct. 24, 1932.
53. "Pan al alcance de todos," *Fantoche*, May 10, 1929.
54. Quoted in Semo, "El cardenismo revisado."
55. Quoted in Ochoa, *Feeding Mexico*, 41.
56. Klarén, "Lost Promise." See critiques of the corporatist interpretation of Cardenismo in Knight, "Cardenismo"; Rubin, "Popular Mobilization and the Myth of State Corporatism."
57. Aziz Nassif, *El estado mexicano y la CTM*; Córdova, *La política de masas del cardenismo*; Anguiano, *El estado y la política obrera del cardenismo*; Knight, "Cardenismo."
58. Jesús Morelos to Lázaro Cárdenas, Mexico City, Nov. 13, 1935, AGN, Presidentes, LCR, caja 637, exp. 521/8.
59. "Dan su apoyo al nuevo comité de panaderos," *El Nacional*, Nov. 10, 1935; "Unificación de panaderos. A pesar de las maniobras del conocido ratero trotzkista Genaro Gómez," *El Machete*, Dec. 19, 1936.
60. "División de un sindicato," *El Nacional*, Nov. 15, 1935; "Los panaderos divididos en dos sindicatos," *El Día*, Dec. 17, 1935; "Emplazamiento de huelga a 2 panaderías," *El Día*, Dec. 22, 1935. Interviews with Alfonso Ortega Ríos, May 27, 2005, Mexico City, and Mario Anguiano Trejo, June 3, 2005, Mexico City.

61. "El monopolio del pan trata de provocar serio conflicto mediante una falsa huelga," *La Prensa*, Apr. 14, 1936.
62. "Podrán trabajar los que no se hallen en huelga," *El Universal*, Apr. 18, 1936.
63. "Los pasteleros asediados ayer por huelguistas," *La Prensa*, Apr. 18, 1936; "Caso de sabotaje en una panadería de la capital," *El Nacional*, Apr. 18, 1936; "Incidentes por la huelga del pan," *El Gráfico*, Apr. 18, 1936.
64. "La huelga de los pambazos. Y que viva el pan inglés," *El Nacional*, Apr. 17, 1936.
65. "El conflicto del pan," *El Nacional*, Apr. 13, 1936.
66. "Faltará el pan por tiempo indefinido," *La Prensa*, Apr. 18, 1936.
67. "Peligro de que además de pan falte la leche," *El Gráfico*, Apr. 17, 1936.
68. "Reglamento de la industria del pan," *Diario Oficial*, June 6, 1936, 26–30; Adolfo Ruiz Cortines to Secretario Particular del Presidente de la República, Mexico City, July 20, 1936, AGN, Presidentes, LCR, caja 637, exp. 521/8.
69. José T. Orrico to Secretario del Presidente de la República, Mexico City, Aug. 4, 1936, AGN, Presidentes, LCR, caja 637, exp. 521/8.
70. María Nieves Gómez Viudad de Rivera to Oficina de Licencias e Inspección Jefe del Departamento Central, Mexico City, Apr. 8, 1936, AGN, Presidentes, LCR, caja 355, exp. 415.2/21.
71. Luis G. García to José T. Orrico and Ramón L. Sánchez, Mexico City, Sept. 18, 1937, AGN, Presidentes, LCR, caja 637, exp. 521/8.
72. "Unificación de tahoneros," *El Nacional*, July 5, 1937.
73. "Un zafarrancho de los obreros de las tahonas," *Excélsior*, Dec. 9, 1937.
74. "Unificación en el gremio de panaderos," *El Nacional*, Dec. 30, 1937.
75. "Se logró la fusión de los panaderos," *El Nacional*, Jan. 21, 1938.
76. "Sangre por la huelga del pan. Un muerto y un herido en una tahona," *El Gráfico*, Jan. 4, 1938.
77. "Continuaron los asaltos a las panaderías, pero esta vez sin que hubiera sangre," *Excélsior*, Jan. 6, 1938.
78. "Cómo acabó la huelga del ramo de panadería," *El Universal*, Jan. 8, 1938.
79. "A qué pesos y precio se venderá pan. Con fecha de ayer entró en vigor el nuevo reglamento para el distrito federal," *El Nacional*, Jan. 20, 1938.
80. "Nuevo amparo de propietarios de panaderías," *El Universal*, Feb. 3, 1938.
81. "Nueva batida a los canasteros. Los expendedores de pan en pequeño fueron detenidos en el mercado," *Excélsior*, Feb. 22, 1938.
82. Sebastián Moreno to Lázaro Cárdenas, Mexico City, Mar. 9, 1938, AGN, Presidentes, LCR, caja 637, exp. 521/8.
83. "Más panaderías se clausuraron ayer," *El Universal*, Apr. 7, 1938; "Diez panaderías más fueron cerradas sólo por vender panes de un peso," *Excélsior*, Apr. 12, 1938; "Cierre en masa de panaderías por vender pan más barato," *Excélsior*, Apr. 15, 1938.
84. "Otro escándalo al ser cerrada ayer una tahona. El propietario de ella, señor Francisco B. Salido, fué golpeado," *Excélsior*, Apr. 21, 1938; "Telescopios para comprar bolillos. Son de tan reducidas proporciones, que no se ven a la simple vista," *Excélsior*, Mar. 24, 1938.

85. "Situación de la industria de panaderos. La abierta actitud de rebeldía asumida por un grupo, la ha perjudicado," *El Nacional*, Mar. 5, 1938.
86. AGN, Presidentes, LCR, caja 637, exp. 521/8; "Trágica muerte de un industrial," *El Nacional*, Aug. 6, 1938; "Industrial asesinado ayer por un líder obrero," *Excélsior*, Aug. 6, 1938.
87. "Trágica muerte de un industrial," *El Nacional*, Aug. 6, 1938; "Manifiesto a la clase productora, a la opinión pública en general," *El Nacional*, Aug. 6, 1938.
88. "Industrial asesinado ayer por un líder obrero," *Excélsior*, Aug. 6, 1938.
89. "Agravantes en el asesinato de conciliación," *Excélsior*, Aug. 7, 1939.
90. "El líder de las tahonas, L. González Uzcaga, es careado con testigos de su crimen," *Excélsior*, Sept. 3, 1938; "Una afrenta a la sociedad," *El Universal*, Jan. 3, 1939.
91. Víctor Díaz to Lázaro Cárdenas, Mexico City, Feb. 24, 1938, AGN, Presidentes, LCR, caja 638, exp. 521/8.
92. Sherman, "Reassessing Cardenismo"; Becker, *Setting the Virgin on Fire*; Dwyer, *The Agrarian Dispute*, 182–88.
93. Gojman de Backal, *Camisas, escudos y desfiles militares*.
94. Hernández García de León, *Historia política del sinarquismo*, 106–20, 181.
95. "Los vendedores de pan barato, perseguidos," *La Prensa*, Jan. 19, 1935.
96. "Se acabaron los 'bolillos' de a dos por cinco," *El Universal*, Jan. 3, 1939; "El pan creció y bajó de peso," *El Universal*, Jan. 3, 1939; "Las panaderías defraudan al consumidor. El pan no tiene el peso que fija el reglamento," *El Nacional*, Jan. 5, 1939.
97. "Festín de mistificadores," *La Prensa*, Jan. 11, 1939.
98. Dr. Jesús Díaz Barriga to Lázaro Cárdenas, Mexico City, Jan. 16, 1939, AGN, Presidentes, LCR, caja 637, exp. 521/8.
99. "Darán garantías a los tahoneros y expendedores," *Excélsior*, Jan. 5, 1939.
100. "Al pueblo de la capital," *El Nacional*, Jan. 5, 1939; "Piden dimitan funcionarios del distrito," *Excélsior*, Jan. 6, 1939.
101. Feliciano Gutiérrez and Vicente Reyes to Lázaro Cárdenas, Mexico City, Jan. 9, 1939, AGN, Presidentes, LCR, caja 637, exp. 521/8; Jesús J. Morales to Lázaro Cárdenas, Mexico City, Jan. 5, 1939, AGN, Presidentes, LCR, caja 637, exp. 521/8; "Considera el gobierno que la reventa del pan es una actividad fuera de la ley," *Excélsior*, Jan. 9, 1939.
102. "La situación es cada vez peor y temen choques," *Excélsior*, Jan. 13, 1939.
103. "Treinta mil piezas de pan fueron decomisadas ayer en tahonas y pequeñas tiendas," *Excélsior*, Jan. 12, 1939; "Más disturbios entre panaderos. Veinte pequeñas tahonas fueron clausuradas ayer por medio de la fuerza," *Excélsior*, Jan. 21, 1939; "Asaltos a las panaderías," *El Universal*, Jan. 21, 1939.
104. "Más disturbios entre panaderos," *Excélsior*, Jan. 21, 1939.
105. "Más quejas de los pequeños panaderos," *Excélsior*, Feb. 19, 1939.
106. "Mediará en la huelga de los panaderos el abogado Villalobos," *El Nacional*, Mar. 31, 1939.
107. "Al incendio y al secuestro recurren los panaderos que se pusieron en huelga," *Excélsior*, Mar. 31, 1939.

108. "Esta madrugada terminó la huelga del pan," *Excélsior*, Apr. 9, 1939.
109. Ibid.
110. "Absurda proposición de los tahoneros ricos. Querían obtener prerrogativas absolutamente ilegales, para consolidar el monopolio," *El Universal*, Mar. 30, 1939.
111. "Carta abierta al ciudadano presidente de la república general de división Lázaro Cárdenas," *El Nacional*, Mar. 31, 1939.
112. "Grave acusación en contra de los grandes tahoneros," *El Nacional*, Sept. 22, 1945; "Más de 100,000 bultos de harina que se fugan," *El Universal*, Oct. 28, 1951; "Descaradamente los tahoneros se enriquecen con la harina," *La Prensa*, Nov. 6, 1951.

Bibliography

Archives

Archivo General de la Nación (AGN)
Archivo General de Notarías del Distrito Federal (AGNDF)
Archivo Histórico Banamex
Archivo Histórico de la Ciudad de México (AHCM)
Archivo Histórico de la Secretaría de Salubridad (AHSS)
Biblioteca Miguel Lerdo de Tejada
Centro de Estudios de Historia de México (CONDUMEX)
Fideicomiso Archivos Plutarco Elías Calles y Fernando Torreblanca
Fototeca de la Coordinación Nacional de Monumentos Históricos, Instituto Nacional de Antropología e Historia (CNMN)
Fototeca Nacional del Instituto Nacional de Antropología e Historia (INAH)
Hemeroteca Nacional

Newspapers

Acción Mundial
Boletín Republicano
Diario del Hogar
Diario Oficial
El Chisme
El Combate

El Correo Español
El Demócrata
El Día
El Gráfico
El Hijo del Ahuizote
El Imparcial
El Machete
El Monitor
El Monitor Republicano
El Municipio Libre
El Nacional
El Popular
El Pueblo
El Radical
El Tiempo
El Universal
Excélsior
La Iberia
La Patria
La Prensa
La Sociedad
La Voz de México
Le Courrier du Mexique
Le Trait d'Union
Mexican Herald
Siglo Diez y Nueve

Printed Materials

Agostoni, Claudia. "Discurso médico, cultura higiénica y la mujer en la ciudad de México al cambio de siglo (XIX–XX)." *Mexican Studies/Estudios Mexicanos* 18, no. 1 (2002): 1–22.

Aguirre, Carlos. *The Criminals of Lima and Their Worlds: The Prison Experience, 1850–1935*. Durham, NC, and London: Duke University Press, 2005.

———. "Violencia y control social: Esclavos y panaderías en Lima, siglo XIX." *Pasado y Presente* 1, no. 1 (1988): 27–37.

Alcázar, Ricardo de. *El gachupín, problema máximo de México*. Mexico City: Private edition, 1934.

Alday Garay, Alberto. "La comunidad baztanesa en la ciudad de México en los siglos XIX y XX." In *Los vascos en las regiones de México siglos XVI a XX*, vol. 2, edited by Amaya Garritz, 87–102. 6 vols. Mexico City: Universidad Nacional Autónoma de México, Ministerio de Cultura del Gobierno Vasco, Instituto Vasco-Mexicano de Desarrollo, 1996.

―――. "Presencia baztanesa en las regiones de México, siglos XIX y XX." In *Los vascos en las regiones de México siglos XVI a XX*, vol. 1, edited by Amaya Garritz, 65–84. 6 vols. Mexico City: Universidad Nacional Autónoma de México, Ministerio de Cultura del Gobierno Vasco, Instituto Vasco-Mexicano de Desarrollo, 1996.

Aldrich, Howard, and Roger D. Waldinger. "Ethnicity and Entrepreneurship." *Annual Review of Sociology* 16 (1990): 11–35.

Anderson, Rodney. *Outcasts in Their Own Land: Mexican Industrial Workers, 1906–1911*. DeKalb: Northern Illinois University Press, 1976.

Anguiano, Arturo. *El estado y la política obrera del cardenismo*. Mexico City: Ediciones Era, 1975.

Anna, Timothy E. *The Fall of the Royal Government in Mexico City*. Lincoln and London: University of Nebraska Press, 1978.

Arcelus Iroz, Pilar. *Presencia de Navarra en México, 1870–1950*. Pamplona: Gobierno de Navarra, Departamento de Presidencia, Justicia e Interior, 2001.

Arrillaga, Basilio José, ed. *Recopilación de leyes, decretos y circulares de los supremos poderes de los Estados-Unidos Mexicanos. Enero a diciembre 1828*. Mexico City: Imprenta de J. M. Fernández de Lara, 1838.

―――. *Recopilación de leyes, decretos y circulares de los supremos poderes de los Estados-Unidos Mexicanos. Enero a diciembre 1829*. Mexico City: Imprenta de J. M. Fernández de Lara, 1838.

―――. *Recopilación de leyes, decretos y circulares de los supremos poderes de los Estados-Unidos Mexicanos. Enero a diciembre 1834*. Mexico City: Imprenta de J. M. Fernández de Lara, 1835.

―――. *Recopilación de leyes, decretos y circulares de los supremos poderes de los Estados-Unidos Mexicanos. 1837*. Mexico City: Imprenta de J. M. Fernández de Lara, 1839.

Arriola Ortiz, Alejandro. *Recordando otros tiempos*. Mexico City: Private edition, 1944.

Arrom, Silvia M. "Popular Politics in Mexico City: The Parián Riot, 1828." *Hispanic American Historical Review* 68, no. 2 (1988): 245–68.

―――. *The Women of Mexico City, 1790–1857*. Stanford, CA: Stanford University Press, 1985.

Artís E., Gloria. "La organización del trabajo en los molinos de trigo (siglo XVIII)." In *Trabajo y sociedad en la historia de México. Siglos XVI–XVIII*, edited by Gloria Artís E., Brígida Von Mentz, Luz María Mohar Betancourt, Clara Elena Suárez A., and Beatriz Scharrer Tamm, 182–201. Mexico City: CIESAS, 1992.

―――. *Regatones y maquileros. El mercado de trigo en la ciudad de México (siglo XVIII)*. Mexico City: CIESAS, 1986.

Auslander, Leora. *Taste and Power: Furnishing Modern France*. Berkeley: University of California Press, 1996.

Auster, Ellen, and Howard Aldrich. "Small Business Vulnerability, Ethnic Enclaves and Ethnic Enterprise." In *Ethnic Communities in Business: Strategies for Economic Survival*, edited by Robin Ward and Richard Jenkins, 39–54. Cambridge and New York: Cambridge University Press, 1984.

Azcona Pastor, José Manuel. *Possible Paradises: Basque Emigration to Latin America*. Reno: University of Nevada Press, 2004.

Aziz Nassif, Alberto. *El estado mexicano y la CTM*. Mexico City: CIESAS, 1989.
Baeza Paz, Guillermina. "La confederación general de trabajo (1921–1931)." *Revista Mexicana de Ciencias Políticas y Sociales* 83 (1976): 113–86.
Banco de México. *La estructura industrial de México en 1950*. Mexico City: Banco de México, S.A., 1950.
———. *La estructura industrial de México en 1960*. Mexico City: Banco de México, S.A., 1967.
Barker, Nancy Nichols. "The French Colony in Mexico, 1821–61: Generator of Intervention." *French Historical Studies* 9, no. 4 (1976): 596–618.
Barrio Lorenzot, Francisco del. "Autos de panaderos de 1761: Sobre que se permita dar excesiva ganancia en las puertas de panaderías." In *El control de precios en la Nueva España. Documentos para su estudio recopilados por Luis Chávez Orozco*, edited by Luis Chávez Orozco. Mexico City: Banco Nacional de Crédito Agrícola y Ganadero, S.A., 1953.
———. *El trabajo en México durante la época colonial. Ordenanzas de gremios en la Nueva España*. Mexico City: Dirección de Talleres Gráficos, 1921.
Barros, Cristina, and Marco Buenrostro. *Panaderías de Tlaxcala, ayer y hoy*. Tlaxcala: Gobierno del Estado de Tlaxcala, 2004.
———, and Mónica del Villar. *El santo olor de la panadería*. Mexico City: Procuraduría Federal del Consumidor, Fernández Cueto Editores, 1992.
Basurto, Jorge. *La clase obrera en la historia de México: Del avilacamachismo al alemanismo*, edited by Pablo González Casanova. Mexico City: Siglo XXI, 1984.
Bauer, Arnold J. *Goods, Power, History: Latin America's Material Culture*. Cambridge and New York: Cambridge University Press, 2001.
———. "La cultura material." In *Para una historia de América*. Vol. 1, *Las estructuras*, edited by Marcello Carmagnani, 404–97. 2 vols. Mexico City: Fondo de Cultura Económica/Colegio de México, 1999.
———. "Millers and Grinders: Technology and Household Economy in Meso-America." *Agricultural History* 64, no. 1 (1990): 1–17.
———. *Treaders and Flailers. Mediterranean Culture in New World Conditions: Elements in the Transferral of Wheat to the Indies*. Working Papers of the Agricultural History Center 44. Davis: University of California–Davis, 1987.
Baz, Gobernador el Sr. D. Juan J. "Panaderías y tocinerías. Bando de 27 de noviembre de 1867." In *Colección de bandos, disposiciones de policía y reglamentos municipales de administración del Distrito Federal*, edited by José M. del Castillo Velasco, 24–27. Mexico City: Imprenta de la V. G. Torres, á cargo de M. Escudero, 1869.
Bazant, Jan. "The Basques in the History of Mexico." *Journal of European Economic History* 12, no. 1 (1983): 5–27.
Becker, Marjorie. *Setting the Virgin on Fire: Lázaro Cárdenas, Michoacán Peasants, and the Redemption of the Mexican Revolution*. Berkeley: University of California Press, 1995.
Benson, Nettie Lee. *The Provincial Deputation in the Harbinger of Political Autonomy, Independence, and Federalism*. Austin: University of Texas Press, 1992.

Bergquist, Charles. *Labor in Latin America: Comparative Essays on Chile, Argentina, Venezuela, and Colombia.* Stanford, CA: Stanford University Press, 1986.
Beriain, Josetxo. *La identidad colectiva: Vascos y navarros.* Alegia, Spain: Consejo Social de la Universidad Pública de Navarra, Ediciones Oria S. L. Haranburu Editor, 1998.
Bernecker, Walther L. *De agiotistas y empresarios. En torno a la temprana industrialización mexicana (siglo XIX).* Translated by Perla Chinchilla Pawling. Mexico City: Universidad Iberoamericana, 1992.
Bewig, Matthew S. "*Lochner v. The Journeymen Bakers of New York*: The Journeymen Bakers, Their Hours of Labor, and the Constitution; A Case Study in the Social History of Legal Thought." *American Journal of Legal History* 38, no. 4 (1994): 413–51.
Blidstein, Marcelo. "Política y caudillismo en el congreso constituyente mexicano de 1917." *Mexican Studies/Estudios Mexicanos* 16, no. 1 (2000): 39–78.
Blum, Ann S. "Conspicuous Benevolence: Liberalism, Public Welfare, and Private Charity in Porfirian Mexico City, 1877–1910." *Americas* 58, no. 1 (2001): 7–38.
Böker, Luise. "Keeping House in Revolutionary Mexico City." In *Mexico Otherwise: Modern Mexico in the Eyes of Foreign Observers*, edited by Jürgen Buchenau, 165–70. Albuquerque: University of New Mexico Press, 2005.
Boletín Mensual del Departamento del Trabajo. "Fábricas de pan y bizcochos." February 1922: 20–23.
Bonacich, Edna. "Theory of Middlemen Minorities." *American Sociological Review* 38, no. 5 (1973): 583–94.
———, and John Modell. *The Economic Basis of Ethnic Solidarity: Small Business in the Japanese American Community.* Berkeley: University of California Press, 1980.
Booker, Jackie R. *Veracruz Merchants, 1770–1829: A Mercantile Elite in Late Bourbon and Early Independent Mexico.* Boulder, CO: Westview Press, 1993.
Bortz, Jeffrey. "The Genesis of the Mexican Labor Relations System: Federal Labor Policy and the Textile Industry, 1925–1940." *Americas* 52, no. 1 (1995): 43–69.
———. "The Revolution, the Labour Regime and Conditions of Work in the Cotton Textile Industry in Mexico, 1910–1927." *Journal of Latin American Studies* 32, no. 3 (2000): 671–703.
———. *Revolution Within the Revolution: Cotton Textile Workers and the Mexican Labor Regime.* Stanford, CA: Stanford University Press, 2008.
Brachet-Marquez, Viviane. *The Dynamics of Domination: State, Class, and Social Reform in Mexico, 1910–1990.* Pittsburgh, PA: University of Pittsburgh Press, 1994.
Bracho, Julio. *De los gremios al sindicalismo: Genealogía corporativa.* Mexico City: Instituto de Investigaciones Sociales, Universidad Nacional Autónoma de México, 1990.
Brading, D. A. *Miners and Merchants in Bourbon Mexico, 1763–1810.* Cambridge: Cambridge University Press, 1971.
Branch, H. N., and L. S. Row. "The Mexican Constitution of 1917 Compared to the Constitution of 1857." *Annals of the American Academy of Political and Social Science* 71, supplement (1917): i–v, 1–116.
Brandes, Stanley H. "On Basque Migration." *American Anthropologist* 75 (1973): 299–302.

Braudel, Fernand. *The Structures of Everyday Life: Civilization and Capitalism, 15th–18th Century.* New York: Harper & Row, 1981.
Bringas, Guillermina, and David Mascareño. *Esbozo histórico del la prensa obrera en México.* Mexico City: Universidad Nacional Autónoma de México, 1988.
Buchenau, Jürgen. *The Last Caudillo: Alvaro Obregón and the Mexican Revolution.* Malden, MA: Wiley-Blackwell, 2011.
———, ed. *Mexico Otherwise: Modern Mexico in the Eyes of Foreign Observers.* Albuquerque: University of New Mexico Press, 2005.
———. *Plutarco Elías Calles and the Mexican Revolution.* Lanham, MD: Rowman & Littlefield, 2007.
———. *Tools of Progress: A German Merchant Family in Mexico City, 1865–Present.* Albuquerque: University of New Mexico Press, 2004.
Buffington, Robert M., and William E. French. "The Culture of Modernity." In *The Oxford History of Mexico*, edited by Michael Meyer and Willam H. Beezley, 373–405. Oxford, MA: Oxford University Press, 2000.
Bulmer-Thomas, Victor. *The Economic History of Latin America Since Independence.* Cambridge: Cambridge University Press, 1994.
Bunker, Steven B. "Transatlantic Retailing: The Franco-Business Model of Fin-de-siècle Department Stores in Mexico City." *Journal of Historical Research in Marketing* 2, no. 1 (2010): 41–60.
Bustamante, Carlos María de. *Apuntes para la historia del gobierno del general D. Antonio López de Santa-Anna, desde principios de octubre de 1841 hasta 6 de diciembre de 1844, en que fué depuesto del mando por uniforme voluntad de la nación.* Mexico City: J. M. Lara, 1845.
Busto, Emiliano. *Estadística de la república mexicana. Estado que guardan la agricultura, industria, minería y comercio. Resúmen y análisis de los informes rendidos á la secretaría de hacienda por los agricultores, mineros, industriales y comerciantes de la república y los agentes de México en el exterior, en respuesta á las circulares de 10. de agosto de 1877*, vol. 1. 3 vols. Mexico City: Impr. de I. Cumplido, 1880.
Calderón, Francisco. *La república restaurada. La vida económica.* Historia Moderna de México, edited by Daniel Cosío Villegas. Mexico City: Editorial Hermes, 1965.
Calderón de la Barca, Fanny. *Life in Mexico.* Berkeley and Los Angeles: University of California Press, 1982.
Camarena Ocampo, Mario. *Jornaleros, tejedores y obreros. Historia social de los trabajadores de San Angel (1850–1930).* Mexico City: Plaza y Valdés, 2001.
Camelo, Rosa. "La importancia de la comida como identificación de un pueblo." In *Herencia española en la cultura material de las regiones de México*, edited by Rafael Diego Fernández, 518–40. Zamora, Mexico: El Colegio de Michoacán, 1993.
Campos Salas, Octaviano. "La intervención del estado en el mercado del trigo y la harina." BA thesis, Economía, Universidad Nacional Autónoma de México, 1944.
Cárcer y Disidier, Mariano de. *¿Qué cosa es gachupín?* Mexico City: Librería de Manuel Porrúa, S.A., 1949.
Cardona, Adalberto. *México y sus capitales.* Paris: Tip. de J. Aguilar Vera, 1904.
Cardoso, Ciro. "Características fundamentales del período 1821–1880." In *México en el siglo XIX (1812–1910). Histórica económica y de la estructura social*, edited by Ciro Cardoso, 41–64. Mexico City: Nueva Imagen, 1980.

———, ed. *México en el siglo XIX (1812-1910). Histórica económica y de la estructura social*. Mexico City: Nueva Imagen, 1980.
Carmagnani, Marcello. *Estado y mercado: La economia pública del liberalismo mexicano, 1850-1911*. Mexico City: El Colegio de México, Fondo de Cultura Económica, 1994.
Carr, Barry. "The Casa del Obrero Mundial, Constitutionalism and the Pact of February 1915." In *El trabajo y los trabajadores en la historia de México*, edited by Elsa Cecilia Frost, Michael Meyer, and Josefina Zoraida Vázquez, 603-32. Mexico City and Tucson: El Colegio de México, University of Arizona Press, 1979.
———. "Marxism and Anarchism in the Formation of the Mexican Communist Party, 1910-1919." *Hispanic American Historical Review* 63, no. 2 (1983): 277-305.
———. *Marxism & Communism in Twentieth-Century Mexico*. Lincoln: University of Nebraska Press, 1992.
Carrera Stampa, Manuel. *Gremios mexicanos. La organización gremial en la Nueva España, 1521-1861*. Mexico City: Cámara Nacional de las Industrias de Transformación, Ibero-Americana de Publicaciones, S.A., 1954.
Carrillo, Ana María. "Economía, política y salud pública en el México porfiriano (1876-1910)." *História, Ciências, Saúde—Manguinhos* 9 (2002): 67-87.
Carson, W. E. *Mexico: The Wonderland of the South*. New York: Macmillian, 1914.
Casado Navarro, Arturo. *Geraldo Murillo. El Dr. Atl*. Mexico City: Universidad Nacional Autónoma de México, 1984.
Castilleja, Aida. "Asignación del espacio urbano: El gremio de los panaderos, 1770-1793." In *ciudad de México: Ensayo de construcción de una historia*, edited by Alejandra Moreno Toscano, 37-46. Mexico City: Instituto Nacional de Antropología e Historia, 1978.
Castillejos Ortiz, Armando. "Los sindicatos obreros en Mexico." BA thesis, Escuela de Jurisprudencia, Universidad Nacional Autónoma de México, 1946.
Castillo Velasco, Jose M. del, ed. *Colección de bandos, disposiciones de policía y reglamentos municipales de administración del Distrito Federal*. Mexico City: Imprenta de la V. G. Torres, á cargo de M. Escudero, 1869.
———. *Coleccion de leyes, supremas órdenes, bandos, disposiciones de policia y reglamentos municipales de administracion del Distrito Federal*, Mexico City: Castillo Velasco e Hijos, 1874.
Castro Gutiérrez, Felipe. *La extinción de la artesanía gremial*. Mexico City: Universidad Nacional Autónoma de México, 1986.
Centro de Estudios Históricos del Movimiento Obrero Mexicano. *La mujer y el movimiento obrero mexicano en el siglo XIX. Antología de la prensa obrera*. Mexico City: Centro de Estudios Históricos del Movimiento Obrero Mexicano, 1975.
Cerutti, Mario. "Empresarios de origen vasco en el norte de México: Entre Monterrey y el Bravo (1850-1915)." In *Los vascos en las regiones de México siglos XVI a XX*, vol. 1, edited by Amaya Garritz, 295-343. 6 vols. Mexico City: Universidad Nacional Autónoma de México, Ministerio de Cultura del Gobierno Vasco, Instituto Vasco-Mexicano de Desarrollo, 1996.
———. *Empresarios españoles y sociedad capitalista en México (1840-1920)*. Colombres, Spain: Fundación Archivo de Indios, 1995.
Chambers, Sarah. *From Subjects to Citizens: Honor, Gender, and Politics in Arequipa, Peru, 1780-1854*. University Park: Pennsylvania State University Press, 1999.

Chambers Gooch, Fanny. *Los mexicanos vistos de cerca*. Mexico City: Banco de México, 1993.

Chowning, Margaret. "The Contours of the Post-1810 Depression in Mexico: A Reappraisal from a Regional Perspective." *Latin American Research Review* 27, no. 2 (1992): 119–50.

Cisneros Sosa, Armando. *La ciudad que construimos. Registro de la expansión de la ciudad de México (1920–1976)*. Mexico City: Universidad Autónoma Metropolitana, 1993.

Clark, Marjorie. *La organización obrera en México*. Mexico City: Era, 1979.

Clark, Robert P. *The Basques: The Franco Years and Beyond*. Reno: University of Nevada Press, 1979.

Clifton, Judith. "On the Political Consequences of Privatisation: The Case of Teléfonos de México." *Bulletin of Latin American Research* 19, no. 1 (2000): 63–79.

Coatsworth, John. "Anotaciones sobre la producción de alimentos durante el porfiriato." *Historia Mexicana* 26, no. 2 (1976): 167–87.

———. "Obstacles to Economic Growth in Nineteenth-Century Mexico." *American Historical Review* 83, no. 1 (1978): 80–100.

Cobas, José A. "Ethnic Enclaves and Middleman Minorities: Alternative Strategies of Immigrant Adaptation?" *Sociological Perspectives* 30, no. 2 (1987): 143–61.

Código penal para el Distrito Federal y territorio de la Baja-California: Sobre delitos del fuero común, y para toda la republica sobre delitos contra la federación. Mexico City: Imprenta del Gobierno en Palacio, 1871.

Coello Salazar, Ermilo. "El comercio interior." In *Historia moderna de México. El porfiriato. Vida económica*, edited by Daniel Cosío Villegas, 766–67. Mexico City: Editorial Hermes, 1965.

Collado Herrera, María del Carmen. *Empresarios y políticos, entre la restauración y la revolución, 1920–1924*. Mexico City: Instituto Nacional de Estudios Históricos de la Revolución Mexicana, 1996.

Collier, Ruth Berins, and David Collier. *Shaping the Political Arena: Critical Junctures, the Labor Movement, and Regime Dynamics in Latin America*. Princeton, NJ: Princeton University Press, 1991.

Conniff, Michael L. "Introduction: Toward a Comparative Definition of Populism." In *Latin American Populism in Comparative Perspective*, edited by Michael L. Conniff, 3–28. Albuquerque: University of New Mexico Press, 1982.

Cooper, Patricia A. *Once a Cigar Maker: Men, Women, and Work Culture in American Cigar Factories, 1900–1919*. Urbana and Chicago: University of Illinois Press, 1987.

Cope, R. Douglas. *The Limits of Racial Domination: Plebeian Society in Colonial Mexico City, 1660–1720*. Madison: University of Wisconsin Press, 1994.

Córdova, Arnaldo. *La política de masas del cardenismo*. Mexico City: Ediciones Era, 1974.

———. *La revolución en crisis: La aventura del maximato*. Mexico City: Cal y Arena, 1995.

Costeloe, Michael P. *The Central Republic in Mexico, 1835–1846*. Cambridge: Cambridge University Press, 1993.

———. *Response to Revolution: Imperial Spain and the Spanish American Revolutions, 1810–1840*. Cambridge: Cambridge University Press, 1986.

Cuéllar, José T. de. *Chucho el ninfo*. Mexico City: Porrúa, 1947.

Deans-Smith, Susan. *Bureaucrats, Planters, and Workers: The Making of the Tobacco Monopoly in Bourbon Mexico*. Austin: University of Texas Press, 1992.
Departamento de la Estadística Nacional. *Censo de población 1930. Distrito Federal*. Mexico City: Departamento de la Estadística Nacional, 1930.
———. *Censo general de habitantes, 1921. Distrito Federal*, Mexico City: Talleres Gráficos de la Nación "Diario Oficial," 1925.
———. *Primer censo industrial, 1930. Resúmenes generales por industrias*. Mexico City: Departamento de la Estadística Nacional, 1930.
Díaz, María Elena. "The Satiric Penny Press for Workers in Mexico, 1900–1910: A Case Study in the Politicisation of Popular Culture." *Journal of Latin American Studies* 22, no. 3 (1990): 497–526.
Díaz, Porfirio. "Planes de la Noria y Tuxtepec." In *Mexico en el siglo XIX. Antología de fuentes e interpretaciones históricas*, edited by Alvaro Matute. Mexico City: Universidad Nacional Autónoma de México, 1993.
Directorio de la colonia española 1937. Mexico City: F. Villar Guerra, 1937.
Dorantes, Aureliano. "El trabajo en México. La industria del pan en la ciudad de México." *Boletín Mensual del Departamento del Trabajo* (February 1922): 5–14.
Douglass, William A. "Reply to Brandes." *American Anthropologist* 75 (1973): 300–302.
———. "Reply to Kasdan and Brandes." *American Anthropologist* 75 (1973): 304–6.
———, and Jon Bilbao. *Amerikanuak: Basques in the New World*. Reno: University of Nevada Press, 1975.
Dublán, Manuel, and José María Lozano, eds. *Legislación mexicano ó colección completa de las disposiciones legislativas*, vol. 1. 42 vols. Mexico City, Imprenta de Comercio, 1876.
Dusenberry, William H. "The Regulation of Meat Supply in Sixteenth-Century Mexico City." *Hispanic American Historical Review* 28, no. 1 (1948): 38–52.
Dwyer, John J. *The Agrarian Dispute: The Expropriation of American-Owned Rural Land in Postrevolutionary Mexico*. Durham, NC, and London: Duke University Press, 2008.
Elena, Eduardo. "Peronist Consumer Politics and the Problem of Domesticating Markets in Argentina, 1943–1955." *Hispanic American Historical Review* 87, no. 1 (2007): 111–49.
Escobedo Mansilla, Ronald, Ana de Zaballa Beascoechea, and Oscar Alvarez Gila, eds. *Emigración y redes sociales de los vascos en América*. Vitoria-Gasteiz, Spain: Servicio Editorial Universidad del País Vasco, 1996.
Estados Unidos Mexicanos. *Estadística gráfica: Progreso de los Estados Unidos Mexicanos: Presidencia del Sr. General Don Porfirio Díaz*. Mexico City: Estadística Gráfica Empresa de Ilustraciones, 1896.
Estados Unidos Mexicanos. *Constitución política de los Estados Unidos Mexicanos. "Artículo 123—Derecho al trabajo digno y socialmente útil."* 1917.
———. *Sexto censo de población. 1940. Distrito Federal*. Mexico City: Secretaría de la Economía Nacional, Dirección General de Estadística, 1943.
Estrada, Baldomero. "Causas de la emigración y tipología de los emigrantes." In *Historia general de la emigración española a Iberoamérica*, edited by Carmen Martínez Gimeno, 219–40. Madrid: Fundación CEDEAL, Historia 16, 1999.

Falcón, Romana. *Las rasgaduras de la descolonización. Españoles y mexicanos a mediados del siglo XIX*. Mexico City: El Colegio de México, 1996.

Fernández, Ramón. *Colección de leyes y disposiciones*. Mexico City: Secretaría del Ayuntamiento Constitucional de México, 1871.

Fernández y Fernández, Ramón. *El trigo en Mexico. El comercio*. 2 vols. Mexico City: Banco Nacional de Crédito Agrícola, S.A., 1939.

Figueroa Doménech, J. *Guía general descriptiva de la república mexicana; Historia, geografía, estadítica, etc., etc., con triple directorio del comercio y la industria, autoridades, oficinas públicas, abogados, médicos, hacendados, correos, telégrafos y ferrocarriles, etc.* Vol. 1, *El Distrito Federal*. 2 vols. Mexico City and Barcelona: R. de S. N. Araluce, 1899.

Fisher, John. "Imperial 'Free Trade' and the Hispanic Economy, 1778–1796." *Journal of Latin American Studies* 13, no. 1 (May 1981): 21–56.

Flores Caballero, Romeo. *Counterrevolution: The Role of Spaniards in the Independence of Mexico*. Translated by Jaime E. Rodríguez. Lincoln: University of Nebraska Press, 1974.

———. "Del libre cambio al proteccionismo." *Historia Mexicana* 19, no. 4 (1970): 492–512.

Florescano, Enrique. "La formación de los trabajadores en la época colonial, 1521–1750." In *La clase obrera en la historia de México. De la colonia al imperio*, edited by Enrique Florescano, 9–124. Mexico City: Siglo Veintiuno, 1981.

———. *Precios del maíz y crisis agrícolas en México (1708–1910)*. Mexico City: El Colegio de México, 1969.

Flores Garza, Marisela. "El desarrollo de la clase trabajadora en la industria de pan y pasteles en México en el periodo 1960–1975." Tesis de licenciatura, Economía, Universidad Nacional Autónoma de México, 1981.

Fowler, Will. *Santa Anna of Mexico*. Lincoln and London: University of Nebraska Press, 2007.

———. "Valentín Gómez Farías: Perceptions of Radicalism in Independent Mexico, 1821–1847." *Bulletin of Latin American Research* 15, no. 1 (1996): 39–62.

French, John D. "The Laboring and Middle-Class Peoples of Latin America and the Caribbean: Historical Trajectories and New Research Directions." In *Global Labour History: A State of the Art*, edited by Jan Lucassen, 289–334. Bern: Peter Lang AG, 2006.

———. "The Origin of Corporatist State Intervention in Brazilian Industrial Relations, 1930–1934: A Critique of the Literature." *Lusa-Brazilian Review* 28, no. 2 (1991): 13–26.

French, William E. *A Peaceful and Working People: Manners, Morals, and Class Formation in Northern Mexico*. Albuquerque: University of New Mexico Press, 1996.

Gaarder, Lorin R. "The Basques of Mexico: An Historical and Contemporary Portrait." PhD diss., Anthropology, University of Utah, 1976.

Gallego, José Andrés, ed. *Navarra y América*. Madrid: Editorial Mapfre, 1992.

Gálvez, D. Joseph de. *Reglamento del gremio de panaderos de esta capital para su abasto*. Mexico City: Imprenta de la Biblioteca Mexicana del Lic. D. Joseph Jáuregui, 1770.

Gamboa Ojeda, Leticia. "La constancia mexicana. De la fábrica, sus empresarios y sus conflictos laborales hasta los años de la posrevolución." *Tzintzun* 39 (January–June 2004): 93–112.

———. *La urdimbre y la trama. Historia social de los obreros textiles de Atlixco, 1899–1924.* Mexico City: Fondo de Cultura Económica, Benemérita Universidad Autónoma de Puebla, 2001.

Gamboa Ramírez, Ricardo. "Las finanzas municipales de la ciudad de México. 1800–1850." In *La ciudad de México en la primera mitad del siglo XIX*, edited by Regina Hernández Franyuti, 11–63. Mexico City: Instituto de Investigaciones Dr. José María Luis Mora, 1994.

García Acosta, Virginia. *Las panaderías, sus dueños y trabajadores. Ciudad de México. Siglo XVIII.* Mexico City: CIESAS, 1989.

———. *Los precios del trigo en la historia colonial de México.* Mexico City: CIESAS, 1988.

García Cubas, Antonio. *El libro de mis recuerdos.* Mexico City: Porrúa, 1986.

García Venero, Maximiano. *Historia del nacionalismo vasco.* Madrid: Editorial Nacional, 1969.

Garner, Paul H. *Porfirio Díaz.* Harlo and New York: Longman, 2001.

Garritz, Amaya, ed. *Aportaciones e integración de los vascos a la sociedad mexicana en los siglos XIX–XX.* Mexico City: Universidad Nacional Autónoma de México, Instituto de Investigaciones Históricas, Centro Vasco Euskal Etxea, Ministerio de Cultura del Gobierno Vasco, 2008.

———. *Los vascos en las regiones de México siglos XVI a XX.* 6 vols. Mexico City: Universidad Nacional Autónoma de México, Ministerio de Cultura del Gobierno Vasco, Instituto Vasco-Mexicano de Desarrollo, 1996.

Gayón Córdova, María. *Condiciones de vida y de trabajo en la ciudad de México en el siglo XIX.* Mexico City: Instituto Nacional de Antropología e Historia, 1988.

———. "Extranjeros en la ciudad de México en 1848." In *Imágenes de los inmigrantes en la ciudad de México, 1753–1910*, edited by Delia Salazar, 137–76. Mexico City: Instituto Nacional de Antropología e Historia, Plaza y Valdés, 2002.

Génin, Augusto. *Notes sur le Mexique.* Mexico City: Imprenta Lacaud, 1910.

Gil Lázaro, Alicia. "Estranjeros perniciosos. Infractores y delincuentes españoles en la ciudad de México (1910–1936)." *Revista de Indias* 63, no. 228 (2003): 477–94.

———. "Hispanofobia en el norte de México durante la revolución mexicana." In *Xenofobia y xenofilia en la historia de México, siglos XIX y XX. Homenaje a Moisés González Navarro*, edited by Delia Salazar, 105–34. Mexico City: SEGOB/Instituto Nacional de Migración, Instituto Nacional de Antropología e Historia, DGE Ediciones S.A. de C.V., 2006.

Gil Sánchez, Mercedes. *Trigo, tiempo y memoria. Molineros carranzanos de México.* Mexico City: Miscelánea Gráfica, S.A. de C.V., 1998.

———, and Roberto Sandoval Zarauz. "Molineros carranzanos de México en el siglo XX." In *Los vascos en las regiones de México siglos XVI a XX*, vol. 6, edited by Amaya Garritz, 123–37. 6 vols. Mexico City: Universidad Nacional Autónoma de México, Ministerio de Cultura del Gobierno Vasco, Instituto Vasco-Mexicano de Desarrollo, 1996.

Gojman de Backal, Alicia. *Camisas, escudos y desfiles militares. Los dorados y el antisemitismo en México (1934–1940)*. Mexico City: Fondo de Cultura Económica, Universidad Nacional Autónoma de México, 2000.

Gómez Galvarriato, Aurora, and Emilio Kourí, "La reforma económica: Finanzas públicas, mercados y tierras." In *Nación, constitución y reforma, 1821–1908*, edited by Erika Pani, 62–119. Mexico City: Fondo de Cultura Económica, 2010.

Gómez Gerardo, Víctor. "Los molinos de trigo del valle de México en el siglo XIX." *Revista de Seminario de Historia Mexicana* 1, no. 4 (1999): 51–67.

———. "Tradicionalismo e innovaciones tecnológicas en la producción de harina en el valle de México en el siglo XIX." Paper presented at the 7° Coloquio de Tacubaya en la Historia: Pasado y Presente, Mexico City, July 7, 2010.

Gonzales, Michael J. "U.S. Copper Companies, the Mine Workers' Union, and the Mexican Revolution, 1910–1920." *Hispanic American Historical Review* 76, no. 3 (1996): 503–34.

González, Alicia Maria. "'El pan de cada día': The Symbols and Expressive Culture of Wheat Bread in Greater Mexico." PhD diss., University of Texas, 1986.

González, Luis. "El liberalismo triunfante." In *Historia general de México*, edited by El Colegio de México, 635–705. Mexico City: El Colegio de México, 1994.

González Angulo, Jorge. "Los gremios de artesanos y la estructura urbana." In *Ciudad de México, ensayo de construcción de una historia*, edited by Alejandra Moreno Toscano, 25–36. Mexico City: Instituto Nacional de Antropología e Historia, 1978.

González Angulo Aguirre, Jorge. *Artesanado y ciudad a finales del siglo XVII*. Mexico City: Fondo de Cultura Económica, 1983.

———, and Roberto Sandoval Zarauz. "Los trabajadores industriales de Nueva España, 1750–1810." In *La clase obrera en la historia de México. De la colonia al imperio*, edited by Enrique Florescano, 173–238. Mexico City: Siglo Veintiuno, 1981.

González Casanova, Pablo. *La clase obrera en la historia de México. En el primer gobierno constitucionalista (1917–1920)*. Mexico City: Siglo Veintiuno, 1980.

González H., Gonzalo. *El trigo en México. Análisis estadístico de la producción*. Mexico City: Banco Nacional de Crédito Agrícola, S.A., 1938.

González Loscertales, Vicente. "Bases para el análisis socioeconómico de la colonia española de México en 1910." *Revista de Indias* 39 (1979): 267–95.

González Navarro, Moisés. *Historia moderna de México. El porfiriato. Vida social*. Mexico City: Editorial Hermes, 1957.

———. *Las ideas políticas de Lucas Alamán*. Mexico City: El Colegio de México, 1952.

———. *Los extranjeros en México y los mexicanos en el extranjero*. 2 vols. Mexico City: El Colegio de México, 1993.

González Peña, Carlos. *El nicho iluminado*. Mexico City: Editorial Stylo, 1947.

Gortari Rabiela, Hira de, and Regina Hernández Franyuti. *La ciudad de México y el Distrito Federal. Una historia compartida*. Mexico City: Departamento del Distrito Federal, Instituto de Investigaciones Dr. José María Luis Mora, 1988.

———, eds. *Memoria y encuentro: La ciudad de México y el Distrito Federal (1824–1928)*. 4 vols. Mexico City: Departamento del Distrito Federal, Instituto de Investigaciones Dr. José María Luis Mora, 1988.

Guemez Pacheco de Padilla Horcasitas y Aguayo, D. Juan Vicente de Conde de Revilla Gigedo. *Instrucción reservada que el Conde de Revilla Gigedo dio á su succesor en el mando, Marqués de Branciforte, sobre el gobierno en este continente en el tiempo que fué su virrey*. Mexico City: Imprenta de la Calle de las Escalerillas, 1831.

Guerra, François-Xavier. "El soberano y su reino. Reflexiones sobre la génesis del ciudadano en América Latina." In *Ciudadanía política y formación de las naciones: Perspectivas históricas de América Latina*, edited by Hilda Sábato, 33–61. Mexico City: Fondo de Cultura Económica, 1999.

———. *México: Del antiguo régimen a la revolución*. 2 vols. Mexico City: Fondo de Cultura Económica, 1988.

———, and Annick Lempérière, eds. *Los espacios públicos en Iberoamérica. Ambigüedades y problemas. Siglos XVIII–XIX*. Mexico City: Centro Francés de Estudios Mexicanos y Centroamericanos, Fondo de Cultura Económica, 1998.

Gutiérrez, Florencia. "De panaderos y panaderías. Condiciones de trabajo y conflictividad laboral a finales del siglo XIX en la ciudad de México." *Secuencia* 66 (2006): 9–34.

Haber, Stephen H. *Industry and Underdevelopment: The Industrialization of Mexico, 1890–1940*. Stanford, CA: Stanford University Press, 1989.

———. "Political Institutions and Financial Development: Evidence from the Political Economy of Bank Regulation in Mexico and the United States." In *Political Institutions and Financial Development*, edited by Stephen H. Haber, Douglass Cecil North, and Barry R. Weingast, 10–59. Stanford, CA: Hoover Institute, 2008.

———. Armando Razo, and Noel Maurer. *The Politics of Property Rights: Political Instability, Credible Commitments, and Economic Growth in Mexico, 1876–1929*. Cambridge and New York: Cambridge University Press, 2003.

Hale, Charles A. *The Transformation of Liberalism in Late Nineteenth-Century Mexico*. Princeton, NJ: Princeton University Press, 1989.

Hall, Linda B. *Alvaro Obregón: Power and Revolution in Mexico, 1911–1920*. College Station: Texas A&M University Press, 1981.

Hamilton, Nora. *The Limits of State Autonomy: Post-revolutionary Mexico*. Princeton, NJ: Princeton University Press, 1982.

Hart, John M. "Nineteenth Century Urban Labor Precursors of the Mexican Revolution: The Development of an Ideology." *Americas* 30, no. 3 (1974): 291–318.

———. *Revolutionary Mexico: The Coming and Process of the Mexican Revolution*. Berkeley: University of California Press, 1997.

———. "The Urban Working Class and the Mexican Revolution: The Case of the Casa del Obrero Mundial." *Hispanic American Historical Review* 58, no. 1 (1978): 1–20.

Helstosky, Carol. *Garlic and Oil: Politics and Food in Italy*. Oxford and New York: Oxford University Press, 2004.

Hernández, Salvador. "Tiempos libertarios. El magonismo en México: Cananea, Río Blanco y Baja California." In *La clase obrera en la historia de México. De la dictadura porfirista a los tiempos libertarios*, edited by F. S. Cardoso, Francisco Hermosillo G., and Salvador Hernández, 101–233. Mexico City: Siglo Veintiuno, 1980.

Hernández Franyuti, Regina, ed. *La ciudad de México en la primera mitad del siglo XIX*. 2 vols. Mexico City: Instituto de Investigaciones Dr. José María Luis Mora, 1994.

Hernández García de León, Héctor. *Historia política del sinarquismo, 1934–1944*. Mexico City: Universidad Iberoamericana, Miguel Angel Porrúa, 2004.

Herrero B., Carlos. *Braulio Iriarte. De la tahona al holding internacional cervecero, cuadernos de historia empresarial*. Mexico City: Universidad Autónoma Metropolitana Iztapalapa, 2002.

———. *Los empresarios mexicanos de origen vasco y el desarrollo del capitalismo en México, 1880–1950*. Mexico City: Universidad Autónoma Metropolitana, Plaza y Valdés, 2004.

Hiebert, Daniel. "Jewish Immigrants and the Garment Industry of Toronto, 1901–1931: A Study of Ethnic and Class Relations." *Annals of the Association of American Geographers* 83, no. 2 (1993): 243–71.

Hobsbawm, Eric, and Joan Wallach Scott. "Political Shoemakers." In *Uncommon People: Resistance, Rebellion and Jazz*, edited by Eric Hobsbawm, 18–42. New York: W. W. Norton, 1998.

Horowitz, Roger, Jeffrey M. Pilcher, and Sydney Watts. "Meat for the Multitudes: Market Culture in Paris, New York City, and Mexico City over the Long Nineteenth Century." *American Historical Review* 109, no. 4 (2004): 1005–83.

Hufton, Olwen H. *Women and the Limits of Citizenship in the French Revolution*. Toronto: University of Toronto Press, 1992.

Huitrón, Jacinto. *Orígenes e historia del movimiento obrero en México*. Mexico City: Editores Mexicanos Unidos, S.A., 1974.

Humboldt, Alexander von. *Political Essay on the Kingdom of New Spain*. Translated by John Black. 2nd ed. London: Longman, Hurst, Rees, Orme and Brown, 1814.

Hünefeldt, Christine. *Paying the Price of Freedom: Family and Labor Among Lima's Slaves, 1800–1854*. Berkeley and Los Angeles: University of California Press, 1994.

Idoate Ezquieta, Carlos J. *Emigración navarra del valle de Baztán a América durante el siglo XIX*. Estella, Spain: Gobierno de Navarra–Departamento de Educación y Cultura, Dirección General de Cultura–Institución Príncipe de Viana, 1989.

Iglesias, Sonia, and Samuel Salinas Alvarez. *El pan nuestro de cada día: Sus orígenes, historia, y desarrollo en México*. Mexico City: CANAINPA, 1997.

Illades, Carlos. *Hacia la república del trabajo: La organización artesanal en la ciudad de México, 1853–1876*. Mexico City: El Colegio de México, Centro de Estudios Históricos, Universidad Autónoma Metropolitan-Iztapalapa, 1996.

———. *Presencia española en la revolución mexicana (1910–1915)*. Mexico City: UNAM–Instituto Mora, 1991.

———. "Propietarios españoles y la revolución mexicana." In *Una inmigración privilegiada: Comerciantes, empresarios y profesionales españoles en México en los siglos XIX y XX*, edited by Clara E. Lida, 170–89. Madrid: Alianza Editorial, 1994.

Iriani, Marcelino. "Los vascos y las cadenas migratorias (1840–1880)." *Secuencia* 33 (1995): 5–26.

Johns, Michael. *The City of Mexico in the Age of Díaz*. Austin: University of Texas Press, 1997.

Kaplan, David H. "The Creation of an Ethnic Economy: Indochinese Business Expansion in Saint Paul." *Economic Geography* 73, no. 2 (1997): 214-33.

Kaplan, Steven L. *The Bakers of Paris and the Bread Question, 1700-1775.* Durham, NC: Duke University Press, 1996.

———. *Provisioning Paris: Merchant and Millers in the Grain and Flour Trade During the Eighteenth Century.* Ithaca, NY, and London: Cornell University Press, 1984.

Kasdan, Leonard. "Family Structure, Migration and the Entrepreneur." *Comparative Studies in Society and History* 7 (1965): 345-57.

———, and Stanley H. Brandes. "Basque Migration Again." *American Anthropologist* 75 (1973): 302-4.

Katz, Friedrich. *The Life and Times of Pancho Villa.* Stanford, CA: Stanford University Press, 1998.

Kaufman, Stuart Bruce. *A Vision of Unity: The History of the Bakery and Confectionary Workers International Union.* Chicago: University of Illinois Press, 1986.

Kenny, Michael, Virginia García Acosta, Carmen Icazuriaga Montes, Clara Elena Suárez A., and Gloria Artís E. *Inmigrantes y refugiados españoles y México.* Mexico City: CIESAS, 1979.

Kinsbruner, Jay. *The Colonial Spanish-American City: Urban Life in the Age of Atlantic Capitalism.* Austin: University of Texas Press, 2005.

———. *Petty Capitalism in Spanish America: The Pulperos of Puebla, Mexico City, Caracas, and Buenos Aires.* Boulder, CO, and London: Westview Press, 1987.

Kizca, John E. *Colonial Entrepreneurs: Families and Business in Bourbon Mexico City.* Albuquerque: University of New Mexico Press, 1983.

———. "The Great Families of Mexico: Elite Maintenance and Business Practices in Late Colonial Mexico City." *Hispanic American Historical Review* 62, no. 3 (1982): 429-57.

Klarén, Peter F. "Lost Promise: Explaining Latin American Underdevelopment." In *Promise of Development: Theories of Change in Latin America*, edited by Peter F. Klarén, 3-33. Boulder, CO: Westview Press, 1986.

Knight, Alan. "Cardenismo: Juggernaut or Jalopy." *Journal of Latin American Studies* 26, no. 1 (1994): 73-107.

———. "El liberalismo mexicano desde la reforma hasta la revolución (una interpretación)." *Historia Mexicana* 34, no. 1 (1985): 59-92.

———. *The Mexican Revolution.* 2 vols. Cambridge: Cambridge University Press, 1986.

———. "The Mexican Revolution: Bourgeois? Nationalist? Or Just a 'Great Rebellion'?" *Bulletin of Latin American Research* 4, no. 2 (1985): 1-37.

———. "Populism and Neo-Populism in Latin American, Especially Mexico." *Journal of Latin American Studies* 30, no. 2 (1998): 223-48.

———. "The Working Class and the Mexican Revolution, c. 1900-1920." *Journal of Latin American Studies* 16, no. 1 (1984): 51-79.

Koreniewicz, Roberto P. "Labor Unrest in Argentina, 1887-1907." *Latin American Research Review* 24, no. 3 (1989): 71-98.

Kurlansky, Mark. *The Basque History of the World.* New York: Walker, 1999.

La Botz, Dan. "American 'Slackers' in the Mexican Revolution: International Proletarian Politics in the Midst of a National Revolution." *Americas* 62, no. 4 (2006): 563-90.

Latrobe, Charles Joseph. *The Rambler in Mexico: 1834*. London: R. B. Seeley and W. Burnside, 1836.

Lau Jaiven, Ana. "Retablo constumbrista: Vida cotidiana y mujeres durante la primera mitad del siglo XIX mexicano según viajeros anglosajones." In *La ciudad de México en la primera mitad del siglo XIX*, edited by Regina Hernández Franyuti, 365-410. Mexico City: Instituto de Investigaciones Dr. José María Luis Mora, 1994.

Leal, Juan Felipe. *Agrupaciones y burocracias sindicales en México: 1906-1938*. Mexico City: Editorial Terra Nova, S.A., 1985.

Lear, John. "Del mutualismo a la resistencia: Las organizationes laborales en la ciudad de México de fines del porfiriato a la revolución." In *Ciudad de México: Instituciones, actores sociales y conflicto político, 1774-1931*, edited by Carlos Illades and Ariel Rodríguez Kuri, 275-309. Zamora and Azcapotzalco: El Colegio de Michoacán and Universidad Autónoma Metropolitana-Iztapalapa, 1996.

———. "Mexico City: Space and Class in the Porfirian Capital, 1884-1910." *Journal of Urban History* 22, no. 4 (1996): 454-92.

———. *Workers, Neighbors, and Citizens: The Revolution in Mexico City*. Lincoln: University of Nebraska Press, 2001.

Lee, Raymond L. "Grain Legislation in Colonial Mexico, 1575-1585." *Hispanic American Historical Review* 27, no. 4 (1947): 647-60.

Lewis, Oscar. *Pedro Martínez: A Mexican Peasant and His Family*. New York: Random House, 1964.

Lhandé, Pierre. *L'émigration basque*. Paris: Nouvelle Librarie Nationale, 1910.

Lida, Clara E. "El perfil de una inmigración: 1821-1939." In *Una inmigración privilegiada: Comerciantes, empresarios y profesionales españoles en México en los siglos XIX y XX*, edited by Clara E. Lida, 25-51. Madrid: Alianza Editorial, 1994.

———. "Los españoles en el México independiente: 1821-1950. Un estado de la cuestión." *Historia Mexicana* 56, no. 2 (2006): 613-50.

———. "Los españoles en México. Del porfiriato a la post-revolución." In *Españoles hacia América. La emigración en masa, 1880-1930*, edited by Nicolás Sánchez Albornoz, 322-42. Madrid: Alianza Editorial, 1988.

———, ed. *Una inmigración privilegiada: Comerciantes, empresarios y profesionales españoles en México en los siglos XIX y XX*. Madrid: Alianza Editorial, 1994.

Light, Ivan, and Edna Bonacich. *Immigrant Entrepreneurs: Koreans in Los Angeles, 1965-1982*. Berkeley, Los Angeles, and London: University of California Press, 1988.

López de Gómara, Francisco. *Historia de las Indias y conquista de México*. Historiadores Primitivos de Indias, edited by Enrique de Vedia. Madrid: Imprenta de M. Rivadeneyra, 1852.

López Monjardín, Adriana. "El espacio de la producción: Ciudad de México, 1850." In *Ciudad de México: Ensayo de construcción de una historia*, edited by Alejandra Moreno Toscano, 45-62. Mexico City: Instituto Nacional de Antropología e Historia, 1978.

López Mora, Rebeca. *El molino de Santa Mónica: Historia de una empresa colonial.* Zinacantepec, Mexico: El Colegio Mexiquense, Fundación Cultural Antonio Haghenbeck y de la Lama, I.A.P., 2000.

López Rosado, Diego G. *Comercialización de granos alimenticios en México.* Mexico City: Secretaría de Comercio, 1981.

———. *Historia del abasto de productos alimenticios en la ciudad de México.* Mexico City: Fondo de Cultura Económica, 1988.

Ludlow, Leonor. "Empresarios y banqueros: Entre el porfiriato y la revolución." In *Una inmigración privilegiada: Comerciantes, empresarios y profesionales españoles en México en los siglos XIX y XX,* edited by Clara E. Lida, 142-69. Madrid: Alianza Editorial, 1994.

Lyon, G. F. *Journal of a Residence and Tour in the Republic of Mexico in the Year 1836.* London: John Murray, 1838.

MacGregor, Josefina. *México y España: Del porfiriato a la revolución.* Mexico City: Instituto Nacional de Estudios Históricos de la Revolución Mexicana, 1992.

———. *Revolución y diplomacia: México y España 1913-1917.* Mexico City: Instituto Nacional de Estudios Históricos de la Revolución Mexicana, 2002.

Maillefert, Eugenio. *Directorio del comercio del imperio mexicano para el año de 1867.* Mexico City: Instituto de Investigaciones Dr. José María Luis Mora, 1992.

Marcos, Desiderio. *México y los españoles.* Mexico City: Tipografía El Automóvil en México, S.A., 1915.

Marichal, Carlos. "Avances recientes en la historia de las grandes empresas y su importancia para la historia económica de México." In *Historia de las grandes empresas en México, 1850-1930,* edited by Carlos Marichal and Mario Cerutti, 9-38. Mexico City: Universidad Autónoma de Nuevo León and Fondo de Cultura Económica, 1997.

———, and Mario Cerutti, eds. *Historia de las grandes empresas en México, 1850-1930.* Mexico City: Universidad Autónoma de Nuevo León, Fondo de Cultura Económica, 1997.

Marroquí, José María. *La ciudad de México.* 3 vols. Mexico City: Jesús Medina Editor, 1969.

Marti, Luis. "Lucas Alamán, Pioneer of Mexican Historiography: An Interpretative Essay." *Americas* 32, no. 2 (October 1975): 239-56.

Matute, Alvaro, ed. *Mexico en el siglo XIX. Antología de fuentes e interpretaciones históricas.* Mexico City: Universidad Nacional Autónoma de México, 1993.

Marx, Karl. *Capital: A Critique of Political Economy.* 2 vols. London: Penguin, 1976.

Maurer, Noel. *The Power and the Money: The Mexican Financial System, 1876-1932.* Stanford, CA: Stanford University Press, 2002.

Medin, Tzvi. *El minimato presidencial: Historia política del maximato (1928-1935).* Mexico City: Ediciones Era, 1982.

———. *El sexenio alemanista: Ideología y praxis política de Miguel Alemán.* 1st ed. Mexico City: Ediciones Era, 1990.

Memorial del departamento del Distrito Federal, septiembre 1937-agosto 1938. Mexico City: Departamento del Distrito Federal, 1938.

Mena Brito S., Bernardino. "Política monopolista en México." BA thesis, Facultad de Derecho y Ciencas Sociales, Universidad Nacional Autónoma de México, 1945.

Merla, Pedro. *El costo de la vida obrera en México.* Mexico City: Secretaría del Trabajo y Previsión Social, 1942.

Mestre Ghigliazza, Manuel. *Efemérides biográficas.* Mexico City: Imp. Aldina, Robredo y Rosell, 1945.

Meyer Cosio, Rosa María. "Empresarios españoles después de la independencia." In *El poder y el dinero. Grupos y regiones mexicanos en el siglo XIX*, edited by Beatriz Rojas, 218–55. Mexico City: Instituto Mora, 1994.

Meyer, Jean. "Los obreros en la revolución mexicana: Los 'Batallones Rojos.'" *Historia Mexicana* 21, no. 1 (1971): 1–37.

Meyer, Lorenzo. *El conflicto social y los gobiernos del Maximato.* Mexico City: El Colegio de México, 1978.

Middlebrook, Kevin J. *The Paradox of Revolution: Labor, the State, and Authoritarianism in Mexico.* Baltimore, MD: Johns Hopkins University Press, 1995.

Ministerio de Fomento, Dirección General de Estadística. *Censo general de la república mexicana, 1895. Distrito Federal.* Mexico City: Oficina Tipográfica de la Secretaría de Fomento, 1898.

Miño Gijalva, Manuel. "Estructura social y ocupación de la población en la ciudad de México, 1790." In *La población de la ciudad de México en 1790. Estructura social, alimentación y vivienda*, edited by Manuel Miño Gijalva and Sonia Pérez Toledo, 147–92. Mexico City: Universidad Autónoma Metropolitana, 2004.

———. "Población y abasto de alimentos en la ciudad de México, 1730–1838." In *Núcleos urbanos mexicanos. Siglos XVIII y XIX*, edited by Manuel Miño Gijalva, 19–140. Mexico City: El Colegio de México, 2006.

Mintz, Sidney. *Sweetness and Power: The Place of Sugar in Modern History.* New York: Viking, 1985.

Miranda Pacheco, Sergio. *Historia de la desaparición del municipio en el Distrito Federal.* Mexico City: Unidad Obrera y Socialista, APN; Frente del Pueblo; Sociedad Nacional de Estudios Regionales, 1998.

Moats, Leone B. *Thunder in Their Veins: A Memoir of Mexico.* New York and London: Century, 1932.

Morales, Luz Marina. "Pan, familia y ayuntamiento. El poder de las élites en la ciudad de Puebla." In *Economía y sociedad en las regiones de México, siglo XIX*, edited by Jaime Olveda, 117–31. Guadalajara: El Colegio de Jalisco, 1996.

Morales, María Dolores. "Espacio, propiedad y órganos de poder en la ciudad de México en el siglo XIX." In *Ciudad de México: Instituciones, actores sociales y conflicto político, 1774-1931*, edited by Carlos Illades and Ariel Rodríguez Kuri, 155–90. Zamora and Azcapotzalco, Mexico: El Colegio de Michoacán and Universidad Autónoma Metropolitana–Iztapalapa, 1996.

———. "La expansión de la ciudad de México en el siglo XIX. El caso de los fraccionamientos." In *Investigaciones sobre la historia de la ciudad de México*, edited by Alejandra Moreno Toscano et al., 76–85. Mexico City: Instituto Nacional de Antropología e Historia, 1974.

———. "La población extranjera de la ciudad de México en 1882." In *Imágenes de los inmigrantes en la ciudad de México, 1753-1910*, edited by Delia Salazar, 177–214. Mexico City: Instituto Nacional de Antropología e Historia, Plaza y Valdés, 2002.

Morales-Moreno, Humberto. "Los molinos de la Asunción y San Miguel en Tecamacalco y Acatzingo, Estado de Puebla." *Apuntes* 21, no. 1 (2008): 136–45.

Moreno Sánchez, Carlos. "Vida de trabajo en la panificadora 'El Antiguo Fénix': El caso de los bizcocheros." Tesis de licenciatura, Escuela Nacional de Antropología e Historia, 1990.

Moreno Toscano, Alejandra. "Los trabajadores y el proyecto de industrialización, 1810–1867." In *La clase obrera en la historia de México. De la colonia al imperio*, edited by Enrique Florescano, 302–50. Mexico City: Siglo Veintiuno, 1981.

Morgan, Tony. "Proletarians, Politicos, and Patriarchs: The Use and Abuse of Cultural Customs in the Early Industrialization of Mexico City, 1880–1910." In *Rituals of Rule, Rituals of Resistance: Public Celebrations and Popular Culture in Mexico*, edited by William H. Beezley, Cheryl English Martin, and William E. French, 151–72. Wilmington, DE: SR Books, 1994.

Mörner, Magnus. "Inserción del fenómeno vasco en la emigración europea a América." In *Emigración y redes sociales de los vascos en América*, edited by Ronald Escobedo Mansilla, Ana de Zaballa Beascoechea, and Oscar Alvarez Gila, 15–30. Vitoria-Gasteiz, Spain: Servicio Editorial Universidad del País Vasco, 1996.

Moya, José C. "A Continent of Immigrants: Postcolonial Shifts in the Western Hemisphere." *Hispanic American Historical Review* 86, no. 1 (2006): 1–28.

———. *Cousins and Strangers: Spanish Immigrants in Buenos Aires, 1850-1930*. Berkeley, Los Angeles, and London: University of California Press, 1998.

Mraz, John. "'En calidad de esclavas': Obreras en los molinos de nixtamal, México, diciembre, 1919." *Historia Obrera* 6, no. 24 (1982): 2–14.

Nebel, Carl. *Viaje pintoresco y arqueológico sobre la parte más interesante de la república mexicana*. Translated by Aza Zats. Mexico City: Porrúa, 1829.

Negri, Ramón P. de. *Official Statement Regarding the Food Situation in Mexico City After the Constitutionalista Occupation*. San Francisco: Consul General of Mexico, 1915.

Newton, Ronald C. "Natural Corporatism and the Passing of Populism in Spanish America." In *Promise of Development: Theories of Change in Latin America*, edited by Peter F. Klarén, 219–33. Boulder, CO: Westview Press, 1986.

Niemeyer, E. V. *Revolution at Querétaro: The Mexican Constitutional Convention of 1916–1917*. Austin and London: University of Texas Press, 1974.

Novelo, Victoria. "Los trabajadores mexicanos en el siglo XIX ¿Obreros o artesanos?" In *Comunidad, cultura y vida social: Ensayos sobre la formación de la clase obrera*, edited by Seminario de Movimiento Obrero y Revolución Mexicana, 15–51. Mexico City: Instituto Nacional de Antropología e Historia, 1991.

Ochoa, Enrique C. *Feeding Mexico: The Political Uses of Food Since 1910*. Wilmington, DE: Scholarly Resources, 2000.

Orozco y Berra, Manuel. *Historia de la ciudad de México desde su fundación hasta 1854*. Mexico City: SepSesentas, 1973.

Otondo y Dufurrena, Agustín. *Diccionario histórico biográfico del valle de Baztán (Navarra)*. Pamplona: Gobierno de Navarra, 2002.

Pani, Erika. "Cultural nacional, cánon español." In *España y el imperio de Maximiliano. Finanzas, diplomacia, cultura e inmigración*, edited by Clara E. Lida, 215–60. Mexico City: El Colegio de México, 1999.

———. "De coyotes y gallinas: Hispanidad, identidad nacional y comunidad políticas durante la expulsión de españoles." *Revista de Indias* 63, no. 228 (2003): 355–74.

Payne, James. *Labor and Politics in Peru*. New York: Yale University Press, 1965.

Peralta Flores, Araceli. *La hacienda de Santa Mónica, Tlalnepantla, Estado de México. Su historia y arquitectura*. Mexico City: Instituto Nacional de Antropología e Historia, 2005.

Pérez Herrero, Pedro. "Algunas hipótesis de trabajo sobre la inmigración española a México: Los comerciantes." In *Tres aspectos de la presencia española en México durante el porfiriato*, edited by Manuel Miño Grijalva, Pedro Pérez Herrero, and María Teresa Jarquín, 103–39. Mexico City: El Colegio de México, 1981.

Pérez Montfort, Ricardo. *Hispanismo y falange. Los sueños imperiales de la derecha española*. Mexico City: Fondo de Cultura Económica, 1992.

Pérez Toledo, Sonia. *Los hijos del trabajo. Los artesanos de la ciudad de México, 1780–1853*. Mexico City: El Colegio de México, Universidad Autónoma Metropolitana-Iztapalapa, 1996.

Pérez Vejo, Tomás. "La conspiración gachupina en *El Hijo del Ahuizote*." *Historia Mexicana* 54, no. 4 (2005): 1105–53.

Pescador, Juan Javier. *The New World Inside a Basque Village: The Oiartzun Valley and Its Atlantic Emigrants, 1550–1800*. Reno: University of Nevada Press, 2003.

Piccato, Pablo. *City of Suspects: Crime in Mexico City, 1900–1930*. Durham, NC, and London: Duke University Press, 2001.

———. "'El Paso de Venus por el disco del sol': Criminality and Alcoholism in Late Porfiriato." *Mexican Studies/Estudios Mexicanos* 11, no. 2 (1995): 203–41.

———. "Politics and the Technology of Honor: Dueling in Turn-of-the-Century Mexico." *Journal of Social History* 33, no. 2 (1999): 331–54.

Pilcher, Jeffrey M. *¡Que Vivan los Tamales! Food and the Making of Mexican Identity*. Albuquerque: University of New Mexico Press, 1998.

Pimentel, Francisco. *Memoria sobre las causas que han originado la situación actual de la raza indígena de México y medios de remediarla*. Mexico City: Andrade y Escalante, 1864.

Pi-Suñer Llorens, Antonia. "Negocios y política a mediados del siglo XIX." In *Una inmigración privilegiada. Comerciantes, empresarios y profesionales españoles en México en los siglos XIX y XX*, edited by Clara E. Lida, 75–96. Madrid: Alianza Editorial, 1994.

Pla Brugat, Dolores, and Guadalupe Zárate M. "Extranjeros en la ciudad de México: 1895–1930." In *La ciudad y el campo en la historia de México. Memoria de la VII reunión de historiadores mexicanos y norteamericanos*, edited by Ricardo Sánchez, Eric Van Young, and Gisela von Wobeser, 399–408. Mexico City: Universidad Nacional Autónoma de México, 1992.

Polt, John H. R. *Gaspar Melchor de Jovellanos*. New York: Twayne, 1971.

Porter, Susie S. *Working Women in Mexico City: Public Discourses and Material Conditions, 1879–1931*. Tucson: University of Arizona Press, 2003.

Portes, Alejandro. "The Social Origins of the Cuban Enclave Economy of Miami." *Sociological Perspectives* 30, no. 4 (1987): 340–72.

Potash, Robert A. *Mexican Government and Industrial Development in the Early Republic: The Banco de Avío*. Amherst: University of Massachusetts Press, 1983.

Prantl, Adolfo, and José L. Grosso. *La ciudad de México. Novísima guía universal de la capital de la República Mexicana*. Mexico City: Libreria Madrileña, 1901.

Prieto, Guillermo. *Memorias de mis tiempos*. Mexico City: Porrúa, 1996.

Prothero, Iorwerth. *Radical Artisans in England and France, 1830–1870*. Cambridge: Cambridge University Press, 1997.

Puga, J. "Higiene de la habitación. La habitación obrera en la Ciudad de México" *Boletín Mensual del Departamento del Trabajo* (February 1922): 14–21.

Raat, William D. "Agustin Aragon and Mexico's Religion of Humanity." *Journal of Inter-American Studies* 11, no. 3 (July 1969): 441–57.

Ramírez Plancarte, Francisco. *La ciudad de México durante la revolución constitucionalista*. Mexico City: Impresores Unidos S de R. L., 1940.

Reed, John. *Insurgent Mexico*. New York: International, 1969.

Reid, Donald. *Paris Sewers and Sewermen: Realities and Representations*. Cambridge, MA: Harvard University Press, 1991.

Reyna, Maria del Carmen. *La prensa censurada durante el siglo XIX*. Mexico City: SEPsesenta, 1976.

———. "Las condiciones del trabajo en las panaderías de la ciudad de México durante la segunda mitad del siglo XIX." *Historia Mexicana* 31, no. 3 (1982): 431–48.

Richmond, Douglas W. "Confrontation and Reconciliation: Mexicans and Spaniards During the Mexican Revolution, 1910–1920." *Americas* 41, no. 2 (1984): 215–28.

———. "Nationalism and Class Conflict in Mexico, 1910–1920." *Americas* 43, no. 3 (1987): 279–303.

Riedlander, Judith. *Being Indian in Hueyapán: A Study of Forced Identity in Contemporary Mexico*. New York: Saint Martin's Press, 1975.

Rivera Castro, José. *En la presidencia de Plutarco Elias Calles (1924–1928)*. Mexico City: Siglo Veintiuno Editores, 1983.

Rivera-Garza, Cristina. "Dangerous Minds: Changing Psychiatric Views of the Mentally Ill in Porfirian Mexico, 1876–1911." *Journal of the History of Medicine* 56 (2001): 36–67.

Rodríguez Kuri, Ariel. "Desabasto, hambre y respuesta política, 1915." In *Instituciones y ciudad. Ocho estudios históricos sobre la ciudad de México*, edited by Carlos Illades and Ariel Rodríguez Kuri, 133–65. Mexico City: Ediciones ¡UníoS!, 2000.

———. "El año cero: El ayuntamiento de México y las facciones revolucionarias (agosto 1914–agosto 1915)." In *Ciudad de México: Instituciones, actores sociales y conflicto político, 1774–1931*, edited by Carlos Illades and Ariel Rodríguez Kuri, 191–220. Zamora and Azcapotzalco: El Colegio de Michoacán and Universidad Autónoma Metropolitana–Iztapalapa, 1996.

———. *Historia del desasosiego. La revolución en la ciudad de México, 1911–1922*. Mexico City: El Colegio de México, 2010.

Romano, Ruggiero. *Mecanismo y elementos del sistema colonial americano, siglos XVI–SXIII*. Translated by Jaime Riera Rehren. Mexico City: El Colegio de México, Fondo de Cultura Económica, 2004.

Rosenzweig, Fernando. "Moneda y bancos." In *Porfiriato. Vida económica*, edited by Francisco Calderón, 789–885. Mexico City: Editorial Hermes, 1965.

Roumagnac, Carlos. *Los criminales en México. Por los mundos del delito. Ensayo de psicología criminal*. Mexico City: Tipografía "El Fénix," 1904.

Roxborough, Ian. "The Analysis of Labour Movements in Latin America: Typologies and Theories." *Bulletin of Latin American Research* 1, no. 1 (1981): 81–95.

Rubin, Jeffrey W. "Popular Mobilization and the Myth of State Corporatism." In *Popular Movements and Political Change in Mexico*, edited by Joe Foweraker and Ann L. Craig, 247–70. Boulder, CO, and London: Lynne Rienner, 1990.

Rudé, George. *The Crowd in History: A Study of Popular Disturbances in France and England, 1730–1848*. New York: John Wiley & Sons, 1964.

Ruiz, Ramón Eduardo. *The Great Rebellion: Mexico, 1905–1924*. New York: Norton, 1980.

———. *Labor and the Ambivalent Revolutionaries, Mexico, 1911–1923*. Baltimore, MD, and London: Johns Hopkins University Press, 1976.

Ruiz de Gordejuela Urquijo, Josu. "Cincuenta años de presencia vasca en México, 1800–1850." Unpublished paper, II Congreso Euskal Herria Mugas, Vitoria-Gasteiz, 2005. Electronic document, www.euskosare.org, accessed February 1, 2012.

Sáenz, Aarón. *Informe presidencial y memoria del departamento del Distrito Federal de julio de 1932 a junio de 1933*. Mexico City: Departamento del Distrito Federal, 1933.

Salazar, Delia. "Extraños en la ciudad. Un acercamiento a la inmigración internacional a la ciudad de México, en los censos de 1890, 1895, 1900 y 1910." In *Imágenes de los inmigrantes en la ciudad de México, 1753–1910*, edited by Delia Salazar, 225–50. Mexico City: Instituto Nacional de Antropología e Historia, Plaza y Valdés, 2002.

Salazar, Roberto. *El empresario industrial. Patrones tradicionales de constitución y sucesión empresarial*. Mexico City: El Colegio de México, Centro de Estudios Económicos y Demográficos, 1971.

Salazar, Rosendo, and José G. Escobedo. *Las pugnas de la gleba (Los albores del movimiento obrero en México)*. Mexico City: Editorial Avante, 1923.

Salvucci, Richard J. *Textiles and Capitalism in Mexico: An Economic History of the Obrajes, 1539–1840*. Princeton, NJ: Princeton University Press, 1987.

Sánchez Alonso, Blanca. *Las causas de la emigración española, 1880–1930*. Madrid: Alianza Editorial, 1995.

Sánchez de Tagle, Esteban. "El inicio de la reforma borbónica en la ciudad de México." *Relaciones* 73 (Winter 1998): 273–80.

———. "Las reformas del siglo XVIII al gobierno; La ciuidad, su hacienda, su policía, su ejército." In *Las reformas borbónicas, 1750–1808*, edited by Clara García Ayluardo, 164–224. Mexico City: Fondo de Cultura Económica, 2010.

Sánchez Ruiz, Gerardo G. "Planificación y urbanismo en la ciudad de México del siglo XX. La etapa de los orígenes, 1917–1928." In *Construcción y arquitectura moderna*, edited by Gerardo G. Sánchez Ruiz, 2.1–2.22. Mexico City: Universidad Autónoma Metropolitana, 2000.

San Juan Victoria, Carlos, and Salvador Velázquez Ramírez. "La formación del estado y las políticas económicas (1821–1880)." In *México en el siglo XIX (1812–1910). Histórica económica y de la estructura social*, edited by Ciro Cardoso, 65–88. Mexico City: Nueva Imagen, 1980.

Schell, William, Jr. *Integral Outsiders: The American Colony in Mexico City, 1876–1911*. Wilminton, DE: Scholarly Resources, 2001.

Scott, Joan Wallach. *The Glassworkers of Carmaux: French Craftsmen and Political Action in a Nineteenth-Century City*. Cambridge, MA: Harvard University Press, 1974.

Secretaría de Fomento, Colonización e Industria. *Censo general de la república mexicana, 1900. Distrito Federal*. Mexico City: Oficina Tipográfica de la Secretaría de Fomento, 1901.

———. *Censo general de la república mexicana, verificado el 28 de octubre de 1900. Distrito Federal*. Mexico City: Oficina Tipográfica de la Secretaría de Fomento, 1901.

Secretaría de la Economía Nacional, Departamento de Estudios Económicos. *Estadísticas sociales del porfiriato, 1877–1910*. Mexico City: Talleres Gráficos de la Nación, 1956.

———. *La industria harinera. Materia prima, molienda y transportes*. Mexico City: Talleres Gráficos de la Nación, 1934.

———. *Resumen general del censo industrial de 1935*. Mexico City: Talleres Gráficos de la Nación, 1941.

———. *Segundo censo industrial, 1935. Panaderías y pastelerías*. Mexico City: Secretaría de Economía Nacional, Dirección General de Estadística, 1937.

Semo, Ilán. "El cardenismo revisado: La tercera vía y otras utopías incertas." *Revista Mexicana de Sociología* 55, no. 2 (1993): 197–223.

Sendra de Servitje, Josefina. *Vivir es luchar*. Mexico City: Private edition, 1977.

Sesto, Julio. *La ciudad de los palacios*. Mexico City: El Libro Español, 1917.

Shaw, Frederick John, Jr. "Poverty and Politics in Mexico City, 1824–1854." PhD diss., University of Florida, 1975.

Sherman, John W. "Reassessing Cardenismo: The Mexican Right and the Failure of a Revolutionary Regime, 1934–1940." *Americas* 54, no. 3 (1998): 357–78.

Silva Herzog, Jesús. *El mexicano y su morada*, Cuadernos americanos. Mexico City: Universidad Nacional Autónoma de México, 1960.

Silva Riquer, Jorge. "La organización de las tiendas pulperas en la ciudad de México, siglo XVIII." In *La población de la ciudad de México en 1790. Estructura social, alimentación y vivienda*, edited by Manuel Miño Gijalva and Sonia Pérez Toledo, 281–310. Mexico City: Universidad Autónoma Metropolitana, 2004.

Sims, Harold. *The Expulsion of Mexico's Spaniards, 1821–1836*. Pittsburgh, PA: University of Pittsburgh Press, 1990.

Skidmore, Thomas E. "Workers and Soldiers: Urban Labor Movements and Elite Responses in Twentieth-Century Latin America." In *Elites, Masses, and Modernization in Latin America, 1850–1930*, edited by E. Brandford Burns and Thomas E. Skidmore, 79–126. Austin and London: University of Texas Press, 1979.

Sociedad Económica de Madrid. *Informe sobre la ley agraria*. Madrid: Instituto de Estudios Políticos, 1955.

Speckman, Elisa. "Las tablas de la ley en la era de la modernidad. Normas y valores en la legislación porfiriana." In *Modernidad, tradición y alteridad. La ciudad de México en el cambio de siglo (XIX–XX)*, edited by Claudia Agostoni and Elisa Speckman, 241–70. Mexico City: Universidad Nacional Autónoma de México, 2001.

Steen, Herman. *Flour Milling in America*. Minneapolis, MN: T. S. Denison, 1963.

Stein, Stanley J. "Bureaucracy and Business in the Spanish Empire, 1759–1804: Failure of a Bourbon Reform in Mexico and Peru." *Hispanic American Historical Review* 61, no. 1 (1981): 2–28.

———, and Barbara H. Stein. *Apogee of Empire: Spain and New Spain in the Age of Charles III, 1759–1789*. Baltimore, MD, and London: Johns Hopkins University Press, 2003.

Storck, John, and Walter Dorwin Teague. *Flour for Man's Bread*. Minneapolis: University of Minnesota Press, 1952.

Suárez, Clara Elena. *La política cerealera en la economía novohispana. El caso del trigo*. Mexico City: CIESAS, 1985.

Super, John C. *Food, Conquest, and Colonization in Sixteenth-Century Spanish America*. Albuquerque: University of New Mexico Press, 1988.

Taibo II, Paco Ignacio. *Bolshevikis. Historia narrativa de los orígenes del comunismo en México (1919–1925)*. Mexico City: Joaquín Mortiz, 1986.

———. "Inquilinos del DF a colgar la rojinegra." *Revista Rebeldía* 30 (May 2005): 48–61.

———, ed. *La huelga de los sombrereros, México 1875*. Mexico City: Centro de Estudios Históricos del Movimiento Obrero Mexicano, 1980.

———, and Rogelio Vizcaíno. *Memoria roja. Las luchas sindicales de los años 20*. Mexico City: Ediciones Leega/Júcar, 1984.

Taylor, Lynne. "Food Riots Revisited." *Journal of Social History* 30, no. 2 (winter 1996): 483–96.

Teichman, Judith A. *The Politics of Freeing Markets in Latin America: Chile, Argentina, and Mexico*. Chapel Hill and London: University of North Carolina Press, 2001.

Teitelbaum, Vanesa. "La corrección de la vagancia. Trabajo, honor y solidaridades en la ciudad de México, 1845–1853." In *Trabajo, ocio y coación. Trabajadores urbanos en México y Guatemala en el siglo XIX*, edited by Clara E. Lida and Sonia Pérez Toledo. Mexico City: Universidad Autónoma Metropolitana, Miguel Angel Porrúa, 2001.

Tejada, Luis. *La cuestión del pan. El anarcosindicalismo en el Perú 1880–1919*. Lima: Instituto Nacional de Cultura, Banco Industrial del Perú, 1988.

Tenenbaum, Barbara A. "Streetwise History: The Paseo de la Reforma and the Porfirian State, 1876–1910." In *Rituals of Rule, Rituals of Resistance*, edited by William Beezley et al., 127–50. Wilmington, DE: SR Books, 1994.

Tenorio-Trillo, Mauricio. "1910 Mexico City: Space and Nation in the City of the Centenario." *Journal of Latin American Studies* 28, no. 1 (1996): 5–104.

Thomas, Hugh. *The Spanish Civil War*. New York: Harper & Brothers, 1961.

Thompson, E. P. "The Moral Economy of the English Crowd in the Eighteenth Century." *Past and Present* 50 (1971): 76–136.

———. "Time, Work-Discipline, and Industrial Capitalism." *Past and Present* 38 (1967): 56–97.

Thompson, Ruth. "The Limitations of Ideology in the Early Argentine Labour Movement: Anarchism in the Trade Unions, 1890–1920." *Journal of Latin American Studies* 16, no. 1 (1984): 81–99.

Thomson, Guy P. C. "Popular Aspects of Liberalism in Mexico, 1848–1888." *Bulletin of Latin American Research* 10, no. 3 (1991): 265–92.

———. *Puebla de los Angeles: Industry and Society in a Mexican City, 1700–1850*. Boulder, CO: Westview Press, 1989.

Tilly, Charles. "Food Supply and Public Order in Modern Europe." In *The Formation of National States in Western Europe*, edited by Charles Tilly, 380–455. Princeton, NJ: Princeton University Press, 1975.

Torres, Mariano. "Una empresa agroindustrial: El Molino de San Mateo de Atlixco, Puebla, 1853–1910." In *Historia de las grandes empresas en México, 1850–1930*, edited by Carlos Marichal and Mario Cerutti, 275–90. Mexico City: Universidad Autónoma de Nuevo León, Fondo de Cultura Económica, 1997.

Trigueros, Ignacio. *Memoria de los ramos municipales correspondiente al semestre de presentada a S.M. el emperador por el alcalde municipal de la ciudad de México, D. Ignacio Trigueros*. Mexico City: Imprenta Económica, 1866.

Twinam, Anne. "Jew to Basque: Ethnic Myths and Antioqueño Entrepreneurship." *Journal of Interamerican Studies and World Affairs* 22, no. 1 (February 2001): 81–107.

Ulloa, Berta. "La lucha armada." In *Historia general de México*, edited by Daniel Cosio Villegas, 757–821. Mexico City: El Colegio de México, 1994.

Valadés, José C. *Memorias de un joven rebelde*. 2 vols. Culiacán: Universidad Autónoma de Sinaloa, 1986.

Valle-Arizpe, Artemio de. *Calle vieja y calle nueva*. Mexico City: Editorial Diana–Departamento del Distrito Federal, 1980.

Vanderwood, Paul J. *Disorder and Progress: Bandits, Police, and Mexican Development*. Lincoln: University of Nebraska Press, 1981.

Van Young, Eric. *Hacienda and Market in Eighteenth-Century Mexico*. Berkeley and Los Angeles: University of California Press, 1981.

Vázquez, Josefina Zoraida. "Los primeros tropiezos." In *Historia general de México*, vol. 2, edited by Daniel Cosio Villegas, 525–82. Mexico City: El Colegio de México, 1998.

Villalobos Calderón, Liborio, ed. *"La convención radical obrera." Antología de la prensa obrera*. Mexico City: Centro de Estudios Históricos del Movimiento Obrero Mexicano, 1978.

Villegas, Abelardo. *Positivism y porfirismo*. Mexico City: Sepsetentas, 1972.

Viqueira Albán, Juan Pedro. ¿*Relajados o reprimidos?: Diversiones públicas y vida social en la ciudad de México durante el siglo de las luces*. Mexico City: Fondo de Cultura Económica, 1987.

Voss, Stuart F. *Latin America in the Middle Period, 1750–1929*. Wilmington, DE: Scholarly Resources, 2001.

Waldinger, Roger D. "Immigrant Enterprise: A Critique and Reformulation." *Theory and Society* 15, no. 1/2 (1986): 249–85.

———. *Through the Eye of the Needle: Immigrants and Enterprise in New York's Garment Trades*. New York and London: New York University Press, 1986.

Walker, David W. *Kinship, Business, and Politics: The Martínez del Río Family in Mexico, 1824–1867*. Austin: University of Texas Press, 1986.

———. "Porfirian Labor Politics: Working Class Organizations in Mexico City and Porfirio Díaz, 1876–1902." *Americas* 37, no. 3 (1981): 257–89.

Weiner, Richard. *Race, Nation, and Market: Economic Culture in Porfirian Mexico*. Tucson: University of Arizona Press, 2004.

Whipp, Richard. "'A Time for Every Purpose': An Essay on Time and Work." In *The Historical Meanings of Work*, edited by Patrick Joyce, 210–36. Cambridge: Cambridge University Press, 1987.

Wright, Thomas C. "The Politics of Urban Provisioning in Latin American History." In *Food, Politics, and Society in Latin America*, edited by John C. Super and Thomas C. Wright, 24–45. Lincoln: University of Nebraska Press, 1985.

Yankelevich, Pablo. "Hispanofobia y revolución: Españoles expulsados de México (1911–1940)." *Hispanic American Historical Review* 86, no. 1 (2006): 29–59.

Yoma Medina, María Rebeca, and Luis Alberto Martos López. *Dos mercados en la historia de la ciudad de México: El Volador y La Merced*. Mexico City: Instituto Nacional de Antropología e Historia, 1990.

Zamacois, Niceto de. *Historia de Méjico desde sus tiempos mas remotos hasta nuestros dias*, vol. 12. Barcelona and Mexico City: J. F. Parres, 1877–1882.

Zanolli Fabila, Betty Luisa. "Inversiones mercantiles en el agro yucateco a finales de la época colonial." *Estudios Agrarios de la Procuraduría Agraria* 31 (2006): 67–76. Electronic document, www.pa.gob.mx/publica/rev_31/betty%20Zanolli.pdf, accessed December 20, 2011.

Zarco, Francisco. *Crónica del congreso extraordinario constituyente, 1856–1857*. Mexico City: El Colegio de México, 1957.

Index

Abelardo L. Rodríguez Market, 140, 147, 149
Acordada Revolt, 25, 25, 30
adulteration, 4, 5, 90, 120, 124, 135, 149
Agrupación de Fabricantes Mexicanos de Pan y Bizcochos del Distrito Federal. *See* Association of Mexican Bakery Owners of Mexico City
Albaitero, Pedro, 58, 60, 62, 64, 71, 74, 80, 98, 102, 119, 125, 148; arrival in Mexico, 48; marriage, 48–50; nephews, 51, 53. *See also* La Florida; Los Gallos
Albaitero García Rejón, Cipriana, 49
Albaitero García Rejón, Mercedes, 48, 51, 53
alcabalas, 32
Alcázar, Ricardo de, 45, 46
American Red Cross, 89, 92, 104
anarchism, 76, 111; contrast with Constitutionalists, 108; influence on Casa del Obrero Mundial, 102; influence on union demands, 100–101, 112–13. *See also* anarchists; Casa del Obrero Mundial; Confederación General de Trabajadores
anarchists, 80, 86, 100, 101, 103, 107, 110, 111, 112, 113, 121; conflicts with communists, 108, 111, 116; founding of CGT, 115–16. *See also* anarchism; Casa del Obrero Mundial; Confederación General de Trabajadores
anticlericalism, 39, 102, 141
anti-gachupinismo, 59–60, 149; after independence, 29, 46; response from *El Correo Español*, 94; during revolution, 92, 93–94, 102–3. *See also* Anti-Spanish League of Mexico; Dr. Atl
Anti-Reelection Clubs, 80
Anti-Spanish League of Mexico, 93
anti-Spanish sentiment. *See anti-gachupinismo*
Armenta, Eloy, 86
Arrache, José, 50, 51, 52, 53, 62, 64, 71, 74, 77, 79, 81, 86, 88, 94, 104
Association of Bakery Owners of Mexico City, 118
Association of Mexican Bakery Owners of Mexico City, 88, 90, 118
Ávila Camacho, Manuel, 145

bakery regulations: in colonial era, 12–13; connections to collective contract, 8, 128, 131, 132, 150; failures of, 15–18; and free-market reforms, 21; and paternalism, 14–15; regulations of 1929, 128–31
bakery strikes, 30, 74–79, 77–78, 81–82, 114–17, 122–23, 132, 135–37

INDEX

Barberena Urrutia, Andrés, 54, 90, 105, 117
Basagoiti y Arteta, Antonio, 60
Basques, 47, 60, 63, 65, 120, 128, 148;
    as attractive immigrants, 46, 47;
    dominance in bread and flour trades,
    51, 55, 106, 127; entrepreneurial
    acumen, 49; importance of nephews,
    51; partnerships with Mexican owners,
    118–19, 125; primogeniture, 47, 51;
    scholarship of, 6. *See also* Baztán
    Valley; Navarre
Baz, Juan José, 36, 39, 41, 42, 63
Baztán Valley, 46–48, 51, 53, 55, 119, 125,
    148. *See also* Basques; Navarre
Belem Prison, 42, 20, 74, 78, 106
bizcocheros, 15, 116
bizcochos, 4, 154n13
bolillos, 1, 37, 90, 111, 116; diminishing
    weight of, 87, 134, 141, 151;
    impediments to mechanization, 105;
    subsidized flour for, 145
Bonaparte, Napoleon, 20
Bourbon authorities, 15, 17, 18, 19, 24
Buerba, Antonio, 34, 35, 75, 77
Bureau of Conciliation and Arbitration,
    105, 110, 114, 116
Bustamante, Anastasio, 26
Bustamante, Carlos María de, 27

Calles, Plutarco Elías, 121, 129, 135, 147
Camisas Doradas (Golden Shirts), 141
Cananea Mine Strike, 82
canasteros, 127; meeting with Lázaro
    Cárdenas, 142; persecution of, 138,
    140, 143, 144, 147, 151. *See also* peddlers
Cárdenas, Lázaro: foundation of CTM,
    135–36; opposition to, 141–45
Carr, Barry, 112
Carranza, Venustiano, 84, 85, 92, 93, 94,
    104, 112, 113, 149; assassination of, 115,
    129; and Constitution of 1917, 109–10;
    relations with Casa del Obrero
    Mundial, 101–3, 107–9, 110
Casa del Obrero Mundial, 86, 87, 89, 98,
    110; alliance with Constitutionalists,
    101–2, 104, 106; closure of, 109, 112;
    internal divisions, 108; strike, 108–9
Castañeda Hospital, 106
Castellano, Raúl, 144
Caste War, 49
cemitas, 5, 69
Centro Vasco, 53, 54, 84, 102
CGT. *See* Confederación General de
    Trabajadores
Chao, Manuel, 87
Charles III, 17, 18
Chucho el ninfo (José T. de Cuéllar), 4
clandestine bakeries, 60, 120, 127, 132, 139;
    hygiene in, 127–28
clerks: working conditions of, 55–56;
    opportunities, 56
Colado, José, 86, 87, 101
collective contract, 8, 117, 124, 133, 138,
    144, 150, 151; and shifts, 132; signing
    of, 122; and small producers, 125–26,
    128, 131; and union rivalries, 136–37;
    workers' demands for, 113, 116
comisión mixta. *See* mixed commission
Committee for the Relief of the Poor, 93
communism, 108, 111, 112, 113, 135, 141, 144.
    See also communists
Communist Party of Mexico, 111
communists, 101, 110, 111; accusations
    against Genaro Gómez and
    Victoriano Muñoz, 136; in CGT, 115;
    conflicts with anarchists, 108, 116.
    See also communism; Communist
    Party of Mexico
Compañía Molinera de Toluca, 55, 91
Confederación de Trabajadores de
    México (CTM), 143, 144; foundation
    of, 135; and internal divisions in
    bakers' union, 136, 138; and Leandro
    González Uzcanga, 139, 140. *See also*
    Sindicato Único
Confederación General de Trabajadores
    (CGT): founding of, 115–16;
    government support of 121; internal
    divisions, 116; separation of bakers'
    union from, 121–22; streetcar workers,

117. *See also* anarchism; anarchists; communism; communists
Confederación Regional de Obreros de México (CROM), 110, 111, 115, 116, 121
Confederación Sindical Unitaria de México (CSUM), 116
Constitutionalists, 83, 111, 112; alliance with Casa del Obrero Mundial, 101–2, 104, 106, 107, 108, 109; contracts with bakery owners, 94, 97; occupation of Mexico City, 84–85, 89, 92, 93; social equilibrium, 110; support for CROM, 110. *See also* Carranza, Venustiano; Obregón, Álvaro
Constitution of 1917: Article 5, 134; Article 27, 109; Article 28, 109, 130, 134; Article 33, 134; Article 123, 109–10, 113, 114, 121, 122; Constitutional Convention (Querétaro), 109
Conventionists: formation of, 85; occupation of Mexico City, 85, 86, 87, 88, 89, 90, 92
Convention of Aguascalientes, 85
copper coins. *See* currency
Córdoba, Florencio, 53, 79, 81, 94, 104, 106, 114
corn. *See* maize
Cortés, Hernán, 11, 28, 49
Costeloe, Michael, 22
CROM. *See* Confederación Regional de Obreros de México
CSUM. *See* Confederación Sindical Unitaria de México
CTM. *See* Confederación de Trabajadores de México
currency, 5; copper coins, 27; and credit for bakeries, 87; devalued currency and real estate purchases, 91; and food crisis, 109

Díaz, Félix, 93
Díaz, Porfirio: and 1871 revolt, 50, 76; immigration policy of, 44, 50; and infrastructure projects, 52, 80; and labor policies, 7, 66–67, 76; opposition to, 80, 82; overthrow of, 84, 100; and police vigilance, 67–68; and promotion of foreign businesses, 60–61, 65, 69, 84, 99, 102, 125, 148; rise to power of, 50, 53; as symbol of Spanish colonialism, 148
Díez Fernández, Pablo, 54, 85
differentiation, 69–70
Dr. Atl (Gerardo Murillo), 93, 102, 109

Echandi, Fermín, 54, 77
echea, 47
Elena, Eduardo, 7
El Eúskaro flour mill, 54, 55, 117, 119
empeño. *See* working conditions in bakeries
encierros. *See* working conditions in bakeries
Enríquez, Ignacio C., 83, 92, 94, 96, 97, 101
Espinosa Suquilvide, Anastasio, 125
esquiroles. *See obreros libres*
expendios, 129, 180n35

fascism, 142
Federation of Workers and Peasants (FROC), 136, 143
Fernández y Fernández, Ramón, 4
Fiel Ejecutoría, 12–14, 19, 21, 25, 129; *fieles repesadores*, 13
Figueroa, Luis, 92
Flores, Rita, 62
Flores Magón brothers, 80
flour mills: decline of, after independence, 27–28, 30; establishment in Mexico, 11; importance in *gremio*, 19. *See also* El Eúskaro flour mill; La Florida
flour subsidies, 145, 152
food crises: in colonial era, 12; in 1840s, 25–27, 28; during revolution, 89–90; during war of independence, 21. *See also* hoarding
Franco, Manuel, 68
free market: *comercio libre* versus *libertad de comercio*, 33–34; influence of

18th-century liberalism, 14, 20, 21–22; late-colonial reforms, 20–23
FROC. *See* Federation of Workers and Peasants
Fuenclara, Count of, 16
Fuentes, Eduardo, 93

gachupín. *See anti-gachupinismo*
Gallardo, José Mariano, 40, 42
Galnares, Gerónimo, 34, 35, 77
Gálvez, José de, 17, 18
Ganastachua, Simón, 78
García, Pedro, 68, 71
García, Telésforo, 59, 85
García Acosta, Virginia, 4
García Menocal, Mario, 111
García Rejón, Joaquín, 49
García Rejón, Manuel, 49
García Rejón y Piñón, Andrés, 49
García Rejón y Piñón, Luisa, 49
García Rejón y Piñón, María de la Luz, 49
Gasca, Celestino, 116
Georges, Pablo des, 83–84, 94, 96, 98–99, 101, 104
Girón, León, 93
Golden Shirts. *See* Camisas Doradas
Gómez, Genaro, 111, 116, 121, 136, 137, 138, 152
Gonzaga Vierya, Luis, 26
González, Pedro, 71, 73
González Uzcanga, Leandro: murder of Argimiro López Fernández, 139–40, 144
Gran Cuerpo Central de Trabajadores, 110, 175n43
gremio, 12, 15, 25, 30, 31, 33, 40, 148–49, 151; and conflicts with colonial government, 18–20; end of, 21; foundation of, 16. *See also* monopoly
Gual, Francisco, 35
Gutiérrez, Eulalio, 87, 88

Helstosky, Carol, 3
Hidalgo, Miguel, 21, 93
hispanismo, 45, 50, 61

hoarding, 15, 88, 89, 90, 98, 103, 149
House of Tiles. *See* Palacio de Azulejos
Huerta, Victoriano, 84, 86, 102, 109
Humboldt, Alexander von, 3, 4, 11
hunger. *See* food crises
hygiene: in bakeries, 52, 72, 119; in "clandestine" bakeries, 127–28; and 1922 health code, 119–20; and persecution of small producers, 128, 131; sanitary inspections, 119, 179n11

Iniestra, Marcelo, 62, 63, 66
Iriarte, Esperanza Moreno, 54
Iriarte, Leonor Moreno, 54
Iriarte Goyeneche, Braulio, 53, 58, 60, 77, 78, 80, 85, 88, 90, 102, 113, 117, 119, 125; and *encierros*, 74; family of, 54; founding of El Eúskaro, 54; founding of Leviatán y Flor, 54; importance of nephews to, 54–55; real estate purchases by, 91; settlement in Mexico, 53–54. *See* El Eúskaro flour mill; Modelo Beer Factory
Irigoyen Echartea, Juan, 51, 53, 54, 60
Irigoyen Echartea, Pedro, 53, 88; friendship with Alvaro Obregón, 98
Iturrigaray, José de, 17

Jáuregui Iriarte, Agustín, 54
Jockey Club, 102
Jovellanos, Gaspar Melchor de, 14, 21
Juárez, Benito, 41, 50, 76

La Florida: founding of, 51; and technological innovations, 51–52
Laguna, Pedro, 86, 118, 119
Lama, Ángel de la, 36, 161n56
Larregui Iriarte, Bautista, 55, 91
Larregui Iriarte, José, 55, 91
Larregui Iriarte, Miguel, 55, 91
Lasa, Gregorio, 35
Latin American Bureau of the Third International, 111
La Vasconia, 54
Lerdo de Tejada, Sebastián, 50

liberals (19th century), 32, 33, 39, 45, 48, 76; and labor reform, 41–42, 66
Lombardo Toledano, Vicente, 138, 144
Loperena Ilarregui, Victoriano, 87, 125
López de Gómara, Francisco, 11
López de Lara, César, 105, 107
López Fernández, Argimiro, 139, 140
Los Gallos, 53, 64, 78, 81, 94, 96, 97, 105, 119; and technological innovations, 52

Madero, Francisco I., 80, 82, 84, 129
Madrigal, Onofre, 120
maize, 3, 4, 11, 21, 22, 28, 53, 90, 98, 104
Marat, Jean Paul, 103
Marx, Karl, 63, 112
Maximilian (of Hapsburg), 34, 36, 38, 39; and arrival of foreign bakery owners, 34
meat: and commerce, 21; and market reforms, 21–23; scarcity of, 21, 28, 90
mechanization: disincentives to, 58; owners' bluff of, 105–6, 115, 173n21. *See also* La Florida; Los Gallos
Mendieta, Aquilino, 33
Mexican Communist Party. *See* Communist Party of Mexico
Mexican Young Red Socialists, 111. *See also* Communist Party of Mexico
Minondo Rota, Segundo, 54, 113
mixed commission, 129, 130, 132, 134, 138, 139, 144; cancelation of, 145
Moats, Leone, 84
Modelo Beer factory, 54, 125
Molina Enríquez, Andrés, 4
monopoly: colonial regulations against, 12, 15; meaning of, 60, 153n1; postrevolutionary rhetoric against, 130. *See also* Constitution of 1917; *gremio*; Spanish monopoly
Montellano, B. O. (Bernardo Ortiz), 63, 77
Moreno, Angela, 54
Moreno, Sebastián, 133
Morones, Luis, 110, 115, 121
Moya, José, 47

Muñoz, Victoriano, 136
Murillo, Gerardo. *See* Dr. Atl

National Revolutionary Party (Partido Revolucionario Nacional), 129
National Union of Small Bread Producers (URPI), 133
Navarre, 44, 46, 47; and Carlista Wars, 47, 53, 54, 125. *See also* Baztán Valley
Negri, Ramón P. de, 92
nota roja, 68, 69, 70
Nuño de Guzmán, Antonio, 11

Obregón, Álvaro, 118; and accusations against foreign merchants, 90, 93, 149; and alliance with Casa del Obrero Mundial, 101; assassination of, 121, 129, 149; and battle of Celaya, 109; and friendship with Pedro Irigoyen, 98; and occupation of Mexico City, 85, 89, 90, 98, 101; and presidential election of 1920, 115; and ties with Luis Morones, 115, 121
obreros libres, 81, 114, 116, 117
Oliver, Pedro Pascual, 46
Ortiz de Montellano, Manuel, 33
Oteiza, Juan, 54, 77
Oyamburu, Martín, 91

Palacio de Azulejos (House of Tiles), 53, 84, 102, 103, 104, 109
Palacio de Hierro, 60
pambazos, 5, 13, 21, 37
pan frío, 5, 135
Partido de la Revolución Institucional (PRI), 152
Partido Laborista, 115
Partido Revolucionario Nacional. *See* National Revolutionary Party
Pastry War, 26
peddlers: conflicts with bakery owners and, 36–39, 58, 86. See also *canasteros; tendejones*
Penal Code (1871), 41
Pérez, Adolfo, 71, 73

Pimentel, Francisco, 41
popular liberalism, 76
Portes Gil, Emilio, 121, 129
positivism, 66
pósito, 17, 18
postura, 13, 19, 21
PRI. *See* Partido de la Revolución Institucional
prices of bread: liberalism and, 14; ounces per cost of, 13, 21, 26, 37–38; and political legitimacy, 4, 5, 25; price fixing under colonialism and, 12, 13, 14, 17, 19. See also *bolillos*; *postura*
Prieto, Francisco, 35, 161n56
Prieto, Guillermo, 4, 28
pulque, 22, 71, 78, 79

Red Battalions, 101, 106, 174n25
Redorta, Mariano, 180n35
regulations. *See* bakery regulations
Revillagigedo, Second Count of, 19, 20
Revolution of Ayutla, 33
Rincón Gallardo, Pedro, 75, 77, 82
Río Blanco strike, 82
Rivera, Diego, 68, 140
Robles Domínguez, Alfredo, 85
Rodríguez, Abelardo L., 129, 130, 132, 147
Roumagnac, Carlos, 71
Royal Basque Society of Friends of the Country, 48
Rubio, José, 175n49
Ruiz, Manuel, 68, 70

Sahagún, Bernardino de, 11
Saint Brigit Convent, 102
Sánchez, Florencio, 96, 104
San José flour mill, 125
Santa Anna, Antonio López de, 22, 26, 27, 28, 32
Santa Mónica flour mill, 28, 30
Santiago Tlaltelolco House of Corrections, 42
Santo Domingo flour mill, 11, 27, 28, 49, 51
San Vicente, Sebastián, 175n48, 175n49
Segura, José, 88, 120

shifts: measure by time versus by volume of production, 79, 113–14
Sinarquismo, 141
Sindicato de Obreros y Obreras en el Ramo de la Panadería, 98
Sindicato de Trabajadores de la Industria del Pan del Distrito Federal, 122
Sindicato Único, 138
small producers, 5, 8, 9, 19, 20; and alliance with Genaro Gómez, 136; and collective contract, 126, 130, 132, 151; distinctions from larger Mexican bakeries, 120, 127; and *gremio*, 16, 18; marginalization after mid-19th century, 31, 33, 34, 39, 43, 58; and meeting with Lázaro Cárdenas, 142; as nonunion businesses, 118, 127, 128; opportunities for, after independence, 24, 25, 30, 31, 40; persecution of, 130, 131, 132, 133, 134, 135, 137–39, 140, 144, 145, 146; as reactionary threat, 141, 142–43; relations with "Spanish monopoly," 87–88, 96, 119; and *tendejones*, 127. See also clandestine bakeries; URPI
Smith, Adam, 14
social equilibrium, 108, 110, 123, 124, 142, 144, 147, 151
socialism, 107, 108, 112
socialist bakeries, 101, 104, 106, 107
Soviet Union, 135
Spanish monopoly, 2, 5, 9, 44, 47, 50, 60, 98, 124, 125, 134, 138, 139, 141, 146, 148, 150, 151, 152
Special Commission of Food Items, 88
strikes. *See* bakery strikes
sweet bread. See *bizcochos*

Tacubaya: river, 11; town, 49, 50, 51
tariffs. *See* wheat
tendejones, 127, 133, 137. *See also* peddlers
Terán, Antonio, 68, 70
Texas War of Secession, 26, 27
tlalchiches. *See* clandestine bakeries; small producers

tortillas, 3, 4, 127, 133, 137; price increases of, due to bread strikes, 75, 104, 137; scarcity of, 90; as signs of backwardness, 5, 133

Ugalde, José, 68, 70
Union and Friendship Mutualist Society, 64
Unión de Propietarios de Panaderías del Distrito Federal. *See* Association of Bakery Owners of Mexico City
Unión Nacional de Pequeño Industrial de Pan (URPI). *See* National Union of Small Bread Producers, 133
United States, 32, 33, 45, 48, 51, 53, 114

Valadés, José, 111
Venegas, Francisco Xavier, 21
Villa, Pancho, 84, 85, 87, 101, 149
Villegas, Amado, 136–38
violence in bakeries, 69–72.
See also *nota roja*

Weis, Teodoro, 36, 161n56
wheat, 3, 4, 12, 13, 19, 28, 30, 31, 43, 44, 52, 53, 54, 55; introduction to Mexico, 11; purchase by millers, 55; tariffs, 31
wheat-flour-bread complex, 28, 31, 55, 63
Wilson, Woodrow, 103, 104
women, 22, 45, 59, 103, 122, 134; food riots and, 83, 85, 90, 91, 149; as retailers, 36; as workers in bakeries, 81–82
working conditions in bakeries, 5, 6, 22, 41, 43, 62–66; *empeño* and, 16–17, 22, 30, 31; *encierro* and, 74, 75, 80; improvement of, after independence, 30–31

Zamacois, Niceto de, 27
Zapata, Emiliano, 84, 85, 87, 101
Zapatistas, 86, 91, 95, 96, 102, 107, 109. *See also* Conventionists; Zapata, Emiliano
Zarco, Francisco, 41
Zermeño, Narciso, 76
Zugarramundi, Marcelo, 105